FRENCH/ ENGLISH-FRENCH BEGINNER'S DICTIONARY

A Beginner's Guide in Words and Pictures

FOURTH EDITION

By Gladys C. Lipton

Director
National FLES Institute,
Kensington, MD

BARRON'S

Dedicated to Benny, Emma, Maya, Nina, and Shane

The author would like to express appreciation to Josée Dufour, Harriet Saxon, Nancy Carlson, and Elaine Wolfire for their advice and for their excellent suggestions.

All inquiries should be addressed to:
Barron's Educational Series, Inc.
250 Wireless Boulevard
Hauppauge, NY 11788
www.barronseduc.com

ISBN-13: 978-0-7641-3975-8
ISBN-10: 0-7641-3975-4
Library of Congress Control Number: 2008934847

Printed in Canada
9 8 7 6 5 4 3 2 1

Table of Contents

Table des Matières

Introduction

Learning another language can be fun for everybody! This *French–English/English–French Beginner's Dictionary* is a book that will be both interesting and useful to you. If you enjoy discovering new words and sentences in French and English, if you like trying to pronounce new sounds and looking at pictures, this book will bring many hours of enjoyment.

This fourth edition contains many new and expanded features, including new words and expressions, particularly in technology. There are new Cultural Notes scattered throughout the book, reflecting both French and American cultures. And there is also a For Travelers supplement to assist you when you travel to the many French-speaking countries around the world. And the French and English pronunciation keys will help you solve some of the mysteries of foreign language pronunciation

Last, but not least, by looking up words and expressions in both languages, you will have an opportunity to compare them and gain some insights into French and American cultures.

Welcome to the world of languages!

Gladys C. Lipton

Introduction

L'apprentissage d'une nouvelle langue peut être amusant pour tout le monde! Le dictionnaire bilingue pour débutants Français/Anglais Anglais/Français est un ouvrage à la fois agréable et fonctionnel. Grâce à lui, tous ceux qui aiment regarder des images, ceux qui se délectent à prononcer de nouveaux sons ainsi que ceux qui apprécient de découvrir la lecture en français et en anglais pourront passer des heures à le feuilleter en s'amusant.

Cette 4ème édition contient de nouvelles caractéristiques avancées. Ainsi, tout au long de l'ouvrage, vous découvrirez un grand nombre de nouveaux mots et expressions d'usage contemporain, issus en particulier du domaine de la technologie. De nombreuses notes culturelles sont également parsemées au fil des pages, faisant référence à la fois aux cultures française et américaine. Il y a aussi un supplément "pour les voyageurs" destiné à assister les personnes voyageant dans n'importe quel pays francophone ou anglophone. La clé de prononciation anglaise et française, vous aidera à résoudre des mystères des langues étrangères.

Enfin, en cherchant des mots ou des expressions dans les deux langues, vous aurez l'occasion de comparer les mots, les expressions et la culture en français et en anglais.

Bienvenue au monde des langues!

Gladys C. Lipton

French-English

(Français-Anglais)

French Pronunciation Key

(La Clef de la Prononciation Française)

Notes

1. Some French sounds do not have any English equivalent. (Shown by —)

2. Capital letters indicate the syllable that receives the emphasis. For example:

a-bree-KOH.

3. Note difference between consonant "w" and phonemic symbol "w̱" for vowel sound for "oi" and "oui."

4. The sound systems of English and French are quite different. The pronunciation key is an attempt to approximate comparative sounds.

CONSONANTS

French Spelling	Phonemic Symbol
b	b
c	k, s
ç	s
ch	sh
d	d, t
f, ph	f
g	g, zh
h	—
j	zh
k	k
l	l
m	m
n	n
gne	n or N (as in *onion*)
p	p
qu, q	k
r	r
s	s, z
t, th	t
tion	syohn
v	v
w	v
x	gs, ks, s, z
y, ille	y (as in *yes*)
z, s, x	z

VOWELS			
French Spelling	French Example	Phonemic Symbol	Sounds something like English word
a	(la)	a	at
â	(bâton)	ah	father
è, êt, ais	(mais, près)	eh	shelf
é, ai, er, ez	(école, j'ai)	ay	day (but it is a *very short* sound in French)
i, y	(si, pyjama)	ee	see
o	(robe)	uh	hut
ô	(hôtel)	oh	open
u	(mur)	~~ew~~	—
ou	(sous)	oo	too
eu	(deux)	eoh	—
e	(me)	é	the (book)
eu	(fleur)	euh	sir
an, am, en, em	(sans)	ahń	—
in, im, aim, ain, ein	(cinq)	aiń	—
on	(son)	ohń	—
un	(un)	uhń	—
oi	(bois)	wa	was
ui, oui	(bruit)	~~ew~~/ee	—

A

à [A] preposition   **at, in, to**
Ils vont à Paris.
They are going to Paris.

---

l'abeille [a-BAY] noun, fem.   **bee**
L'abeille aime la fleur.
The bee likes the flower.

---

l'abricot [a-bree-KOH] noun, masc.   **apricot**
L'abricot est délicieux.
The apricot is delicious.

---

absent [ab-SAHN] adjective, masc.   **absent**
absente [ab-SAHNT] fem.

Georges est absent aujourd'hui.
George is absent today.

---

accord [a-KUHR] noun, masc.   **agreement**
d'accord! [da-KUHR] idiomatic expression   **agreed!, O.K.,**
Veux-tu jouer avec moi? D'accord!   **all right**
Do you want to play with me? O.K.!

---

acheter [a-SHTAY] verb   **to buy**
  j'achète   nous achetons
  tu achètes   vous achetez
  il, elle achète   ils, elles achètent

Le garcon achète une balle.
The boy is buying a ball.

---

l'acteur [ak-TEUHR] noun, masc.   **actor**
l'actrice [ak-TREES] fem.   **actress**
L'acteur est beau.
The actor is handsome.

---

l'addition [a-dee-SYOHN] noun, fem.   **addition; check**
Après le dîner, papa demande l'addition.   **(in restaurant)**
After dinner, Dad asks for the check.

---

l'adresse [a-DREHS] noun, fem.   **address**
Quelle est votre adresse?
What is your address?

---

l'aéroport [a-ay-ruh-PUHR] noun, masc.   **airport**

Il y a tant d'avions à l'aéroport!
There are so many airplanes at the airport!

---

l'âge [AHZH] noun, masc.   **age (used with**
Quel âge as-tu? J'ai huit ans.   **"How old...?")**
How old are you? I am eight (years old). (See **avoir**)

---

l'agent (de police)   **police officer**
[a-ZHAHN-dé-puh-LEES] noun, masc.
L'agent de police dirige la circulation.
The police officer directs traffic.

---

agréable [a-gray-ABL] adjective   **pleasant, nice**
Le printemps est une saison agréable.
Spring is a pleasant season.

aider [eh-DAY] verb   **to help, to aid**

   j'aide   nous aidons

   tu aides   vous aidez

   il, elle aide   ils, elles aident

Jean aide sa soeur à porter les livres.
John helps his sister carry the books.

---

l'aiguille [ay-GWEEY] noun, fem.   **needle**

Voici une aiguille à coudre.
Here is a sewing needle. (See **coudre**)

---

l'aile [EHL] noun, fem.   **wing**

L'avion a deux ailes.
The airplane has two wings.

---

aimer [eh-MAY] verb   **to like, to love**

   j'aime   nous aimons

   tu aimes   vous aimez

   il, elle aime   ils, elles aiment

Maman aime ses enfants.
Mother loves her children.

---

ainsi [ain-SEE] adverb   **(in) this way**

Ainsi dansent les petites marionettes.
The little marionettes dance this way.

---

l'air [EHR] noun, masc.   **air, appearance, look**

Le tigre a l'air féroce.
The tiger has a ferocious look.

7

aller [a-LAY] verb   **to go (also used**
  je vais   nous allons   **with exp. of health)**
  tu vas   vous allez
  il, elle va   ils, elles vont

Où allez-vous? Je vais chez moi.
Where are you going? I'm going home.

Comment allez-vous? Je vais très bien, merci.
How are you? I'm very well, thank you.

---

l'allumette [a-lew-MEHT] noun, fem.   **match**

Les allumettes sont dangereuses pour les enfants.
Matches are dangerous for children.

---

l'alphabet [al-fa-BEH] noun, masc.   **alphabet**

Il y a vingt-six lettres dans l'alphabet français.
There are twenty-six letters in the French alphabet.

---

l'ambulance [ahń-bew-LAHŃS] noun, fem.   **ambulance**

L'ambulance va à l'hôpital.
The ambulance is going to the hospital.

---

amener [am-NAY] verb   **to bring (people)**
  j'amène   nous amenons
  tu amènes   vous amenez
  il, elle amène   ils, elles amènent

Le garçon amène sa soeur à la maison.
The boy brings his sister home.

---

américain [a-may-ree-KAIŃ] adjective, masc.   **American**
américaine [a-may-ree-KEHN] fem.

C'est un avion américain.
It's an American airplane.

---

l'ami [a-MEE] noun, masc.   **friend**
l'amie fem.

Je suis ton amie.
I am your friend.

---

l'amour [a-MOOR] noun, masc.   **love**
Le garçon a un grand amour pour son chien.
The boy loves his dog.

---

amusant [a-mew-ZAHN] adjective, masc.   **amusing, funny**
amusante [a-mew-ZAHNT] fem.
Le clown est amusant.
The clown is funny.

---

s'amuser [sa-mew-ZAY] verb   **to have a good time**
  je m'amuse   nous nous amusons
  tu t'amuses   vous vous amusez
  il, elle s'amuse   ils, elles s'amusent

Je mamuse au cirque.
I have a good time at the circus.

---

l'an [AHN] noun, masc.   **year**
J'ai neuf ans.
I'm nine years old.

le Jour de l'An   **New Year's Day** (See **jour**)

---

l'ananas [a-na-NA] noun, masc.   **pineapple**
L'ananas est gros.
The pineapple is big.

---

l'âne [AHN] noun, masc.   **donkey**
L'âne a deux longues oreilles.
The donkey has two long ears.

---

l'anglais [ah-GLEH] noun, masc.   **English**

On parle anglais aux Etats-Unis.
They speak English in the United States.

---

l'animal [a-nee-MAL] noun, masc.   **animal**
les animaux [a-nee-MOH] pl.

Les animaux sont dans la forêt.
The animals are in the forest.

l'animal favori   **pet** (See **favori**)

---

l'anneau [a-NOH] noun, masc.   **ring**

Quel joli anneau!
What a pretty ring! (See **bague**)

---

l'année [a-NAY] noun, fem.   **year**

Il y a douze mois dans une année.
There are twelve months in a year.

---

l'anniversaire [a-nee-vehr-SEHR] noun, masc.   **birthday,**
                                                                                          anniversary
Joyeux anniversaire! Quel âge as-tu?
Happy Birthday! How old are you?

---

août [oo] noun, masc.   **August**

En août il fait chaud.
In August it is hot.

---

l'appareil photo [a-pa-RAY-fuh-TOH] noun, masc.   **camera**

Regarde mon appareil. Il est nouveau.
Look at my camera. It is new.

le caméscope [KAH-meh-skohp] noun, fem.   **video camera**

---

l'appartement [a-par-té-MAHX] noun, masc.   **apartment**

Mon appartement est au deuxième étage.
My apartment is on the third floor.

---

appeler [a-PLAY] verb   **to call**

j'appelle	nous appelons
tu appelles	vous appelez
il, elle appelle	ils, elles appellent

J'appelle mon amie.
I call my friend.

---

s'appeler [sa-PLAY] verb   **to be called, —name is**

je m'appelle	nous nous appelons
tu t'appelles	vous vous appelez
il, elle s'appelle	ils, elles s'appellent

Comment vous appelez-vous? Je m'appelle Henri.
What is your name? My name is Henry.

---

l'appétit [a-pay-TEE] noun, masc.   **appetite**

Bon appétit!
Hearty appetite! (Enjoy your meal!)

---

apporter [a-puhr-TAY] verb   **to bring**

j'apporte	nous apportons
tu apportes	vous apportez
il, elle apporte	ils, elles apportent

Ils apportent des valises à la colonie de vacances.
They bring valises to camp.

11

apprendre [a-PRAHNDR] verb   **to learn**
  j'apprends   nous apprenons
  tu apprends   vous apprenez
  il, elle apprend   ils, elles apprennent
Elle aime apprendre le français.
She likes to learn French.

après [a-PREH] preposition   **after**
Septembre est le mois après août.
September is the month after August.

l'après-midi [a-preh-mee-DEE] noun, masc.   **afternoon**
Il est deux heures de l'après-midi.
It is two o'clock in the afternoon.

> A "gouter" is a children's afternoon snack that
> consists of cookies or juice.
>
> Un goûter pour les enfants, dans l'après-midi,
> consiste des biscuits ou du jus.

l'aquarium [a-kwa-RYUHM] noun, masc.   **aquarium,**
                                      fish tank
Il y a des poissons rouges dans l'aquarium.
There are some goldfish in the fish tank.

l'araignée [a-ray-NAY] noun, fem.   **spider**

Qui a peur d'une araignée?
Who's afraid of a spider?

l'arbre [ARBR] noun, masc.   **tree**

L'arbre a beaucoup de branches.
The tree has many branches.

---

l'arc-en-ciel [ar-kahń-SYEHL] noun, masc.   **rainbow**

J'aime les couleurs de l'arc-en-ciel.
I like the colors of the rainbow.

> The "Arc de Triomphe" is a monument in Paris.
>
> L'Arc de Triomphe est un momument qui se trouve à Paris.

---

l'argent [ar-ZHAHŃ] noun, masc.   **silver; money**

Il n'a pas assez d'argent.
He doesn't have enough money.

en argent [ahń-nar-ZHAHŃ]   **made of silver**

L'épingle est en argent.
The pin is made of silver.

---

l'armée [ar-MAY] noun, fem.   **army**

Les soldats sont dans l'armée.
Soldiers are in the army.

---

l'armoire [ar-MWAR] noun, fem.   **closet, cupboard**

L'armoire est vide.
The cupboard is empty (bare).

---

arranger [a-rahń-ZHAY] verb   **to arrange**

j'arrange	nous arrangeons
tu arranges	vous arrangez
il, elle arrange	ils, elles arrangent

Le professeur arrange ses papiers.
The teacher arranges his papers.

---

arrêter [a-reh-TAY] verb   **to stop; to arrest**

j'arrête	nous arrêtons
tu arrêtes	vous arrêtez
il, elle arrête	ils, elles arrêtent

L'agent de police arrête l'homme.
The policeman arrests the man.

L'agent arrête les autos.
The policeman stops the cars.

---

s'arrêter [sa-reh-TAY] verb   **to stop (oneself; itself)**

je m'arrête	nous nous arrêtons
tu t'arrêtes	vous vous arrêtez
il, elle s'arrête	ils, elles s'arrêtent

Le train s'arrête à la gare.
The train stops at the station.

---

arrière [a-RYEHR] adjective   **back, rear**
en arrière de [ahń-a-RYEHR-deh] preposition   **behind**

Un garçon est en arrière des autres.
One boy is behind the others.

---

arriver [a-ree-VAY] verb   **to arrive; to happen;**
                                                      to come

j'arrive	nous arrivons
tu arrives	vous arrivez
il, elle arrive	ils, elles arrivent

Le facteur arrive à dix heures.
The postman arrives at ten o'clock.

Qu'est-ce qui arrive?
What is happening?

---

l'artiste [ar-TEEST] noun, masc.   **artist**

Mon frère est artiste.
My brother is an artist.

---

l'aspirateur [as-pee-ra-TEUHR]   **vacuum cleaner**
noun, masc.

Pour nettoyer la maison, on emploie l'aspirateur.
We use the vacuum cleaner to clean the house.

---

s'asseoir [sa-SWAR] verb   **to sit down**
   je m'assieds   nous nous asseyons
   tu t'assieds   vous vous asseyez
   il, elle s'assied   ils, elles s'asseyent

Grand-mère s'assied sur une chaise.
Grandmother sits down on a chair.

---

assez [a-SAY] adverb   **enough**

As-tu assez de pommes de terre?
Do you have enough potatoes?

---

l'assiette [a-SYEHT] noun, fem.   **plate**

L'assiette est sur la table.
The plate is on the table.

---

assis [a-SEE] adjective, masc.   **seated**
assise [a-SEEZ] fem.

Il est assis dans un fauteuil.
He is seated in an armchair.

---

assister [a-sees-TAY] verb   **to attend**
   j'assiste   nous assistons
   tu assistes   vous assistez
   il, elle assiste   ils, elles assistent

Nous assistons à un jeu de football.
We attend a soccer game.

---

l'astronaute [a-struh-NUHT] noun, masc.   **astronaut**

L'astronaute fait un voyage en fusée.
The astronaut takes a trip in a spaceship.

---

attendre [a-TAHNDR] verb   **to wait for**

j'attends	nous attendons
tu attends	vous attendez
il, elle attend	ils, elles attendent

Elle attend son amie.
She is waiting for her friend.

---

attention! [a-tahn-SYOHN] interjection   **take care!,**
     be careful!
Le professeur dit: "Attention!"
The teacher says, "Take care!"

Faites attention! [feh-tza-tahn-SYOHN]   **Pay attention!**
idomatic expression   (See **faire**)

---

attraper [a-tra-PAY] verb   **to catch**

j'attrape	nous attrapons
tu attrapes	vous attrapez
il, elle attrape	ils, elles attrapent

Bravo! Jean attrape la balle.
Hurray! John catches the ball.

---

au [OH] masc. (contraction of à + le)   **to the**
à la [a-la] fem.
aux [OH] pl. (contraction of à + les)

La petite fille donne du lait aux chats.
The little girl gives milk to the cats.

---

aujourd'hui [oh-zhoor-DEW/EE] adverb   **today**

Aujourd'hui c'est le douze janvier.
Today is January 12th.

au revoir [uhr-vwar] interjection   **good-bye**
Le matin Papa dit: "au revoir" à sa famille.
In the morning Father says "Good-bye" to his family.

---

aussi [oh-see] adverb   **too, also; as**
Moi aussi, je veux des bonbons!   **(used in comparisons)**
I want some candy too!

Marc est aussi grand que Jacques.
Mark is as tall as Jack.

---

l'auto [uh-toh] noun, fem.   **auto(mobile), car**
L'auto roule sur la route.
The car goes along the road.

en auto [ahń-nuh-toh]   **by car**

---

l'autobus [uh-tuh-bews] noun, masc.   **bus**
Les enfants vont à l'école en autobus.
The children go to school by bus.

---

l'automne [oh-tuhn] noun, masc.   **autumn, fall**
En automne il fait frais.
In autumn it is cool.

---

autour de [oh-toor-deh] adverb   **around**
Je voudrais faire un voyage autour du monde.
I would like to take a trip around the world.

---

autre [ohtr] adjective, pronoun   **other, another**
Voici un autre crayon.
Here is another pencil.

l'autre [ohtr] pronoun, masc., fem.   **the other**
Voici mon mouchoir. Les autres sont sur le lit.
Here is my handkerchief. The others are on the bed.

---

avant [a-VAHN] preposition   **before**

Le professeur arrive avant les étudiants.
The teacher arrives before the students.

---

avec [a-VEHK] preposition   **with**

Marie est à la plage avec ses amies.
Mary is at the beach with her friends.

avec soin   **carefully** (See **soin**)

---

l'avenir [av-NEER] noun, masc.   **future**

Je vais visiter la France dans l'avenir.
In the future I'm going to visit France.

---

l'aventure [a-vahn-TEWR] noun, fem.   **adventure**

J'aime lire les aventures d'Astérix.
I like to read the adventures of Astérix.

---

l'avenue [av-NEW] noun, fem.   **avenue**

L'Avenue des Champs-Elysées est à Paris.
The Avenue des Champs-Elysées is in Paris.

---

aveugle [a-VEUH-gl] adjective   **blind**

Cet homme est aveugle.
This man is blind.

---

l'avion [a-VYOHN] noun, masc.   **airplane**
en avion   **by air**
par avion   **airmail**
l'avion à réaction [a-vyohn-na-ray-a-KSOHN]   **jet plane**
noun, masc.

L'avion à réaction va très vite.
The jet plane goes very fast.

le pilote d'avion   **(airplane) pilot**
                                                                      (See **pilote**)

---

l'avocat [a-vuh-KA] noun, masc.   **lawyer**

Mon oncle est avocat.
My uncle is a lawyer.

---

avoir [a-VWAR] verb   **to have**

j'ai	nous avons
tu as	vous avez
il, elle a	ils, elles ont

Elle a un crayon.
She has a pencil.

Quel âge avez-vous? J'ai onze ans.
How old are you? I am 11 years old.

Qu'avez-vous? J'ai mal à la tête.
What's the matter? I have a headache.

Avez-vous chaud? Oui, j'ai chaud.
Are you warm? Yes, I'm warm.

As-tu peur? Oui, j'ai peur.
Are you afraid? Yes, I'm afraid.

Pauvre bébé, il a sommeil.
The poor baby is sleepy.

Pauvre bébé, il a faim.
The poor baby is hungry.

Nous avons froid.
We are cold.

Marie a soif.
Mary is thirsty.

Papa a raison. Toi, tu as tort.
Father is right. You are wrong.

Elle a honte.
She is ashamed.

il y a [eel-YA]   **there is, there are**
Y a-t-il? [ya-TEEL]   **Is there, are there?**

Il y a trois enfants dans cette famille.
There are three children in this family.

---

avril [a-VREEL] noun, masc.   **April**

Il pleut beaucoup en avril.
It rains a lot in April.

B

les bagages [ba-GAZH] noun, masc., pl.   **baggage, luggage**

Les bagages sont prêts pour le voyage.
The baggage is ready for the trip.

---

la bague [BAG] noun, fem.   **ring**

Hélène porte une jolie bague.
Helen is wearing a pretty ring.

---

le bain [BAIN] noun, masc.   **bath**

Papa donne un bain à l'enfant.
Father is giving the baby a bath.

la salle de bain   **bathroom** (See **salle**)
le bain de soleil   **sunbath** (See **soleil**)

---

le baiser [beh-ZAY] noun, masc.   **kiss**

Maman donne un baiser à l'enfant.
Mother is kissing the child.

---

baisser [beh-SAY] verb   **to lower, to put down**
   je baisse   nous baissons
   tu baisses   vous baissez
   il, elle baisse   ils, elles baissent

Le professeur dit: "Baissez les mains!"
The teacher says, "Put your hands down!"

---

le balai [ba-LAY] noun, masc.   **broom**

On nettoie le plancher avec un balai.
We clean the floor with a broom.

---

la balançoire [ba-lahń-SWAR] noun, fem.   **seesaw; swing**

*Dans le parc les enfants s'amusent sur
les balançoires.*
In the park the children are having a good
time on the swings (seesaws).

---

le balayeur des rues   **street cleaner**
[ba-lay-yeuhr-day-REW] noun, masc.

Le balayeur des rues porte un balai.
The street cleaner is carrying a broom.

---

la balle [BAL] noun, fem.   **ball**

La balle est ronde.
The ball is round.

---

le ballon [ba-LOHN] noun, masc.   **balloon**

"Oh! Je perds mon ballon," crie la petite fille.
"Oh! I'm losing my balloon," cries the little girl.

---

la banane [ba-NAN] noun, fem.   **banana**

La banane est mûre quand elle est jaune.
The banana is ripe when it is yellow.

---

la banque [BAHNK] noun, fem.   **bank**

Avez-vous de l'argent à la banque?
Do you have any money in the bank?

---

la barbe [BARB] noun, fem.   **beard**

Mon frère, qui est à l'université, a une barbe.
My brother, who is at the university, has a beard.

---

les bas [BAH] noun, masc.   **stockings**

Les femmes portent des bas de nylon.
Women wear nylon stockings.

---

bas [BAH] adjective, masc.   **low, short**
basse [BAHS] fem.

L'arbre à gauche est bas; l'arbre à droite est haut.
The tree at the left is short; the tree at the right is tall.

à voix basse [a-vwa-BAHS]   **in a low voice**

Ma cousine parle à voix basse.
My cousin speaks in a low voice.

là bas   **down there, over there**

---

le base-ball [behs-BUHL] noun, masc.   **baseball**

Mon frère joue au base-ball.
My brother plays baseball.

---

le basket-ball [bas-keht-BUHL] noun, masc.   **basketball**

Mon camarade joue au basket-ball.
My friend plays basketball.

---

le bateau [ba-TOH] noun, masc.   **boat, ship**
les bateaux pl.

On traverse l'océan en bateau.
You cross the ocean by ship.

---

le bâtiment [bah-tee-MAHN] noun, masc.   **building**

Les bâtiments sont très hauts dans la ville.
The buildings are very tall in the city.

---

le bâton [bah-TOHN] noun, masc.   **stick**

L'agent de police porte un bâton.
The policeman carries a stick.

---

battre [BATR] verb   **to hit**

je bats	nous battons
tu bats	vous battez
il, elle bat	ils, elles battent

Il me bat!
He's hitting me!

(se) battre [BATR] verb   **to fight**

beau [BOH] adjective, masc.   **beautiful, handsome,**
beaux [BOH] masc., pl.   **good-looking**
belle [BEHL] fem.
bel [BEHL] masc., before a vowel

L'acteur est beau; l'actrice est belle.
The actor is handsome; the actress is beautiful.

Il fait beau   **The weather is good** (See **faire**)

---

beaucoup de (d') [boh-KOO-deh] adverb   **much, many,**
                                     a lot (of)
Berthe a beaucoup de livres.
Bertha has a lot of books.

---

le bébé [bay-BAY] noun, masc.   **baby**

Marie joue avec le bébé.
Mary plays with the baby.

---

le bec [BEHK] noun, masc.   **beak**

L'oiseau a un bec jaune.
The bird has a yellow beak.

---

le berceau [behr-SOH] noun, masc.   **cradle**

Ma soeur est dans le berceau.
My sister is in the cradle.

---

besoin, avoir besoin de (d')   **to need**
[bé-ZWAIN], [a-vwar-bé-ZWAIN-dé] idomatic expression
Le poisson a besoin d'eau.
The fish needs water.

---

bête [BEHT] adjective   **silly, stupid**
Le petit chien est bête.
The puppy is silly.

---

la bête [BEHT] noun, fem.   **beast, animal**
Le lion est une bête sauvage.
The lion is a wild animal.

---

le beurre [BUHR] noun, masc.   **butter**
Passez-moi le beurre, s'il vous plaît.
Pass the butter, please.

---

la bibliothèque [bee-blyoh-TEHK] noun, fem.   **library**

*Il y a tant de livres
dans la bibliothèque!*
There are so many books
in the library!

---

la bicyclette [bee-see-KLEHT] noun, fem.   **bicycle**
Quand il fait beau Bernard va à bicyclette.
When the weather is good, Bernard rides his bicycle.

le vélo [vay-LOH] noun, masc.   **bike, bicycle**
As-tu un vélo?
Do you have a bike?

---

bien [BYAIŃ] adverb   **well**

Je vais très bien, merci.
I'm feeling very well, thank you.

bien sûr [byaiń-SEWR] interjection   **of course**
bien entendu [byaiń-ahń-tahń-DEW]   **of course**
interjection

Aimez-vous les bonbons? Bien sûr (Bien entendu!)
Do you like candy? Of course!

bientôt [byahn-TOH] adverb   **soon**

Le facteur arrive bientôt.
The mailman will come soon.

à bientôt [a-byahn-TOH] interjection   **See you soon!**

Je vais faire des emplettes. À bientôt!
I am going shopping. See you soon!

---

le bifteck [beef-TEHK] noun, masc.   **(beef)steak**

Le bifteck est bon.
The steak is good.

---

le bijou [bee-ZHOO] noun, masc.   **jewel, jewelry**
les bijoux pl.

Il y a beaucoup de bijoux dans la malle.
There are many jewels in the trunk.

---

les billes [BEEY] noun, masc., pl.   **marbles**

Les garçons aiment jouer aux billes.
Boys like to play marbles.

le stylo à bille   **ballpoint pen** (See **stylo**)

---

le billet [bee-YAY] noun, masc.   **ticket; note; bill (money)**

Voici mon billet, monsieur.
Here is my ticket, sir.

Je suis riche! J'ai un billet de dix francs!
I am rich! I have a ten-franc note!

---

bizarre [bee-ZAR] adjective   **odd, strange**

Voici un animal bizarre!
Here is a strange animal!

---

blanc [BLAHN] adjective, masc.   **white**
blanche [BLAHNSH] fem.

Mes souliers sont blancs.
My shoes are white.

---

le blé [BLAY] noun, masc.   **wheat**

Je vois le blé dans les champs.
I see wheat in the fields.

---

bleu [BLEOH] adjective, masc.   **blue**
bleue fem.

Le ciel est bleu, n'est-ce pas?
The sky is blue, isn't it?

---

blond [BLOHN] adjective, masc.   **blonde**
blonde [BLOHND] fem.

Avez-vous les cheveux blonds?
Do you have blond hair?

---

boire [BWAR] verb   **to drink**
  je bois   nous buvons
  tu bois   vous buvez
  il, elle boit   ils, elles boivent

L'enfant boit du lait.
The child is drinking milk.

le boisson [bwa-SOHN] noun, masc.   **drink**

Le soda est un boisson.
Soda is a drink.

---

le bois [BWA] noun, masc.   **woods, forest**

Je vais dans le bois.
I am going into the woods.

en bois [ahń-BWA]   **made of wood, wooden**

La table est en bois.
The table is made of wood.

---

la boîte [BWAT] noun, fem.   **box**
la boîte aux lettres [b<u>wa</u>-toh-LEHTR]   **letter box, mailbox**
noun, fem.

Il met la lettre dans la boîte aux lettres.
He puts the letter in the mailbox.

---

bon [BOHŃ] adjective, masc.   **good**
bonne [BUHN] fem.

C'est un livre intéressant; c'est un bon livre.
It is an interesting book; it is a good book.

Bonne chance!   **Good luck!** (See **chance**)
Bonne fête!   **Happy birthday!** (See **fête**)

---

les bonbons [bohn/-BOHŃ] noun, masc., pl.   **candy**

Les enfants aiment les bonbons.
Children like candy.

---

le bonhomme de neige   **snowman**
[buh-NUHM-dé-NEHZH] noun, masc.

Le bonhomme de neige porte un chapeau.
The snowman is wearing a hat.

28

bonjour [bohń-ZHOOR] interjection   **Hello; Good morning; Good afternoon**

"Bonjour, mes enfants," dit le professeur.
"Good morning, children," says the teacher.

---

bon marché [bohń-mar-SHAY]   **cheap(ly), inexpensive(ly)**
adjective, adverb

On vend le pain bon marché; il ne coûte pas cher.
Bread is cheap; it is not expensive.

---

bonne adjective, fem.   (See **bon**)
de bonne heure   (See **heure**)

---

la bonne [BUHN] noun, fem.   **maid, cleaning woman**

La bonne nettoie la maison.
The maid cleans the house.

---

bonsoir [bohń-SWAR] interjection   **Good evening!**

Quand Papa retourne à la maison à neuf heures, il dit: "Bonsoir!"
When Father returns home at nine o'clock, he says, "Good evening!"

---

le bord [BUHR] noun, masc.   **edge; shore**

Je suis assis au bord du lac.
I am seated on the shore of the lake.

---

la botte [BUHT] noun, fem.   **boot**

Quand il neige je mets mes bottes.
When it snows I put on my boots.

---

la bouche [BOOSH] noun, fem.   **mouth**

L'enfant ouvre la bouche quand il pleure.
The child opens his mouth when he cries.

le boucher [boo-SHAY] noun, masc.   **butcher**

Le boucher vend la viande.
The butcher sells meat.

---

la boucherie [boo-SHREE] noun, fem.   **butcher shop**

On va à la boucherie pour acheter de la viande.
You go to the butcher shop to buy meat.

---

la boue [BOO] noun, fem.   **mud**

Mes mains sont couvertes de boue!
My hands are covered with mud!

---

le boulanger [boo-lahń-ZHAY] noun, masc.   **baker**

Le boulanger fait le pain.
The baker makes bread.

---

la boulangerie [boo-lahń-ZHREE] noun, fem.   **bakery**

On va à la boulangerie pour acheter du pain.
You go to the bakery to buy bread.

---

le boulevard [bool-VAR] noun, masc.   **boulevard,**
                                  wide street
*Les étudiants se promènent sur le
boulevard St-Michel à Paris.*
Students walk on the Boulevard St. Michel in Paris.

---

le bouquet [boo-KEH] noun, masc.   **bunch of flowers,**
                                     bouquet
"Voici un bouquet, Marthe," dit François.
"Here is a bunch of flowers, Martha," says Frank.

---

la bouteille [boo-TAY] noun, fem.   **bottle**

Attention! La bouteille est en verre.
Be careful! The bottle is made of glass.

---

la boutique [boo-TEEK] noun, fem.   **small store, shop**

Pardon. Où se trouve la boutique de
monsieur Le Blanc?
Excuse me. Where is Mr. Le Blanc's shop?

---

le bouton [boo-TOHN] noun, masc.   **button; (light)switch;**
                                                        doorknob;
Ce manteau a seulement trois boutons.   **doorbell**
This coat has only three buttons.

Nous voici à la porte de Virginie. Où est le bouton?
Here we are at Virginia's house. Where is the doorbell?

---

la branche [BRAHNSH] noun, fem.   **branch**

L'arbre a beaucoup de branches.
The tree has many branches.

---

le bras [BRA] noun, masc.   **arm**

L'homme a mal au bras.
The man has a sore arm.

---

bravo [bra-VOH] interjection   **Well done! Hurray!**

Arnaud répond bien à la question.
Le professeur dit: "Bravo!"
Arnold answers the question well.
"Well done!" says the teacher.

---

la brioche [BRYUHSH] noun, fem.   **roll**

Susanne prend une brioche pour le petit déjeuner.
Susan eats a roll for breakfast.

---

la brosse [BRUHS] noun, fem.   **brush**

*La brosse à cheveux est plus grande que la
brosse à dents.*
The hairbrush is bigger than the toothbrush.

---

se brosser [sé-bruh-SAY] verb   **to brush (oneself)**

je me brosse	nous nous brossons
tu te brosses	vous vous brossez
il, elle se brosse	ils, elles se brossent

Laure se brosse les cheveux.
Laura is brushing her hair.

---

le brouillard [broo-YAR] noun, masc.   **fog**

Il est difficile de voir à cause du brouillard.
It is difficult to see because of the fog.

---

le bruit [BREW/EE] noun, masc.   **noise**

Le tonnerre fait un grand bruit.
Thunder makes a loud noise.

---

brûler [brew-lay] verb   **to burn**

je brûle	nous brûlons
tu brûles	vous brûlez
il, elle brûle	ils, elles brûlent

On brûle du bois dans la cheminée.
We burn wood in the fireplace.

---

brun [BRUHN] adjective, masc.   **brown**
brune [BREWN] fem.

Le garçon a les cheveux bruns.
The boy has brown hair.

---

le buffet [buh-FEH] noun, masc.   **cupboard, sideboard**

Il y a des assiettes dans le buffet.
There are plates in the cupboard.

---

le bureau [bew-ROH] noun, masc.   **desk; office**

Le bureau du professeur est grand.
The teacher's desk is big.

Voici le bureau d'une grande compagnie.
Here is the office of a large company.

le bureau de poste [bew-ROH-dé-PUHST]   **post office**
noun, masc.

*On va au bureau de poste pour mettre un colis
à la poste.*
You go to the post office to mail a package.

C

ça (See **cela**)

---

la cacahuète [ka-ka-WEHT] noun, fem.   **peanut**

L'éléphant aime manger les cacahuètes.
The elephant likes to eat peanuts.

---

cacher [ka-SHAY] verb   **to hide**

je cache	nous cachons
tu caches	vous cachez
il, elle cache	ils, elles cachent

Le garçon cache les fleurs derrière lui.
The boy is hiding the flowers behind him.

jouer à cache-cache [zhoo-AY-ah-kash-KASH]   **to play**
idiomatic expression   **hide-and-seek**
                                  (See **jouer***)*
Les enfants jouent à cache-cache.
The children are playing hide-and-seek.

---

le cadeau [ka-DOH] noun, masc.   **gift, present**
les cadeaux pl.

Voici un cadeau pour votre anniversaire.
Here is a birthday gift.

---

le café [ka-FAY] noun, masc.   **coffee; café,**
                                 small restaurant
Voulez-vous du café?
Do you want some coffee?

Il y a un café au coin de la rue.
There is a café on the corner.

---

le cahier [ka-YAY] noun, masc.   **notebook**
Elle écrit ses devoirs dans un cahier.
She writes her homework in a notebook.

le calendrier [ka-lah*n*-DRYAY] noun, masc.   **calendar**
Selon le calendrier c'est aujourd'hui le 12 mai.
According to the calendar, today is May 12th.

---

le camarade [ka-ma-RAD] noun, masc.   **close friend, pal**
Mon camarade et moi, nous allons jouer au parc.
My friend and I are going to the park to play.

---

le camion [ka-MYOH*n*] noun, masc.   **truck**
Le camion fait beaucoup de bruit.
The truck makes a lot of noise.

---

la campagne [kah*n*-PA<u>N</u>] noun, fem.   **country**
                                                (opposite of city)
If fait beau. Allons à la campagne!
It's nice weather. Let's go to the country!

---

le canapé [ka-na-PAY] noun, masc.   **sofa**

Le canapé est très confortable.
The sofa is very comfortable.

---

le canard [ka-NAR] noun, masc.   **duck**
Voilà des canards sur le lac.
There are some ducks on the lake.

---

le canif [ka-NEEF] noun, masc.   **pocketknife, jackknife**
Avez-vous un canif?
Do you have a pocketknife? (See **couteau**)

---

le caoutchouc [ka-oo-TSHOO] noun, masc.   **rubber**

Il pleut. Il faut que je mette mes bottes en caoutchouc.
It is raining. I have to put on my rubbers.

en caoutchouc [ahń-ka-oo-TSHOO]   **made of rubber**

---

la capitale [ka-pee-TAL] noun, fem.   **capital**

Savez-vous le nom de la capitale de la France?
Do you know the name of the capital of France?

> Paris is the capital of France.
>
> Paris est la capitale de la France.

---

la carotte [ka-RUHT] noun, fem.   **carrot**

Le lapins mangent des carottes.
Rabbits eat carrots.

---

carré [ka-RAY] adjective, masc.   **square**
carrée fem.

La boite est carrée.
The box is square.

---

la carte [KART] noun, fem.   **map; playing card; postcard; card; menu**

*Avez-vous une carte des routes de
la France?*
Do you have a road map of France?

Savez-vous jouer aux cartes?
Do you know how to play cards?

Ces cartes postales sont jolies.
These postcards are pretty.

---

casser [ka-SAY] verb   **to break**

je casse	nous cassons
tu casses	vous cassez
il, elle casse	ils, elles cassent

Attention! Ne casse pas l'assiette!
Be careful! Don't break the plate!

---

cause [KOHZ] noun, fem.   **cause**
à cause de [a-KOHZ-dé]   **because of**

Je dois rester à la maison à cause de la neige.
I have to stay home because of the snow.

---

la cave [KAV] noun, fem.   **basement, cellar**

Il y a plusieurs paquets dans la cave.
There are several packages in the cellar.

---

le CD [say-day] noun, masc.   **CD**

C'est un nouveau CD?
Is that a new CD?

le lecture CD noun, masc.   **CD player**

---

ce [SE] adjective, masc.   **this**
cette [SEHT] fem.
ces [SAY] masc., pl.
cet [SEHT] masc. form before a vowel

Cette petite fille est sage.
This little girl is well behaved.

c'est [SEH]   **it is, this is**

C'est aujourd'hui mercredi.
Today it is Wednesday.

c'est dommage (See **dommage**)
c'est triste (See **triste**)

---

ceci [sé-SEE] pronoun   **this**

Mmm, ceci est bon!
Mmm, this is good!

---

la ceinture [sain-TEWR] noun, fem.   **belt**

Tiens! Tu portes une nouvelle ceinture!
Well! You're wearing a new belt!

---

cela [SLA]   **that**

Je n'aime pas cela!
I don't like that!

---

célèbre [say-LEHBR] adjective   **famous**

Le président des Etats-Unis est célèbre.
The President of the United States is famous.

> Victor Hugo was a famous French writer of the nineteenth century.
>
> Victor Hugo était un célèbre écrivain français du 19ème siècle.

---

le céleri [sayl-REE] noun, masc.   **celery**

On fait une salade avec du céleri.
We make a salad with celery.

---

celui [sé-LEWEE] pronoun, masc.   **the one that,**
ceux [SEOH] masc., pl.   **the one who**
celle [SEHL] fem.
celles [SEHL] fem., pl.

Voici un stylo rouge. Celui de mon père est jaune.
Here is a red pen. The one that belongs to my father
is yellow.

Voici une règle rouge. Celles qui sont sur la table
sont jaunes.
Here is a red ruler. Those that are on the table
are yellow.

---

cent [SAHN] adjective   **one hundred**

Il y a cent personnes à la foire!
There are a hundred people at the fair!

---

le cerceau [sehr-SOH] noun, masc.   **hoop**

Le garçon roule un grand cerceau.
The boy is rolling a big hoop.

---

le cercle [SEHRKL] noun, masc.   **circle**

Les garçons forment un cercle pour jouer.
The boys form a circle to play.

---

le cerf-volant [sehr-vuh-LAHN] noun, masc.   **kite**
les cerfs-volants pl.

Bon, il fait du vent. Allons jouer avec un cerf-volant.
Good, it's windy. Let's play with a kite.

---

la cerise [sé-REEZN] noun, fem.   **cherry**

Je vais cueillir des cerises.
I am going to pick cherries.

---

chacun [sha-KUHN] pronoun, masc.   **each one**
chacune [sha-KEWN] fem.

Voilà cinq jeunes filles; chacune a une fleur.
Here are five girls; each one has a flower.

> Proverb: Everyone has his or her preference.
>
> Un proverbe: Chacun à son goût.

---

la chaise [SHEHZ] noun, fem.   **chair**

Cette chaise est trop grande pour moi.
This chair is too big for me.

---

la chambre [SHAHMBR] noun, fem.   **bedroom**

Cet appartement a trois chambres.
This apartment has three bedrooms.

---

le champ [SHAHM] noun, masc.   **field**

C'est un champ de blé, n'est-ce pas?
It's a field of wheat, isn't it?

---

la chance [SHAHNS] noun, fem.   **luck**
Bonne chance! [buhn-SHAHNS] interjection! Good luck!

Avant l'examen mon ami dit: "Bonne chance!"
Before the examination my friend says, "Good luck."

avoir de la chance   **to be lucky** (See **avoir**)

Le garçon gagne un prix. Il a de la chance.
The boy wins a prize. He is lucky.

---

le chandail [shahn-DAHY] noun, masc.   **sweater**

Je porte un chandail parce qu'il fait frais.
I am wearing a sweater because it is cool.

40

changer [shahn-ZHAY] verb   **to change**

je change	*nous changeons*
tu changes	*vous changez*
il, elle change	*ils, elles changent*

Il faut changer de train.
We have to change to another train.

---

la chanson [shahn-SOHN] noun, fem.   **song**

Quelle chanson préférez-vous?
Which song do you prefer?

> The "Marseillaise" is the national anthem of France.
>
> La Marseillaise est la chanson nationale de la France.

---

chanter [shahn-TAY] verb   **to sing**

je chante	nous chantons
tu chantes	vous chantez
il, elle chante	ils, elles chantent

Je chante et les oiseaux chantent.
I am singing and the birds are singing.

41

le chapeau [sha-POH] noun, masc.　　　　　　　　**hat**

Quel joli chapeau!
What a pretty hat!

---

chaque [SHAK] adjective　　　　　　　　　**each, every**

Je mets une fourchette à chaque place.
I put a fork at each place.

---

le chasseur [sha-SEUHR] noun, masc.　　　　　　**hunter**

Le chasseur entre dans la forêt.
The hunter goes into the forest.

---

le chat [SHA] noun, masc.　　　　　　　　　　　**cat**

Les chats aiment le lait.
Cats like milk.

> Proverb: When the cat is away, the mice play.
>
> Un proverbe: Quand le chat n'est pas là, les souris dansent.

---

le chaton [sha-TOHN] noun, masc.　　　　　　　**kitten**

le château [sha-TOH] noun, masc.　　　　　**castle, palace**

Le roi habite un grand château.
The king lives in a large palace.

---

chaud [SHOH] adjective, masc.   **hot, warm**
chaude [SHOHD] fem.

Il fait chaud aujourd'hui. Allons nager. (See **faire**)
It's hot today. Let's go swimming.

Le garçon a chaud. Il va nager. (See **avoir**)
The boy is hot. He is going swimming.

---

le chauffeur [shoh-FEUHR] noun, masc.   **driver**

Le chauffeur s'arrête quand le feu est rouge.
The driver stops when the light is red.

---

la chaussette [shoh-SEHT] noun, fem.   **sock**

Je voudrais acheter une paire de chaussettes.
I would like to buy a pair of socks.

---

la chaussure [shoh-SEWR] noun, fem.   **shoe**

Je n'aime pas ces chaussures!
I don't like these shoes!

---

le chef [SHEHF] noun, masc.   **leader**

Mais non! Tu joues toujours le rôle du chef.
No! You're always playing the leader.

---

le chemin [SHMAIN] noun, masc.   **road**

C'est le chemin de la ville?
Is this the road to town?

le chemin de fer [SHMAIN-dé-FEHR] noun, masc.   **railroad**

Pour aller à Marseille, je prends le chemin de fer.
To go to Marseilles, I take the railroad.

---

la cheminée [shé-mee-NAY] noun, fem.   **fireplace; chimney**

Les chaussures sont près de la cheminée.
The shoes are near the fireplace.

---

la chemise [SHMEEZ] noun, fem.   **(man's) shirt**

Le garçon porte une chemise blanche.
The boy is wearing a white shirt.

---

cher [SHEHR] adjective, masc.   **dear; expensive**
chère fem.

Je commence une lettre à Maman avec les mots:
"Chère Maman."
I begin a letter to Mother with the words,
"Dear Mother."

Cette bicyclette est trop chère.
This bicycle is too expensive.

---

chercher [shehr-SHAY] verb   **to look for**
  je cherche   nous cherchons
  tu cherches   vous cherchez
  il, elle cherche   ils, elles cherchent

Papa cherche toujours ses clefs.
Father is always looking for his keys.

---

le cheval [SHVAL] noun, masc.   **horse**
les chevaux [SHVOH] pl.

Le soldat monte à cheval.
The solider rides on a horse.

---

le cheveu [SHVEOH] noun, masc.   **hair**
les cheveux pl.

Les étudiants à l'université aiment les cheveux longs.
Students at the university like long hair.

---

la chèvre [SHEHVR] noun, fem.   **goat**

Le fermier a une chèvre.
The farmer has a goat.

---

chez [SHAY] preposition   **to (or at) the house of**

Je vais manger chez mon oncle.
I am going to eat at my uncle's house.

chez moi [shay-MWA] idiomatic expression   **to (or at) my house**

Viens chez moi tout de suite.
Come to my house immediately.

---

le chien [SHYAIN] noun, masc.   **dog**

As-tu un chien?
Do you have a dog?

le petit chien [ptee-SHYAIN] noun, masc.   **puppy**

le chocolat [shuh-kuh-LA] noun, masc.   **chocolate**

Comment? Tu n'aimes pas les chocolats?
What? You don't like chocolates?

choisir [shwa-ZEER] verb   **to choose**

je choisis	nous choisissons
tu choisis	vous choisissez
il, elle choisit	ils, elles choisissent

Dans l'examen, choisissez la réponse correcte.
On the examination, choose the correct answer.

la chose [SHOHZ] noun, fem.   **thing**

On vend toutes sortes de choses dans cette boutique.
They sell all kinds of things in this store.

le chou [SHOO] noun, masc.   **cabbage**

Préférez-vous le chou ou les carottes?
Do you prefer cabbage or carrots?

le ciel [SYEHL] noun, masc.   **sky**

Je vois la lune dans le ciel.
I see the moon in the sky.

la cigarette [see-ga-REHT] noun, fem.   **cigarette**

Est-ce que ton oncle fume des cigarettes?
Does your uncle smoke cigarettes?

le cinéma [see-nay-MAH] noun, masc.   **movies, film**

Il y a un bon film au cinéma.
There is a good film at the movies.

cinq [SAID̸, SAID̸K] adjective   **five**

La main a cinq doigts. [SAID̸]
The hand has five fingers.

Voici cinq enfants. [SAID̸K]
Here are five children.

J'en ai cinq. [SAID̸K]
I've got five.

cinquante [saiń-KAHŃT] adjective   **fifty**

Il y a cinquante états dans le Etats-Unis.
There are fifty states in the United States.

la circulation [seer-kew-la-SYOHŃ] noun, fem.   **traffic**

La circulation s'arrête au feu rouge.
The traffic stops for the red light.

le cirque [SEERK] noun, masc.   **circus**

Il ya a beaucoup d'animaux au cirque.
There are many animals at the circus.

les ciseaux [see-ZOH] noun, masc., pl.   **scissors**

Je coupe le papier avec les ciseaux.
I cut the paper with scissors.

le citron [see-TROHÑ] noun, masc.   **lemon**

Les citrons sont jaunes.
Lemons are yellow.

---

la citrouille [see-TROOY] noun, fem.   **pumpkin**

C'est une grosse citrouille.
This is a big pumpkin.

---

clair [KLEHR] adjective, masc.   **light, clear**
claire fem.

Quelle belle journée claire!
What a beautiful, clear day!

---

la classe [KLAS] noun, fem.   **class**
la salle de classe noun, fem.   **classroom** (See **salle**)

Nous sommes dans la salle de classe.
We are in the classroom.

---

la clef [KLAY] noun, fem. (sometimes spelled **clé**)   **key**

Où est ma clef?
Where is my key?

---

la cloche [KLUHSH] noun, fem.   **bell**

A midi la cloche sonne.
The bell rings at noon.

---

le clou [KLOO] noun, masc.   **nail (metal)**

Mon frère joue avec des clous et un marteau.
My brother plays with nails and a hammer.

---

le clown [KLOON] noun, masc.   **clown**

Quand je suis au cirque je dis "Bonjour" au clown.
When I am at the circus I say "Hello" to the clown.

---

le cochon [kuh-SHOHN] noun, masc.   **pig**

Le fermier a trois cochons.
The farmer has three pigs.

---

le coeur [KEUHR] noun, masc.   **heart**

Regardez tous les coeurs sur la carte!
Look at all the hearts on the (playing) card!

---

le coin [KWAIN] noun, masc.   **corner**

Il faut traverser la rue au coin.
You must cross the street at the corner.

---

le colin-maillard [kuh-lain-mah-YAR]   **blindman's buff**
noun, masc.

jouer à colin-maillard   **to play blindman's buff**
[kuh-lain-mah-YAR] idiomatic expression   (See **jouer**)

Oui, je voudrais jouer à colin-maillard.
Yes, I'd like to play blindman's buff.

---

le colis [kuh-LEE] noun, masc.   **package**

Ah, bon! Un colis pour moi!
Oh, good! A package for me!

---

coller [kuh-LAY] verb   **to paste, to glue**

je colle	nous collons
tu colles	vous collez
il, elle colle	ils, elles collent

Je colle une image sur une page de mon cahier.
I glue a picture to a page of my notebook.

---

la colonie de vacances   **camp**
[kuh-luh-need-va-KAHNS] noun, fem.

*Mon cousin passe huit semaines à la colonie
de vacances.*
My cousin spends eight weeks at camp.

---

colorier [kuh-luh-ree-AY] verb   **to color**

je colorie	nous colorions
tu colories	vous coloriez
il, elle colorie	ils, elles colorient

Nous colorions avec les crayons de couleur.
We color with crayons.

---

combien [kohn-BYAIN] adverb   **how much, how many**

Combien de jouets as-tu?
How many toys do you have?

---

commander [kuh-mahn-DAY] verb   **to order,
to command**

je commande	nous commandons
tu commandes	vous commandez
il, elle commande	ils, elles commandent

Au restaurant Papa commande le dîner.
In the restaurant Father orders dinner.

---

comme [KUHM] preposition   **for, as**

Comme dessert, elle prend une glace au chocolat.
For dessert she has chocolate ice cream.

---

commencer [kuh-mahń-SAY] verb   **to begin, to start**
  je commence   nous commençons
  tu commences   vous commencez
  il, elle commence   ils, elles commencent

La classe de français commence à neuf heures.
The French class begins at nine o'clock.

---

comment [kuh-MAHŃ] adverb   **how; what?**

Comment allez-vous?
How are you?

Comment?
What?

---

la compagnie [kohń-pa-<u>NEE</u>] noun, fem.   **company**

La Compagnie Bardot se trouve au coin de la rue.
The Bardot Company is located on the corner
(of the street).

---

la compétition [kohń-pay-tee-SYOŃ] noun, fem.   **contest**

Jeanne va gagner la compétition.
Jeanne is going to win the contest.

---

le complet [kohń-PLEH] noun, masc.   **suit**

Papa porte un complet quand il va au travail.
Dad wears a suit when he goes to work.

---

comprendre [kohń-PRAHŃDR] verb   **to understand**
  je comprends   nous comprenons
  tu comprends   vous comprenez
  il, elle comprend   ils, elles comprennent

Tu comprends la leçon d'aujourd'hui?
Do you understand today's lesson?

---

compter [kohⁿ-TAY] verb   **to count**
   je compte   nous comptons
   tu comptes   vous comptez
   il, elle compte   ils, elles comptent

Il sait compter de cinq à un: cinq, quatre,
trois, deux, un.
He knows how to count from five to one: five,
four, three, two, one.

---

le concours noun, masc.   **contest** (See **compétition**)

---

conduire [kohⁿ-DEW/EER] verb   **to drive**
   je conduis   nous conduisons
   tu conduis   vous conduisez
   il, elle conduit   ils, elles conduisent

Hélas! Je suis trop jeune pour conduire l'auto.
Too bad! I am too young to drive the car.

se conduire verb   **to behave**
   je me conduis   nous nous conduisons
   tu te conduis   vous vous conduisez
   il, elle se conduit   ils, elles se conduisent

Les enfants se conduisent bien à table.
The children behave well at the table.

---

la confiture [kohⁿ-fee-TEWR] noun, fem.   **jam**

Donnez-moi un morceau de pain avec de
la confiture aux fraises, s'il vous plaît.
Please give me a piece of bread with strawberry jam.

---

confortable [kohⁿ-fuhr-TABL] adjective   **comfortable**

Mon lit est très confortable.
My bed is very comfortable.

---

le conseiller [kohń-say-YAY] noun, masc.   **counselor**
la consellère [kohń-say-YEHR] fem.

Mon conseiller s'appelle M. Blanc.
My counselor's name is Mr. Blanc.

---

le congé [kohń-ZHAY] noun, masc.   **leave of absence**
un jour de congé   **a day off** (See **jour**)

---

connaître [kuh-NEHTR] verb   **to know** (information),
                                     to be acquainted

je connais	nous connaissons
tu connais	vous connaissez
il, elle connaît	ils, elles connaissent

                                 with

Connais-tu mon maître?
Do you know my teacher?

See also: savoir

---

le conte [KOHŃT] noun, masc.   **story, tale**

Lisez-moi le conte des "Trois petits chatons."
Read me the story of the "Three Little Kittens."

le conte de fées   **fairy tale** (See **la fée**)

---

content [kohń-TAHŃ] adjective, masc.   **happy, glad**
contente [kohń-TAHŃT] fem.

La petite fille n'est pas contente.
The little girl is not happy.

---

continuer [kohn-tee-new-AY] verb   **to continue**

je continue	nous continuons
tu continues	vous continuez
il, elle continue	ils, elles continuent

Je continue à jouer du piano jusqu'à cinq heures.
I will continue to play the piano until five o'clock.

---

contre [KOHⁿTR] preposition   **against**

Henri met le miroir contre le mur.
Henry puts the mirror against the wall.

---

copier [kuh-PYAY] verb   **to copy**

je copie	nous copions
tu copies	vous copiez
il, elle copie	ils, elles copient

Il faut copier les phrases qui sont au tableau noir.
We have to copy the sentences that are on the blackboard.

---

le coq [KUHK] noun, masc.   **rooster**

Le coq se lève de bonne heure.
The rooster gets up early.

---

le coquillage [kuhk-KYAZH] noun, masc.   **shell**

Je cherche des coquillages à la plage.
I am looking for shells at the beach.

---

la corde [KUHRD] noun, fem.   **rope**
sauter à la corde   **to jump rope** (See **sauter**)

Marie, Jeanne, et moi, nous sautons à la corde.
Mary, Joan, and I are jumping rope.

---

correct [kuh-REHKT] adjective, masc.   **correct**
correcte fem.

Le professeur dit: "Ecrivez la réponse correcte."
The teacher says, "Write the correct answer."

le côté [koh-TAY] noun, masc.   **side**

à côté de [a-koh-TAY de/] preposition   **next to,**

Dans le restaurant Pierre est assis   **at the side of**
à côté de Caroline.
At the restaurant Peter is seated next to Carolyn.

---

la côtelette [koh-TLEHT] noun, fem.   **cutlet, chop**

Préfères-tu une côtelette de veau ou de mouton?
Do you prefer a veal cutlet or a lamb chop?

---

le coton [kuh-TOHꟼ] noun, masc.   **cotton**

en coton   **made of cotton**

Il porte une chemise en coton.
He is wearing a cotton shirt.

---

le cou [KOO] noun, masc.   **neck**

Ma grand'mère dit: "J'ai mal au cou."
My grandmother says, "My neck hurts."

---

se coucher [sé-koo-SHAY] verb   **to go to bed;**

je me couche	nous nous couchons	**to set (sun)**
tu te couches	vous vous couchez	
il, elle se couche	ils, elles se couchent	

Je n'aime pas me coucher de bonne heure.
I don't like to go to bed early.

Le soleil se couche.
The sun is setting.

---

coudre [KOODR] verb   **to sew**

je couds	nous cousons
tu couds	vous cousez
il, elle coud	ils, elles cousent

l'aiguille à coudre   **sewing needle** (See **l'aiguille**)

Maman coud avec une aiguille à coudre.
Mother sews with a sewing needle.

la couleur [koo-LEUHR] noun, fem.   **color**

De quelle couleur est la banane?
What color is the banana?

blanc	white
bleu	blue
brun	brown (for hair, eyes)
gris	gray
jaune	yellow
marron	brown
noir	black
orange	orange
rose	pink
rouge	red
vert	green
violet	purple, violet

---

le coup [koo] noun, masc.   **blow; knock**

On frappe deux coups à la porte. Qui est là?
There are two knocks on the door. Who's there?

tout à coup   **suddenly** (See **tout**)
le coup de pied [KOOD-PYAY]   **kick**

Il donne un coup de pied à la balle.
He kicks the ball.

---

couper [koo-PAY] verb   **to cut**

je coupe	nous coupons
tu coupes	vous coupez
il, elle coupe	ils, elles coupent

Papa coupe le pain avec un couteau.
Dad cuts the bread with a knife.

---

courageux [koo-ra-ZHEOH] adjective, masc.   **courageous,**
courageuse [koo-ra-ZHEOHZ] fem.   **brave**

Le prince est courageux quand il sauve la princesse.
The prince is brave when he saves the princess.

---

courir [koo-REER] verb   **to run**

je cours	nous courons
tu cours	vous courez
il, elle court	ils, elles courent

Ils courent à la gare parce qu'ils sont en retard.
They are running to the station because they are late.

---

court [KOOR] adjective, masc.   **short**
courte [KOORT] fem.

Une règle est courte; l'autre est longue.
One ruler is short; the other is long.

---

le cousin [koo-ZAIN] noun, masc.   **cousin**
la cousine [koo-ZEEN] fem.

*Mon cousin Paul a dix ans et ma cousine
Marie a dix-huit ans.*
My cousin Paul is ten years old and my cousin
Mary is eighteen.

---

le couteau [koo-TOH] noun, masc.   **knife**
les couteaux pl.

Elle met un couteau à chaque place sur la table.
She puts a knife at each place at the table.

---

coûter [koo-TAY] verb   **to cost**

il, elle coûte	ils, elles coûtent

Combien coûte ce peigne?
How much does this comb cost?

---

couvert [koo-VEHR] adjective, masc.   **covered**
couverte [koo-VEHRT] fem.

L'arbre est couvert de neige.
The tree is covered with snow.

Il est couvert.
It is cloudy.

---

mettre le couvert   **to set the table** (See **mettre**)

---

la couverture [koo-vehr-TEWR] noun, fem.   **cover, blanket**

En hiver j'aime une couverture chaude sur le lit.
In winter I like a warm blanket on my bed.

---

la craie [KREH] noun, fem.   **chalk**

Le garçon écrit au tableau noir avec la craie.
The boy is writing on the blackboard with chalk.

---

la cravate [kra-VAT] noun, fem.   **tie**

La cravate de Papa est trop grande pour moi.
Daddy's tie is too big for me.

---

le crayon [kray-YOHN] noun, masc.   **pencil**

Donnez-moi un crayon, s'il vous plaît.
Please give me a pencil.

le crayon de couleur   **crayon**
[kray-yohn-dkoo-LEUHR] noun, masc.

Je dessine avec les crayons de couleur.
I draw with crayons.

---

crier [kree-AY] verb   **to shout, to scream**
   je crie   nous crions
   tu cries   vous criez
   il, elle crie   ils, elles crient

Maman crie: "Viens vite!"
Mom shouts, "Come quickly!"

---

croire [KRWAR] verb   **to believe**
   je crois   nous croyons
   tu crois   vous croyez
   il, elle croit   ils, elles croient

Je crois que je peux aller au cinéma.
I believe I can go to the movies.

---

le croissant [krwa-SAHN] noun, masc.   **croissant**

Henriette prend un croissant pour le petit déjeuner.
Harriet has a croissant for breakfast.

---

cueillir [keuh-YEER] verb   **to pick, to gather**
  je cueille   nous cueillons
  tu cueilles   vous cueillez
  il, elle cueille   ils, elles cueillent

Il va cueillir des pommes.
He is going to pick some apples.

---

la cuiller [kew/ee-YEHR] noun, fem.   **spoon**
(sometimes spelled **cuillère**)

Je n'ai pas de cuiller.
I don't have a spoon.

---

le cuir [KEW/EER] noun, masc.   **leather**
en cuir   **made of leather**

La veste de mon frère est en cuir.
My brother's jacket is made of leather.

---

la cuisine [kew/ee-ZEEN] noun, fem.   **kitchen**

La cuisine est petite.
The kitchen is small.

faire la cuisine   **to cook** (See **faire**)

---

curieux [kew-RYEOH] adjective, masc.   **curious**
curieuse [kew-RYEOHZ] fem.

Elle est curieuse. Elle voudrait ouvrir le paquet.
She is curious. She would like to open the package.

D

la dame [DAHM] noun, fem.   **lady**

Qui est cette dame?
Who is this lady?

jouer aux dames   **to play checkers**
(See **jouer**)

---

dangereux [dahń-ZHREOH] adjective, masc.   **dangerous**
dangereuse [dahń-ZHREOHZ] fem.

*Il est dangereux de courir dans la rue pour
attraper une balle.*
It is dangerous to run into the street to catch a ball.

---

dans [DAHŃ] preposition   **in, into**

Ils entrent dans l'école.
They go into the school.

---

danser [dahń-SAY] verb   **to dance**
   je danse   nous dansons
   tu danses   vous dansez
   il, elle danse   ils, elles dansent

Ma soeur aime danser.
My sister likes to dance.

---

la date [DAT] noun, fem.   **date**

Quelle ese la date?
What is the date?

---

de [dé] preposition   **from; of; some;**
                                      any (also shows possession)
du [DEW] masc. (contraction of de + le)
de la fem. [dé-LA]
des [DAY] pl. (contraction of de + les)

Elle vient de Paris.
She comes from Paris.

Voulez-vous du pain?
Do you want any bread?

C'est le ballon de mon frère.
It's my brother's balloon.

Elle va acheter des pommes de terre.
She is going to buy some potatoes.

---

debout [dé-BOO] adverb   **standing**

Dans la salle de classe la maîtresse est debout.
In the classroom the teacher is standing.

---

décembre [day-SAHMBR] noun, masc.   **December**

Il fait froid en décembre.
It is cold in December.

---

décorer [day-kuh-RAY] verb   **to decorate**
  je décore   nous décorons
  tu décores   vous décorez
  il, elle décore   ils, elles décorent

Il décore sa bicyclette.
He is decorating his bicycle.

---

défense de [day-FAHNS-de]   **It is forbidden to,**
idiomatic expression   **No...**

défense d'entrer [day-FAHNS-dahn-TRAY]   **No admittance**
idiomatic expression

Défense d'entrer. Nous ne pouvons pas entrer.
No admittance. We cannot enter.

défense de fumer   **No smoking**
[day-FAHNS-dé-few-MAY] idiomatic expression

Défense de fumer à l'école.
No smoking in school.

---

le défilé [day-fee-LAY] noun, masc.   **parade**

Nous marchons dans le défilé.
We walk in the parade.

---

dehors [dé-UHR] preposition   **outside**

Mon ami m'attend dehors.
My friend is waiting for me outside.

---

déjà [day-ZHA] adverb   **already**

Il est déjà l'heure de partir?
It is already time to leave?

---

le déjeuner [day-zheuh-NAY] noun, masc.   **lunch**

Je prends le déjeuner à midi.
I eat lunch at noon.

le petit déjeuner [ptee-day-zheuh-NAY]　　　**breakfast**
noun, masc.

Je prends le petit déjeuner à sept heures et demie.
I eat breakfast at seven thirty.

---

délicieux [day-lee-SYEOH] adjective, masc.　　　**delicious**
délicieuse [day-lee-SYEOHZ] fem.

Le gâteau est délicieux.
The cake is delicious.

---

demain [dé-MAIN] adverb　　　　　　　　　　**tomorrow**

Demain je vais à la colonie de vacances.
Tomorrow I am going to camp.

---

demander [dé-mahn-DAY] verb　　　　　　　　**to ask**
je demande　　　　　nous demandons
tu demandes　　　　vous demandez
il, elle demande　　　ils, elles demandent

Je demande à Papa: "Je peux aller à la foire?"
I ask Father: "May I go to the fair?"

---

demeurer [dé-meuh-RAY] verb　　　　　　　　**to live**
je demeure　　　　　nous demeurons
tu demeures　　　　vous demeurez
il, elle demeure　　　ils, elles demeurent

Où demeurez-vous?
Where do you live?

See also: habiter, vivre

---

demi [dé-MEE] adjective, masc.　　　　　　　**half**
demie fem.
la demi-heure [dé-mee-EUHR] noun, fem.　　**half an hour**

Voilà une demi-heure que je vous attends!
I have been waiting for you for half an hour!

la dent [DAHИ] noun, fem.   **tooth**

J'ai mal aux dents.
I have a toothache.

---

le dentifrice [dahИ-tee-FREES] noun, masc.   **toothpaste**

Maman, je n'aime pas ce dentifrice.
Mom, I don't like this toothpaste.

---

le dentiste [dahИ-TEEST] noun, masc.   **dentist**

Le dentiste dit: "Ouvre la bouche."
The dentist says, "Open your mouth."

---

dépasser [day-pah-SAY] verb   **to pass**

je dépasse	nous dépassons
tu dépasses	vous dépassez
il, elle dépasse	ils, elles dépassent

L'auto dépasse le camion.
The car passes the truck.

---

se dépêcher [sé-day-peh-SHAY] verb   **to hurry**

je me dépêche	nous nous dépêchons
tu te dépêches	vous vous dépêchez
il, elle se dépêche	ils, elles se dépêchent

Ils se dépêchent parce qu'ils sont en retard.
They hurry because they are late.

depuis [dé-ᴘᴇᴡ/ᴇᴇ] preposition   **for**

Elle attend sa tante depuis une heure.
She has been waiting for her aunt for an hour.

---

de rien   **you're welcome** (See **rien**)

---

dernier [dehr-ɴʏᴀʏ] noun, adjective, masc.   **last one; last**
dernière [dehr-ɴʏᴇʜʀ] fem.

Paul est le dernier à s'asseoir à table.
Paul is the last one to sit down at the table.

C'est mon dernier franc!
It is my last franc!

---

derrière [deh-ʀʏᴇʜʀ] preposition   **behind**

Caroline est derrière la chaise.
Carolyn is behind the chair.

---

descendre [deh-ꜱᴀʜɴᴅʀ] verb   **to go down**
  je descends   nous descendons
  tu descends   vous descendez
  il, elle descend   ils, elles descendent

L'homme descend de la montagne.
The man goes down the mountain.

---

le désert [day-ᴢᴇʜʀ] noun, masc.   **desert**

Le désert est très sec.
The desert is very dry.

---

désirer [day-zee-ʀᴀʏ] verb   **to wish, to want**
  je désire   nous désirons
  tu désires   vous désirez
  il, elle désire   ils, elles désirent

Monsieur désire?
What do you wish, sir?

---

le dessert [deh-SEHR] noun, masc.   **dessert**

Comme dessert je désire une tarte aux fraises.
I would like to have a strawberry tart for dessert.

> There are some famous French desserts such as *chocolate mousse* and *crêpes suzettes.*
>
> Il y a des fameux desserts français comme "la mousse au chocolat," et "les crêpes suzettes."

---

dessiner [deh-see-NAY] verb   **to draw**

je dessine	nous dessinons
tu dessines	vous dessinez
il, elle dessine	ils, elles dessinent

Va au tableau noir et dessine une maison.
Go to the blackboard and draw a house.

---

détester [day-tehs-TAY] verb   **to hate, to detest**

je déteste	nous détestons
tu détestes	vous détestez
ile, elle déteste	ils, elles détestent

Il déteste les épinards.
He hates spinach.

---

deux [DEOH] adjective   **two**

Je vois deux chats.
I see two cats.

deux fois   **twice** (See **la fois**)

---

deuxième [deoh-ZYEHM] adjective   **second**

Quel est le nom du deuxième mois de l'année?
What is the name of the second month of the year?

---

devant [dé-VAHÑ] preposition   **in front of**

Il y a une table devant le canapé.
There is a table in front of the sofa.

---

devenir [dév-NEER] verb   **to become**
  je deviens   nous devenons
  tu deviens   vous devenez
  il, elle devient   ils, elles deviennent

Il voudrait devenir médecin.
He would like to become a doctor.

---

deviner [dé-vee-NAY] verb   **to guess**
  je devine   nous devinons
  tu devines   vous devinez
  il, elle devine   ils, elles devinent

Tu peux deviner combien d'argent j'ai dans la main?
Can you guess how much money I have in my hand?

---

le devoir [dé-VWAR] noun, masc.   **homework; duty**

Nous allons faire nos devoirs ensemble.
We are going to do our homework together.

---

devoir [dé-VWAR] verb   **to have to**
  je dois   nous devons
  tu dois   vous devez
  il, elle doit   ils, elles doivent

Je dois me laver les mains.
I have to wash my hands.

---

le dictionnaire [deek-syohñ-NEHR] noun, masc.   **dictionary**

Ce dictionnaire est très lourd.
This dictionary is very heavy.

---

différent [dee-fay-RAHN] adjective, masc.   **different**
différente [dee-fay-RAHNT] fem.

Ces pains sont différents.
These loaves of bread are different.

---

difficile [dee-fee-SEEL] adjective   **difficult**

Il est difficile de lire cette lettre.
It is difficult to read this letter.

---

le dimanche [dee-MAHNSH] noun, masc.   **Sunday**

Le dimanche nous allons au parc.
We go to the park on Sundays.

---

la dinde [DAIND] noun, masc.   **turkey**

Tu aimes manger la dinde?
Do you like to eat turkey?

---

le dîner [dee-NAY] noun, masc.   **dinner**

Nous prenons le dîner à huit heures.
We eat dinner at eight o'clock.

---

dire [DEER] verb   **to say**

je dis	nous disons
tu dis	vous dites
il, elle dit	ils, elles disent

Le professeur dit "Bonjour" chaque matin.
The teacher says "Good Morning" each morning.

vouloir dire [voo-lwar-DEER] verb   **to mean**

Que veut dire ce mot?
What does this word mean?

diriger [dee-ree-ZHAY] verb   **to direct**
  je dirige   nous dirigeons
  tu diriges   vous dirigez
  il, elle dirige   ils, elles dirigent

Mon frère dirige le jeu.
My brother is directing the game.

---

le disque [DEESK] noun, masc.   **computer disk**
J'utilise des disques pour l'ordinateur   (See **l'ordinateur**)
Apple.
I use disks for the Apple computer.

---

dix [DEES, DEEZ, DEE] adjective   **ten**

Combien de doigts avez-vous? Dix. [DEES]
How many fingers do you have? Ten.

Il a dix abricots. [DEEZ] *(before a vowel)*
He has ten apricots.

Il a dix ballons. [DEE] *(before a consonant)*
He has ten balloons.

---

dix-huit [dee-ZEW/EET] adjective   **eighteen**

Elle a dix-huit ans.
She is eighteen years old.

---

dix-neuf [deez-NEOHF] adjective   **nineteen**

C'est aujourd'hui le dix-neuf septembre.
Today is September 19th.

---

dix-sept [dee-SEHT] adjective   **seventeen**

Neuf et huit font dix-sept.
Nine and eight are seventeen.

---

le docteur [duhk-TEUHR] noun, adjective   **doctor**
Maman dit: "Tu es malade. Je vais appeler le docteur."
Mother says, "You are sick. I am going to call the doctor."

---

le doigt [DWA] noun, masc.   **finger**
Le bébé a dix petits doigts.
The baby has ten little fingers.

---

le dollar [duh-LAR] noun, masc.   **dollar**
Voilà un dollar pour toi.
Here is a dollar for you.

---

les dominos [doh-mee-NOH] noun, masc., pl.   **dominoes**
Mon cousin joue bien aux dominos.
My cousin plays dominoes well.

---

dommage [doh-MAHZH] noun, masc.   **pity**
C'est dommage! [seh-doh-MAHZH]   **That's too bad!**
interjection

Vous n'aimez pas le chocolat?
C'est dommage!
You don't like chocolate?
That's too bad!

---

donner [duh-NAY] verb   **to give**
  je donne   nous donnons
  tu donnes   vous donnez
  il, elle donne   ils, elles donnent

Donne-moi l'appareil, s'il te plaît.
Please give me the camera.

---

dormir [duhr-MEER] verb   **to sleep**
   je dors   nous dormons
   tu dors   vous dormez
   il, elle dort   ils, elles dorment

Tu dors? Je voudrais te parler.
Are you sleeping? I would like to talk to you.

---

le dos [DOH] noun, masc.   **back**

C'est Robert? Je ne sais pas. Je vois seulement son dos.
Is it Robert? I don't know. I see only his back.

---

doucement [doos-MAHИ] adverb   **softly, gently**

Marche doucement. Maman a mal à la tête.
Walk softly. Mother has a headache.

---

la douche [DOOSH] noun, fem.   **shower**

Je prends une douche chaque matin.
I take a shower every. morning.

---

doux [DOO] adjective, masc.   **sweet, soft, gentle**
douce [DOOS] fem.

Ce manteau est très doux.
This coat is very soft.

---

la douzaine [doo-ZEHN] noun, fem.   **dozen**

Elle achète une douzaine de poires.
She is buying a dozen pears.

---

douze [DOOZ] adjective   **twelve**

Il y a douze bananes dans une douzaine.
There are twelve bananas in a dozen.

---

le drapeau [dra-POH] noun, masc.　　　　　　**flag**
les drapeaux pl.

Voilà deux drapeaux dans la salle de classe.
There are two flags in the classroom.

> The French flag has three colors: blue,
> white, and red.
>
> Le drapeau français est tricolore: bleu,
> blanc et rouge.

---

droit [DRWA] adjective, masc.　　　　　　　　**right**
droite [DRWAT] fem.
la main droite [main-DRWAT] noun, fem.　　**right hand**

Je lève la main droite.
I raise my right hand.

à droite [a-DRWAT] preposition　　　　　**to the right**

L'arbre est à droite de la maison.
The tree is to the right of the house.

---

drôle [DROHL] adjective　　　　　　　　**funny; odd**

Les marionnettes sont drôles.
The marionettes are funny.

---

dur [DEWR] adjective, masc.　　　　　　　　**hard**
dure fem.

Cette pomme est trop dure.
This apple is too hard.

---

le DVD [day-vee-day] noun, masc.　　　　　**DVD**

Ce DVD est amusant.
This DVD is amusing.

---

le lecture DVD noun, masc.　　　　　**DVD player**

E

l'eau [OH] noun, fem.   **water**
les eaux pl.

Il y a de l'eau dans la piscine.
There is water in the swimming pool.

échecs [ay-SHEHK] noun, masc., pl.   **chess**
jouer aux échecs   **to play chess** (See **jouer**)

---

l'éclair [ay-KLEHR] noun, masc.   **lightning**
J'ai peur de l'éclair.
I am afraid of lightning.

---

l'école [ay-KUHL] noun, fem.   **school**
Le jeudi nous n'allons pas à l'école.
We don't go to school on Thursdays.

écouter [ay-koo-TAY] verb   **to listen**
  j'écoute   nous écoutons
  tu écoutes   vous écoutez
  il, elle écoute   ils, elles écoutent

Le garçon écoute la radio.
The boy is listening to the radio.

écrire [ay-KREER] verb   **to write**
  j'écris   nous écrivons
  tu écris   vous écrivez
  il, elle écrit   ils, elles écrivent

La maîtresse dit: "Écrivez la date au tableau noir."
The teacher says, "Write the date on the blackboard."

écrivain [eh-kree-VEHN] noun, masc.   **writer**

Charles Perrault was a writer famous for his stories for children.
Charles Perrault était un écrivain célebre pour ses histoires pour les enfants.

---

effacer [eh-fa-SAY] verb   **to erase**
  j'efface   nous effaçons
  tu effaces   vous effacez
  il, elle efface   ils, elles effacent

Oh, une faute! Je dois effacer ce mot.
Oh, a mistake! I have to erase this word.

---

effrayant [eh-fray-YAHN] adjective, masc.   **frightening**
effrayante [eh-fray-YAHNT] fem.

Le tonnerre est effrayant.
Thunder is frightening.

égal [ay-GAL] adjective, masc.   **equal, all the same**
égale fem.
égaux [ay-GOH] pl.

Tu veux la glace ou le gâteau?
Oh, cela m'est égal.
Do you want ice cream or cake?
Oh, it doesn't make any difference.
(Oh, it's all the same to me.)

l'église [ay-GLEEZ] noun, fem.   **church**

Il y a une grande église dans la ville.
There is a big church in the city.

> The Eiffel Tower is an important symbol
> of France.
>
> La Tour Eiffel est un symbole important
> de la France.

électrique [ay-lehk-TREEK] adjective, masc. or fem.   **electric**

Regarde! On vend des machines à écrire électriques.
Look! They sell electric typewriters.

---

l'éléphant [ay-lay-FAHN] noun, masc.   **elephant**

Il y a un grand éléphant dans le jardin zoologique.
There is a big elephant in the zoo.

---

l'élève [ay-LEV] noun, masc. or fem.   **pupil**
les élèves [leh-zay-LEV] pl.

Les élèves sont dans la salle de classe.
The pupils are in the classroom.

---

elle [EHL] pronoun, fem.   **she, her, it**
elles pl.   **they**

Elles sont assises.
They are seated.

Donnez le crayon à elle, pas à moi.
Give the pencil to her, not to me.

Où est ma chaussure? Elle est sous le lit.
Where is my shoe? It's under the bed.

---

un email [ee-mehl] noun, masc.   **e-mail**

Voilà un autre email.
There's another e-mail.

envoyer un message par email verb   **to e-mail**

l'émission [ay-mee-syoń] noun, fem.   **broadcast**

Aimez-vous l'émission de Paris?
Do you like the broadcast from Paris?

l'emplettes [ahń-pleht] noun, fem.   **purchase**
faire des emplettes   **to go shopping** (See **faire**)

employer [ahń-plwa-YAY] verb   **to use**
  j'emploie   nous employons
  tu emploies   vous employez
  il, elle emploie   ils, elles emploient

Elle emploie les ciseaux pour couper le ruban.
She uses scissors to cut the ribbon.

emprunter [ahń-pruhń-TAY] verb   **to borrow**
  j'emprunte   nous empruntons
  tu empruntes   vous empruntez
  il, elle emprunte   ils, elles empruntent

Je peux emprunter la gomme?
May I borrow the eraser?

en [AHŃ] preposition   **in, into**

En juillet nous allons aux Etats-Unis.
In July we are going to the United States.

encore [ahń-KUHR] adverb   **again; more; still**

Lisez la lettre encore une fois.
Read the letter once again.

Tu désires encore du pain?
Do you want more bread?

Es-tu encore à la maison?
Are you still at home?

---

l'enfant [ahń-FAHX] noun, masc. or fem.   **child**
les enfants [leh-zahń-FAHX] pl.   **children**

Les enfants sont au lit.
The children are in bed.

---

enfin [ahń-FAIX] adverb   **finally**

Il fait beau, enfin!
It is good weather, finally!

---

ennuyé [ahń-newee-YAY] adjective, masc.   **annoyed**
ennuyée fem.

Maman est ennuyée quand je fais trop de bruit.
Mother is annoyed when I make too much noise.

---

enseigner [ahń-seh-NYAY] verb   **to teach**
  j'enseigne   nous enseignons
  tu enseignes   vous enseignez
  il, elle enseigne   ils, elles enseignent

Qui enseigne la musique dans cette classe?
Who teaches music to this class?

---

ensemble [ahń-SAHXBL] adverb   **together**

Nous allons à l'épicerie ensemble.
We are going to the grocery store together.

---

ensuite [ahń-sɛw/EET] adverb   **then**

Je lis le livre; ensuite je rends le livre à la bibliothèque.
I read the book; then I return the book to the library.

---

entendre [ahń-TAHŃDR] verb   **to hear**
   j'entends   nous entendons
   tu entends   vous entendez
   il, elle entend   ils, elles entendent

J'entends le téléphone qui sonne.
I hear the telephone ringing.

bien entendu   **of course** (See **bien**)

---

entier [ahń-TYAY] adjective, masc.   **whole**
entière [ahń-TYEHR] fem.

Bien sûr je voudrais manger le gâteau entier!
Of course I would like to eat the whole cake!

---

entre [AHŃTR] preposition   **between**

Quel est le numéro entre quatorze et seize?
What is the number between fourteen and sixteen?

---

l'entrée [ahń-TRAY] noun, fem.   **entrance, admission**

Il faut payer à l'entrée.
One must pay at the entrance.

---

entrer [ahń-TRAY] verb   **to enter, to come into,**
   j'entre   nous entrons   **to go into**
   tu entres   vous entrez
   il, elle entre   ils, elles entrent

Ils entrent dans la maison.
They go into the house.

défense d'entrer   **No admittance**
                             (See **défense de ...**)

---

l'enveloppe [ahń-VLUHP] noun, fem.   **envelope**

Le facteur me donne une enveloppe.
The mailman gives me an envelope.

l'envie [ahn-VEE] noun, fem.   **desire, longing**
avoir envie de [a-vwahr-ahń-VEE-de/]   **to have the wish to**
idiomatic expression

Il a envie de lire.
He feels like reading.

envoyer [ahń-vwa-YAY] verb   **to send**
   j'envoie   nous envoyons
   tu envoies   vous envoyez
   il, elle envoie   ils, elles envoient

Mon oncle va m'envoyer un cadeau.
My uncle is going to send me a present.

épais [ay-PEH] adjective, masc.   **thick**
épaisse [ay-PEHS] fem.

La peau du citron est très épaisse.
The lemon's skin is very thick.

l'épaule [ay-POHL] noun, fem.   **shoulder**

La balle frappe l'épaule de Claude.
The ball hits Claude's shoulder.

l'épicerie [ay-pee-SREE] noun, fem.   **grocery store**

On va à l'épicerie pour acheter du sucre.
You go to the grocery store to buy sugar.

l'épicier [ay-pee-SYAY] noun, masc.   **grocer**

L'epicier vend du sel et de la confiture.
The grocer sells salt and jam.

---

les épinards [ay-pee-NAR] noun, masc., pl.   **spinach**

Les épinards sont verts.
Spinach is green.

---

l'épingle [ay-PAINGL] noun, fem.   **pin**

Quelle jolie épingle en forme de fleurs!
What a pretty flower pin!

épouser [ay-poo-ZAY] verb   **to marry**
  j'épouse   nous épousons
  tu épouses   vous épousez
  il, elle épouse   ils, elles épousent

Le prince épouse la princesse.
The prince marries the princess.

---

l'équipe [ay-KEEP] noun, fem.   **team**

Nous sommes tous membres de la même équipe.
We are all members of the same team.

---

l'escalier [ehs-ka-LYAY] noun, masc.   **staircase**

J'aime sauter la dernière marche de l'escalier.
I like to jump over the last step of the staircase.

---

l'espace [ehs-PAS] noun, masc.   **space**

Les astronautes voyagent dans l'espace.
The astronauts travel in space.

---

espérer [ehs-pay-RAY]   verb   **to hope**
   j'espère   nous espérons
   tu espères   vous espérez
   il, elle espère   ils, elles espèrent

J'espère avoir une bonne note en histoire.
I hope to have a good mark in history.

---

essayer [eh-say-YAY]   verb   **to try**
   j'essaye   nous essayons
   tu essayes   vous essayez
   il, elle essaye   ils, elles essayent

Elle essaye de porter le paquet lourd.
She tries to carry the heavy package.

---

l'essence [eh-SAHNS]   noun, fem.   **gasoline**

Papa dit: "Nous n'avons pas assez d'essence."
Daddy says, "We don't have enough gasoline."

---

l'est [EHST]   noun, masc.   **east**

Quand je vais de Paris à Strasbourg, je vais vers l'est.
When I go from Paris to Strasbourg, I go toward the east.

---

est-ce que [ehs-KUH]   **(one form of asking a question)**

Est-ce que tu viens avec moi?
(or: Tu viens avec moi?)
(or: Viens-tu avec moi?)
Are you coming with me?

---

et [AY]   conjunction   **and**

André et son ami jouent ensemble.
Andrew and his friend are playing together.

---

l'étage [ay-TAZH]   noun, masc.   **floor (of a building)**

À quel étage est votre appartement?
On what floor is your apartment?

---

l'état [ay-TA] noun, masc. **state**

De quel état venez-vous?
From which state do you come?

---

l'été [ay-TAY] noun, masc. **summer**

Préférez-vous l'été ou l'hiver?
Do you prefer summer or winter?

éteindre [ay-TAIℵDR] verb **to turn off**
   j'éteins   nous éteignons
   tu éteins   vous éteignez
   il, elle éteint   ils, elles éteignent

J'éteins la lumière.
I turn off the light.

éternuer [ay-tehr-new/-AY] verb **to sneeze**
   j'éternue   nous éternuons
   tu éternues   vous éternuez
   il, elle éternue   ils, elles éternuent

Tu éternues. Tu as un rhume?
You're sneezing. Do you have a cold?

---

l'étoile [ay-TWAL] noun, fem. **star**

Combien d'étoiles y a-t-il dans le ciel?
How many stars are there in the sky?

étonnant [ay-tuh-NAHℵ] adjective, masc. **surprising**
étonnante [ay-tuh-NAHℵT] fem.

Il est étonnant de recevoir une lettre d'une actrice.
It is surprising to receive a letter from an actress.

étranger [ay-trahń-ZHAY] noun,   **stranger, foreign**
adjective, masc.
étrangère [ay-trahń-ZHEHR] fem.

Maman dit: "Ne parlez pas aux étrangers."
Mother says, "Don't speak to strangers."

C'est un livre étranger.
It is a foreign book.

être [EHTR] verb   **to be**

je suis	nous sommes
tu es	vous êtes
il, elle est	ils, elles sont

Papa, où sommes-nous?
Dad, where are we?

étroit [ay-TRWA] adjective, masc.   **narrow, tight**
étroite [ay-TRWAT] fem.

Le tiroir est trop étroit pour les papiers.
The drawer is too narrow for the papers.

---

l'étudiant [ay-tew-DYAŃ] noun, masc.   **student**
l'étudiante [ay-tew-DYAHŃT] fem.

Mon cousin est étudiant à l'université.
My cousin is a student at the university.

étudier [ay-tew-DYAY] verb   **to study**

j'étudie	nous étudions
tu étudies	vous étudiez
il, elle étudie	ils, elles étudient

Je dois étudier ce soir. J'ai un examen demain.
I have to study this evening. I have an examination
tomorrow.

l'euro [EUH-ROH] noun, masc.   **euro**

J'ai cinq euros dans la poche.
I have five euros in my pocket.

---

eux [EOH] pronoun, masc., pl.   **them**

Je vais à l'école avec eux.
I go to school with them.

---

l'examen [eh-gza-MAIN] noun, masc.   **examination, test**

Tu as une bonne note à l'examen?
Do you have a good mark on the examination?

---

excellent [eh-kseh-LAHN] adjective, masc.   **excellent**
excellente [eh-kseh-LAHNT] fem.

Le professeur dit: "Ce travail est excellent."
The teacher says, "This work is excellent."

---

excusez-moi [eh-kskew-zay-MWA]   **excuse me**
idiomatic expression

Excusez-moi. Voici vos paquets.
Excuse me. Here are your packages.

---

expliquer [eh-ksplee-KAY] verb   **to explain**
   j'explique   nous expliquons
   tu expliques   vous expliquez
   il, elle explique   ils, elles expliquent

Jeanne, tu peux m'expliquer cette phrase?
Joan, can you explain this sentence to me?

---

exprès [eh-KSPREH] adverb   **on purpose, intentionally**

Mon frère me taquine exprès.
My brother teases me on purpose.

---

extraordinaire   **unusual; wonderful;**
[eh-kstra-uhr-dee-NEHR] adjective   **extraordinary**

Nous allons faire un voyage extraordinaire en fusée.
We are going to take an unusual trip in a rocket ship.

F

fâché [fah-SHAY] adjective, masc.   **angry, displeased**
fâchée fem.

Quand je taquine ma soeur, Maman est fâchée.
When I tease my sister, Mom is angry.

---

facile [fa-SEEL] adjective   **easy**

Il est facile de faire mes devoirs.
It is easy to do my homework.

---

le facteur [fak-TUHR] noun, masc.   **mail carrier, postman**

Le facteur apporte des lettres et des paquets.
The mail carrier brings letters and packages.

---

faible [FEHBL] adjective   **weak**

Le pauvre garçon est faible parce qu'il est malade.
The poor boy is weak because he is sick.

---

la faim [FAIN] noun, fem.   **hunger**
avoir faim [a-vwar-FAIN]   **to be hungry**
idiomatic expression

Avez-vous faim? Oui, j'ai faim.
Are you hungry? Yes, I'm hungry. (See **avoir**)

---

faire [FEHR] verb   **to make; to do**

je fais	nous faisons
tu fais	vous faites
il, elle fait	ils, elles font

Il fait ses devoirs.
He does his homework.

faire des emplettes idiomatic expression   **to go shopping**

Maman fait des emplettes.
Mom goes shopping.

faire beau idiomatic expression   **to be nice weather**

Il fait beau aujourd'hui, n'est-ce pas?
It's nice weather today, isn't it?

faire du vent idiomatic expression   **to be windy**

Il fait du vent aujourd'hui.
It's windy today.

faire un voyage idiomatic expression   **to take a trip**

*Je vais faire un voyage dans deux
semaines.*
I am going to take a trip in two weeks.

faire une promenade   **to take a walk**
idiomatic expression

Le soir Papa fait une promenade avec Maman.
In the evening Dad and Mom take a walk.

faire attention idiomatic expression   **to pay attention**

*Quand le professeur dit "Faites attention,"
je ferme le livre.*
When the teacher says "Pay attention," I close the book.

faire la cuisine idiomatic expression   **to cook**

Qui fait la cuisine?
Who is cooking?

(l'addition)

Cinq et huit font treize.
Five and eight are thirteen.

faire un pique-nique (See **pique-nique**)

---

la famille [fa-MEEY] noun, fem.   **family**
Combien de personnes y a-t-il dans votre famille?
How many people are there in your family?

le nom de famille   **family name, surname**
[nohń-dé-fa-MEEY] noun, masc.

---

fatigué [fa-tee-GAY] adjective, masc.   **tired**
fatiguée fem.

Après deux heures de travail dans le jardin,
je suis fatigué.
After two hours of work in the garden, I am tired.

---

faut, il faut [FOH]   **it is necessary;**
idiomatic expression   **one must; you have to**

Il faut aller à l'école.
It is necessary to go to school.
(We have to go to school.)
(Everyone has to go to school.)
(You have to go to school.)

---

la faute [FOHT] noun, fem.   **error, mistake**
Je fais des fautes quand j'écris en français.
I make mistakes when I write in French.

---

le fauteuil [foh-TUHY] noun, masc.   **armchair**
J'aime m'asseoir dans le fauteuil.
I like to sit in the armchair.

---

faux [FOH] adjective, masc.   **false**
fausse [FOHS] fem.

Il a six ans, vrai ou faux?
He is six years old, true or false?

---

favori [fa-voh-REE] adjective, masc.   **favorite**
favorite [fa-voh-REET] fem.

Quel est ton jouet favori?
What is your favorite toy?

l'animal favori [a-nee-mal-fa-voh-REE] noun, masc.   **pet**

Mon chien est mon animal favori.
My dog is my pet.

---

le fax [fahks] noun, masc.   **fax**

Charles faxe un fax.
Charles is sending a fax.

faxer verb   **to fax**

---

la fée [FAY] noun, fem.   **fairy**
le conte de fées [kohn/t-dé-FAY] noun, masc.   **fairy tale**

Lisez-moi ce conte de fées.
Read this fairy tale to me.

---

la femme [FAM] noun, fem.   **woman, wife**

Ces deux femmes vont faire des emplettes.
These two women are going shopping.

---

la fenêtre [fé-NEHTR] noun, fem.   **window**

Le chien aime regarder par la fenêtre.
The dog likes to look out the window.

le fer [FEHR] noun, masc.   **iron; iron (metal)**

Le fer ne marche pas. Je ne peux pas repasser cette robe.
The iron is not working. I can't iron this dress.

en fer [ahń-FEHR]   **made of iron**

Le fourneau est en fer.
The stove is made of iron.

---

la ferme [FEHRM] noun, fem.   **farm**

Il y a des vaches et des chevaux à la ferme.
There are cows and horses on the farm.

l'âne	donkey	la dinde	turkey
le cheval	horse	le lapin	rabbit
la chèvre	goat	le mouton	sheep
le cochon	pig	le poulet	chicken
le coq	rooster	la vache	cow

---

fermer [fehr-MAY] verb   **to close**

je ferme	nous fermons
tu fermes	vous fermez
il, elle ferme	ils, elles ferment

Fermez la fenêtre, s'il vous plaît.
Please close the window.

---

la fermier [fehr-MYAY] noun, masc.   **farmer**

Mon grand-père est fermier.
My grandfather is a farmer.

---

féroce [fay-RUHS] adjective   **ferocious, fierce, wild**

Qui a peur d'un tigre féroce?
Who is afraid of a ferocious tiger?

---

la fête [FEHT] noun, fem.   **holiday; birthday; party**

Le jour de la fête est le dix-huit juillet?
The party is July 18th?

Bonne fête [buhn-FEHT] interjection   **Happy birthday**

---

le feu [FEOH] noun, masc.   **fire; light (traffic)**

Le feu est chaud.
The fire is hot.

On traverse la rue quand on voit le feu vert.
You cross the street when you see the green light.

---

la feuille [FUHY] noun, fem.   **leaf, sheet of paper**

Les feuilles sont vertes en été.
The leaves are green in summer.

Donne-moi une feuille de papier, s'il te plaît.
Give me a sheet of paper, please.

---

février [fay-VRYAY] noun, masc.   **February**

Combien de jours y a-t-il en février?
How many days are there in February?

---

la ficelle [fee-SEHL] noun, fem.   **string**

Je cherche une ficelle pour mon cerf-volant.
I am looking for a string for my kite.

la fièvre [FYEHVR] noun, fem.   **fever**

Je dois rester au lit. J'ai de la fièvre.
I have to stay in bed. I have a fever.

---

la figure [fee-GEWR] noun, fem.   **face**

Elle se lave la figure.
She is washing her face.

---

la fille [FEEY] noun, fem.   **girl; daughter**

La petite fille joue avec sa poupée.
The little girl plays with her doll.

Je vous présente ma fille, Aimée.
I should like to introduce my daughter, Amy.

---

le film [FEELM] noun, masc.   **film, movie**

On joue un bon film au cinéma?
Are they playing a good film at the movies?

---

le fils [FEES] noun, masc.   **son**

Je vous présente mon fils, Georges.
I should like to introduce my son, George.

---

la fin [FAIN] noun, fem.   **end**

C'est la fin de la leçon.
It is the end of the lesson.

---

finir [fee-NEER] verb   **to finish**
   je finis   nous finissons
   tu finis   vous finissez
   il, elle finit   ils, elles finissent

Je vais finir mon travail avant de sortir.
I am going to finish my work before going out.

la fleur [FLUHR] noun, fem.   **flower**

Nous avons beaucoup de fleurs dans le jardin.
We have many flowers in the garden.

---

le foin [FWAIN] noun, masc.   **hay**

Le fermier donne du foin aux chevaux.
The farmer gives hay to the horses.

---

la foire [FWAR] noun, fem.   **fair**

Nous allons à la foire pour nous amuser.
We are going to the fair to have a good time.

---

la fois [FWA] noun, fem.   **time**

On frappe trois fois à la porte.
They knock three times at the door.

encore une fois [ahn-kuh-rewn-FWA]   **again**
idiomatic expression

Répétez encore une fois.
Repeat once again.

---

foncé [fohn-SAY] adjective, masc.   **dark**
foncée fem.

Elle porte une robe bleu foncé.
She is wearing a dark blue dress.

---

le football [fuht-BUHL] noun, masc.   **soccer**

Savez-vous jouer au football?
Do you know how to play soccer?

---

la forêt [fuh-REH] noun, fem.   **forest, woods**

Il y a cent arbres dans la forêt!
There are a hundred trees in the forest!

former [fuhr-MAY] verb **to form, to make**

je forme	nous formons
tu formes	vous formez
il, elle forme	ils, elles forment

Je forme une balle avec la neige.
I make a snowball with the snow.

en forme de (d') [ah*ñ*-fuhrm-d*é*] **in the form of,**
idiomatic expression **shaped like**

Le petit gâteau est en forme d'étoile.
The cookie is in the form of a star.

---

formidable [fuhr-mee-DABL] interjection **Great!,**
Marvelous!,
Tu vas au cirque? Formidable! **Wonderful!**
You are going to the circus? Great!

---

fort [FUHR] adjective, masc. **strong**
forte [FUHRT] fem.

Mon père est très fort.
My father is very strong.

---

fort [FUHR] adverb **loudly**

Il joue trop fort du tambour.
He plays the drum too loudly.

---

fou [FOO] adjective, masc. **mad, crazy**
folle [FUHL] fem.

Le chien est fou.
The dog is mad.

---

la fourchette [foor-SHEHT] noun, fem. **fork**

Je mange la viande avec une fourchette.
I eat meat with a fork.

---

la fourmi [foor-MEE] noun, fem.   **ant**

La fourmi est très petite.
The ant is very small.

---

le fourneau [foor-NOH] noun, masc.   **stove**

Attention! Le fourneau est chaud.
Careful! The stove is hot.

---

frais [FREH] adjective, masc.   **cool; fresh**
fraîche [FREHSH] fem.

Il fait frais à la plage.
It is cool at the beach.

---

la fraise [FREHZ] noun, fem.   **strawberry**

Le fraises sont rouges.
Strawberries are red.

---

français [frahn-SEH] adjective, masc.   **French**
française [frahn-SEHZ] fem.

Je lis un livre français.
I am reading a French book.

---

la France [FRAHNS] noun, fem.   **France**

Voici une carte de la France.
Here is a map of France.

---

frapper [fra-PAY] verb   **to hit; to knock**

Maman, on frappe à la porte.
Mom, someone is knocking at the door.

---

le frère [FREHR] noun, masc.   **brother**

Je suis petit, mais mon frère est grand.
I am little, but my brother is big.

---

le froid [FRWAH] noun, masc.   **cold**

Quand il fait froid en hiver, j'ai froid.
When it is cold in winter, I am cold.

il fait froid   **it is cold** (See **faire**)
avoir froid   **to be cold** (See **avoir**)

---

le fromage [fruh-MAHZH] noun, masc.   **cheese**

Ma soeur prend du fromage comme dessert.
My sister has cheese for dessert.

---

les fruits [FREW/EE] noun, masc.   **fruit**

Voici des fruits. Préférez-vous une poire ou une banane?
Here is some fruit. Do you prefer a pear or a banana?

---

fumer [few-MAY] verb   **to smoke**

je fume	nous fumons
tu fumes	vous fumez
il, elle fume	ils, elles fument

Papa dit qu'il est dangereux de fumer.
Dad says that it is dangerous to smoke.

défense de fumer   **no smoking**
                                                      (See **défense...**)
la fumée [few-MAY] noun, fem.   **smoke**

---

la fusée [few-ZAY] noun, fem.   **spaceship**

On va à la lune en fusée.
They are going to the moon in a spaceship.

---

le fusil [few-ZEE] noun, masc.   **gun**

Le chasseur porte un fusil.
The hunter carries a gun.

G

gagner [ga-NAY] verb   **to earn; to win**
  je gagne   nous gagnons
  tu gagnes   vous gagnez
  il, elle gagne   ils, elles gagnent

C'est notre équipe qui gagne!
Our team wins!

le gagnant [ga-NAHN] noun, masc.   **winner**
la gagnante [ga-NAHNT] fem.

Qui est le gagnant?
Who is the winner?

---

gai [GAY] adjective, masc.   **gay, cheerful**
gaie fem.

Ma soeur est toujours gaie.
My sister is always cheerful.

---

le gant [GAHN] noun, masc.   **glove**

Elle porte des gants blancs.
She is wearing white gloves.

le garage [ga-RAZH] noun, masc.   **garage**

Où est la voiture? Elle n'est pas dans le garage.
Where is the car? It isn't in the garage.

le garçon [gar-SOHN] noun, masc.   **boy; waiter**

Le garçon joue avec sa soeur.
The boy is playing with his sister.

garder [gar-DAY] verb   **to guard; to keep**
  je garde   nous gardons
  tu gardes   vous gardez
  il, elle garde   ils, elles gardent

L'agent de police garde la banque.
The policeman is guarding the bank.

la gare [GAR] noun, fem.   **station**

Le train est en gare.
The train is in the station.

le gâteau [gah-TOH] noun, masc.   **cake**
le petit gâteau [ptee-gah-TOH] noun, masc.   **cookie**

Voici un petit gâteau pour Thérèse et un morceau de gâteau pour Guillaume.
Here is a cookie for Theresa and a piece of cake for William.

gauche [GOHSH] adjective   **left**
la main gauche [main-GOHSH] noun, fem.   **left hand**

Je lève la main gauche.
I raise my left hand.

à gauche [a-GOHSH] idiomatic expression   **to the left**

L'arbre est à gauche de la maison.
The tree is to the left of the house.

le gaz [GAZ] noun, masc.   **gas**

*Tu as une cuisinière à gaz? Nous avons
un fourneau électrique!*
You have a gas stove? We have an electric stove!

le géant [zhay-AHⁿ] noun, masc.   **giant**

Lis-moi le conte "Jacques et le géant."
Read me the story of "Jack and the Giant."

le genou [ZHNOO] noun, masc.   **knee**
les genoux pl.

Tu as mal au genou? C'est triste.
You have a sore knee? That's too bad!

les gens [ZHAHⁿ] noun, masc., pl.   **people**

Beaucoup de gens sont dans le magasin.
Many people are in the store.

gentil [zhahⁿ-TEE] adjective, masc.   **gentle, kind, nice**
gentille [zhahⁿ-TEEY] fem.

La maîtresse est gentille. Elle ne gronde pas.
The teacher is nice. She doesn't scold.

la glace [GLAS] noun, fem.   **ice cream; ice; mirror**

Tu aimes la glace à la vanille?
Do you like vanilla ice cream?

Allons patiner sur la glace.
Let's go ice skating.

Est-ce que vous avez une glace?
Do you have a mirror?

le patin à glace   **ice skate**   (See **patin**)

glisser [glee-SAY] verb   **to slide; to slip**

je glisse	nous glissons
tu glisses	vous glissez
il, elle glisse	ils, elles glissent

Nous glissons sur la glace en hiver.
We slip on the ice in winter.

---

la gomme [GUHM] noun, fem.   **eraser**

Je dois effacer cette phrase avec la gomme.
I have to erase this sentence with the eraser.

---

google [GOO-g l] noun   **Google**

Jean aime chercher sur google.
John likes to use Google.

---

chercher sur google verb   **to use Google**

---

la gorge [GUHRZH] noun, fem.   **throat**

La maîtresse dit doucement: "J'ai mal à la gorge."
The teacher says softly, "I have a sore throat."

---

le goûter [goo-TAY] noun, masc.   **snack**

Bonjour Maman. Tu as un goûter pour nous?
Hello, Mom. Do you have a snack for us?

---

grand [GRAHN] adjective, masc.   **big, tall, high,**
grande [GRAHND] fem.   **large; great**

Voici un grand arbre et un petit arbre.
Here is a big tree and a little tree.

Madame Curie est une grande savante.
Madame Curie is a great scientist.

---

la grand-mère [grahn-MEHR] noun, fem.   **grandmother**

Dimanche nous allons chez ma grand-mère.
We are going to my grandmother's house on Sunday.

le grand-père [grahń-PEHR] noun, masc.   **grandfather**

Mon grand-père aime conduire la voiture.
My grandfather likes to drive the car.

les grands-parents [grahń-pa-RAHŃ]   **grandparents**
noun, masc. and fem., pl.

---

le gratte-ciel [gra-TSYEHL] noun, masc.   **skyscraper**

La ville de New York a beaucoup de gratte-ciel.
New York City has many skyscrapers.

---

gratuit [gra-TWEE] adjective, masc.   **free**
gratuite [gra-TWEET] fem.

L'entrée est gratuite.
Admission is free.

---

la grenouille [gruh-NOOY] noun, fem.   **frog**

J'essaye d'attraper une grenouille.
I am trying to catch a frog.

---

grimper [graiń-PAY] verb   **to climb**
   je grimpe   nous grimpons
   tu grimpes   vous grimpez
   il, elle grimpe   ils, elles grimpent

Le chat grimpe sur l'arbre.
The cat climbs the tree.

---

gris [GREE] adjective, noun   **gray**
grise [GREEZ] fem.

La souris est grise.
The mouse is gray.

---

gronder [grohń-DAY] verb   **to scold**
  je gronde   nous grondons
  tu grondes   vous grondez
  il, elle gronde   ils, elles grondent

Il a honte parce que sa mère le gronde.
He is ashamed because his mother is scolding him.

---

gros [GROH] adjective, masc.   **big, fat**
grosse [GROHS] fem.

L'éléphant est gros.
The elephant is big.

---

la guerre [GEHR] noun, fem.   **war**

Mon oncle est soldat à la guerre.
My uncle is a soldier in the war.

---

la guitare [gee-TAR] noun, fem.   **guitar**

Je sais jouer de la guitare.
I know how to play the guitar.

101

H

s'habiller [sa-bee-YAY] verb   **to get dressed,**
  je m'habille   nous nous habillons   **to dress**
  tu t'habilles   vous vous habillez
  il, elle s'habille   ils, elles s'habillent

Je me lève, je m'habille, je vais à l'école.
I get up, I get dressed, I go to school.

---

habiter [a-bee-TAY] verb   **to live (dwell)**
  j'habite   nous habitons
  tu habites   vous habitez
  il, elle habite   ils, elles habitent

Où habitez-vous?
Where do you live?

See also: demeurer, vivre

---

haricots [a-ree-KOH] noun, masc., pl.   **beans**
les haricots verts [leh-a-ree-koh-VEHR]   **string beans**
noun, masc., pl.

Nous avons des haricots verts pour le dîner.
We have string beans for dinner.

---

haut [OH] adjective, masc.   **high; tall; loud**
haute [OHT] fem.

La Tour Eiffel est très haute.
The Eiffel Tower is very tall.

à haute voix [a-oh-VWA] idiomatic expression   **in a loud**
voice, aloud

La maîtresse dit: "Parlez à haute voix."
The teacher says, "Speak in a loud voice."

en haut [ahń-OH] adverb   **upstairs**

Où es-tu? En haut.
Where are you? Upstairs.

Hélas! [ay-LAHS] interjection   **What a pity!**

Hélas! Tu ne peux pas venir avec moi.
What a pity! You can't come with me.

---

l'hélicoptère [lay-lee-kuhp-TEHR] noun, masc.   **helicopter**

Qu'est-ce que c'est? Un hélicoptère.
What is it? A helicopter.

---

l'herbe [LEHRB] noun, fem.   **grass**

L'herbe est verte.
Grass is green.

---

l'heure [LEUHR] noun, fem.   **hour; o'clock, time**

Quelle heure est-il?
What time is it?

C'est l'heure du dîner. Il est sept heures et demie.
It is dinner time. It is seven thirty.
(It is half past seven.)

de bonne heure [dé-buh-NEUHR] adverb   **early**

Le soleil se lève de bonne heure.
The sun rises early.

la demi-heure (See **demi**)
tout à l'heure   **in a little while** (See **tout**)

---

heureux [uh-REOH] adjective, masc.   **happy, glad,**
heureuse [uh-REOHZ] fem.   **delighted**

Tout le monde est heureux à une fête.
Everyone is happy at a party.

---

le hibou [lé-ee-BOO] noun, masc.   **owl**
hiboux pl.

On entend le hibou pendant la nuit.
You hear the owl during the night.

---

hier [YEHR] adverb   **yesterday**

C'est aujourd'hui le dix mai; hier, le neuf mai.
Today is May 10; yesterday (was) May 9.

---

l'histoire [lees-TWAR] noun, fem.   **story; history**

Tu aimes l'histoire "Les trois ours"?
Do you like the story of "The Three Bears"?

---

l'hiver [lee-VEHR] noun, masc.   **winter**

En hiver il fait froid.
It is cold in winter.

---

l'homme [LUHM] noun, masc.   **man**

L'homme vient pour réparer le téléviseur.
The man comes to fix the television set.

---

l'honneur [luh-NUHR] noun, masc.   **honor**
en l'honneur de [ahń-luh-NUHR-de]   **in honor of**
idiomatic expression

Nous dînons au restaurant en l'honneur de ma fille.
We are dining in a restaurant in honor of my daughter.

---

l'honte [LOHŃT] noun, fem.   **shame**
avoir honte [OHŃT] idiomatic expression   **to be ashamed**

Il a honte parce qu'il est méchant.
He is ashamed because he is naughty.

---

l'hôpital [loh-pee-TAL] noun, masc.   **hospital**

L'infirmière travaille à l'hôpital.
The nurse works at the hospital.

---

l'horloge [luhr-LUHZH] noun, fem.   **clock**

L'horloge sonne deux fois. Il est deux heures.
The clock strikes twice. It is two o'clock.

l'hôtel [loh-TEHL] noun, masc.　　　　　　　　　　**hotel**

Quel est le nom de cet hôtel?
What is the name of this hotel?

---

l'hôtesse [loh-TEHS] noun, fem.　　　　　**flight attendant**

L'hôtesse nous sert un bon repas.
The flight attendant serves us a good meal.

---

l'huile [LEW/EEL] noun, fem.　　　　　　　　　　　**oil**

Maman, tu mets de l'huile dans la salade?
Mother, are you putting oil in the salad?

---

huit [EW/EET] [EW/EE] adjective　　　　　　　　　**eight**

J'ai huit insectes. [EW/EET] *(before a vowel)*
I have eight insects.

Je vois huit cuillers. [EW/EE] *(before a consonant)*
I see eight spoons.

---

humide [ew-MEED] adjective　　　　**humid, moist, damp**

Mon maillot est humide.
My bathing suit is damp.

I

---

ici [ee-SEE] adverb　　　　　　　　　　　　　　　**here**

Viens ici, Pierrot.
Come here, Pierrot.

---

l'idée [ee-DAY] noun, fem.　　　　　　　　　　　**idea**

Quelle bonne idée d'aller nager!
What a good idea it is to go swimming!

---

l'île [EEL] noun, fem.   **island**

La Corse est une île française.
Corsica is a French island.

il [EEL] pronoun, masc.   **he; it**
ils pl.   **they**

Ils sont assis. Il est assis.
They are seated. He is seated.

Voici le crayon. Il est jaune.
Here is the pencil. It is yellow.

il y a [eel-YA]   **there is, there are**
                                 (See **avoir**)

il n'y a pas de quoi   **You're welcome.**
[eel-nee-ya-pa-dé-KWAH] idiomatic expression

l'image [ee-MAHZH] noun, fem.   **picture**
Il y a beaucoup d'images dans ce livre.
There are many pictures in this book.

l'imperméable [ain-pehr-may-ABL] noun, masc.   **raincoat**
Il porte son imperméable parce qu'il pleut.
He is wearing his raincoat because it is raining.

important [ain-puhr-TAHN] adjective   **important**
Il est important de manger des légumes.
It is important to eat vegetables.

importer [aiń-puhr-TAY] verb   **to be of importance**
N'importe! [naiń-PUHRT]   **No matter!—Never mind**

Le train n'est pas en gare? N'importe. Il vient bientôt.
The train is not at the station? Never mind! It will
come soon.

---

impossible [aiń-puh-SEEBL] adjective   **impossible**
Il est impossible de rouler ce rocher.
It is impossible to roll this rock.

---

indiquer [aiń-dee-KAY] verb   **to point to, to indicate**
  j'indique   nous indiquons
  tu indiques   vous indiquez
  il, elle indique   ils, elles indiquent

L'agent de police indique qu'il faut aller par cette route.
The policeman indicates that we must go by this road.

---

l'infirmière [aiń-feer-MYEHR] noun, fem.   **nurse**

Ma voisine est infirmière.
My neighbor is a nurse.

---

l'ingénieur [aiń-zhay-NYUHR] noun, masc.   **engineer**
Je voudrais devenir ingénieur.
I would like to become an engineer.

---

l'insecte [aiń-SEHKT] noun, masc.   **insect**
Je déteste les insectes!
I hate insects!

intelligent [ain-teh-lee-ZHAHN]   **intelligent**
adjective, masc.
intelligente [ain-teh-lee-ZHAHNT] fem.
Le professeur dit: "Quelle classe intelligente!"
The teacher says, "What an intelligent class!"

intéressant [ain-tay-reh-SAHN]   **interesting**
adjective, masc.
intéressante [ain-tay-reh-SAHNT] fem.
Tu trouves que le film est intéressant?
Do you think the film is interesting?

internet [IN-tehr-neht] noun   **Internet**
Internet est intérésant.
The Internet is interesting.
surfer sur internet verb   **surfing the Internet**

un ipod [AI-PAHD] noun, masc.   **i-pod**
Mon ipod est petit.
My i-pod is small.
le podcast [PAHD-kast] noun, masc.   **podcast**

inviter [ain-vee-TAY] verb   **to invite**
  j'invite   nous invitons
  tu invites   vous invitez
  il, elle invite   ils, elles invitent
Ma tante m'invite chez elle.
My aunt invites me to her house.

J

jamais [zha-MEH] adverb   **never**
Je ne veux jamais jouer avec toi!
I never want to play with you!

la jambe [ZHAHNB] noun, fem.   **leg**

*L'homme a deux jambes; l'animal a
quatre pattes.*
Man has two legs; animals have four paws.

---

le jambon [zhahn-BOHN] noun, masc.   **ham**

Vous prenez du jambon dans votre sandwich?
Will you have some ham in your sandwich?

---

janvier [zhahn-VYAY] noun, masc.   **January**

Le six janvier est un jour de fête en France.
January sixth is a holiday in France.

---

le jardin [zhar-DAIN] noun, masc.   **garden**

Le jardin est plein de fleurs au mois de juin.
The garden is full of flowers in June.

le jardin zoologique   **zoo**
[zhar-dain-zuh-uh-luh-ZHEEK] noun, masc.

Les animaux féroces sont au jardin zoologique.
Ferocious animals are at the zoo.

l'éléphant	elephant	**l'ours**	bear
le kangourou	kangaroo	**le renard**	fox
le léopard	leopard	**le serpent**	snake
le lion	lion	**le singe**	monkey
le loup	wolf	**le tigre**	tiger

---

jaune [ZHOHN] adjective   **yellow**

Le maïs est jaune.
Corn is yellow.

---

je [jé] pronoun   **I**

Je parle à mes amis.
I am speaking to my friends.

---

jeter [jé-TAY] verb   **to throw**
  je jette   nous jetons
  tu jettes   vous jetez
  il, elle jette   ils, elles jettent

Il jette une pierre dans l'eau.
He throws a stone into the water.

---

le jeu [ZHEOH] noun, masc.   **game**
les jeux pl.   **games**

Quel jeu préfères-tu?
Which game do you prefer?

---

jeudi [zheoh-DEE] noun, masc.   **Thursday**

Jeudi est mon anniversaire.
My birthday is Thursday.

---

jeune [ZHEUHN] adjective   **young**

Toujours on me dit: "Tu es trop jeune!"
They always say to me, "You're too young!"

---

je vous en prie [zhe-voo-zahn-PREE]   **you're welcome**
idiomatic expression

Merci, mademoiselle. Je vous en prie, monsieur.
Thank you, miss. You're welcome, sir.

---

joli [zhuh-LEE] adjective, masc.   **pretty, good-looking**
jolie fem.

Quel joli chandail! Il est neuf?
What a pretty sweater! Is it new?

---

jouer [zhoo-AY] verb   **to play**

je joue	nous jouons
tu joues	vous jouez
il, elle joue	ils, elles jouent

Jouons à la balle.
Let's play ball.

Laure joue du piano.
Laura plays the piano.

jouer aux dames [zhoo-ay-oh-DAM]   **to play checkers**
idiomatic expression

Mon ami et moi, nous jouons aux dames.
My friend and I play checkers.

jouer aux échecs [zhoo-ay-oh-zay-SHEHK]   **to play chess**
idiomatic expression

Mon père et mon oncle jouent aux échec.
My father and my uncle play chess.

---

le jouet [zhoo-AY] noun, masc.   **toy**

Quelle sorte de jouets as-tu?
What kind of toys do you have?

---

le jour [ZHOOR] noun, masc.   **day**

Quel jour de la semaine est-ce?
What day of the week is it?

un jour de congé [zhoor-dé-kohń-ZHAY]   **a day off**
noun, masc.

Le jeudi est un jour de congé pour les élèves français.
Thursday is a day off for French students.

le Jour de l'An [zhoor-dé-LAHŃ]   **New Year's Day**
noun, masc.

Le premier janvier est le Jour de l'An.
January 1st is New Year's Day.

tous le jours [too-leh-ZHOOR] adverb   **every day**

Je lis tous les jours.
I read every day.

---

le journal [zhoor-NAL] noun, masc.   **newspaper**
les journaux [zhoor-NOH] pl.

Après le dîner mon oncle lit le journal.
After dinner my uncle reads the newspaper.

---

la journée [zhoor-NAY] noun, fem.   **day**

Je vais passer la journée chez ma cousine.
I am going to spend the day at my cousin's house.

---

juillet [zhewee-YAY] noun, masc.   **July**

Le quatorze juillet est la fête nationale française.
July 14th is the French national holiday.

---

juin [ZHWAIN] noun, masc.   **June**

Combien de jours y a-t-il en juin?
How many days are there in June?

---

la jupe [ZHEWP] noun, fem.   **skirt**

Je ne peux pas choisir. Quelle jupe préfères-tu?
I can't choose. Which skirt do you prefer?

---

le jus [ZHEW] noun, masc.   **juice**
le jus d'orange [zhew-duh-RAHNZH]   **orange juice**
noun, masc.

J'aime le jus d'orange.
I like orange juice.

---

jusqu'à [zhew-SKA] preposition   **until**
Nous sommes à l'école jusqu'à trois heures.
We are in school until three o'clock.

---

juste [ZHEWST] adjective   **fair; correct**
Mais c'est mon tour. Ce n'est pas juste!
But it's my turn. It isn't fair!

K

le kangourou [kahn-goo-ROO] noun, masc.   **kangaroo**

Le kangourou est un animal bizarre.
The kangaroo is a strange animal.

---

le kilomètre [kee-loh-MEHTR] noun, masc.   **kilometer**
J'habite à cinq kilomètres de l'école.
I live five kilometers from the school.

113

L

l' adverb	**the** (See **le**)
l'	**it; him** (See **le**)
la	**the** (See **le**)
la	**it; her** (See **le**)
là [LA]	**there**

---

là-bas [la-BA] adverb　　　　**down there; over there**

Tu vois ton frère qui arrive, là-bas?
Do you see your brother coming, down there?

---

le lac [LAK] noun, masc.　　　　　　　　**lake**

Je vais à la pêche au bord du lac.
I go fishing at the lake shore.

---

laid [LEH] adjective, masc.　　　　　　　**ugly**
laide [LEHD] fem.

Je n'aime pas ce chapeau; il est laid.
I don't like this hat; it's ugly.

---

la laine [LEHN] noun, fem.　　　　　　　**wool**
en laine [ahń-LEHN]　　**made of wool, woolen**

Mon manteau est en laine.
My coat is made of wool.

---

laisser [leh-SAY] verb　　　　　**to leave; to let;**
　　　　　　　　　　　　　　　　　　to permit

je laisse	nous laissons
tu laisses	vous laissez
il, elle laisse	ils, elles laissent

Je laisse souvent mes livres chez Michel.
I often leave my books at Michael's house.

Mon frère me laisse laver la voiture.
My brother lets me wash the car.

See also: partir, quitter, sortir

---

le lait [LEH] noun, masc.   **milk**

Je bois du lait et Papa boit du café au lait.
I drink milk and Dad drinks coffee with milk.

---

la laitue [leh-TEW] noun, fem.   **lettuce**

On prépare une salade avec la laitue.
We make a salad with lettuce.

---

la lampe [LAHMP] noun, fem.   **lamp**

La lampe est dans le salon.
The lamp is in the living room.

---

lancer [lahn-SAY] verb   **to throw**
  je lance   nous lançons
  tu lances   vous lancez
  il, elle lance   ils, elles lancent

Il me lance un oreiller!
He's throwing a pillow at me!

---

la langue [LAHNG] noun, fem.   **tongue**

Je me brûle la langue avec la soupe chaude.
I burn my tongue with hot soup.

---

le lapin [la-PAIN] noun, masc.   **rabbit**

Le lapin est mignon.
The rabbit is cute.

---

large [LARZH] adjective   **broad, wide**

Le boulevard est une rue large.
The boulevard is a wide street.

---

la larme [LARM] noun, fem.   **tear**

Grand-père dit: "Assez de larmes!"
Grandpa says, "Enough tears!"

le lavabo [la-va-BOH] noun, masc.   **washstand,**
Le lavabo est dans la salle de bain.   **bathroom sink**
The washstand is in the bathroom.

---

laver [la-VAY] verb   **to wash**
  je lave   nous lavons   **(something or**
  tu laves   vous lavez   **someone)**
  il, elle lave   ils, elles lavent

Nous lavons le chien.
We are washing the dog.

se laver [sé-la-VAY] verb   **to wash (oneself)**
  je me lave   nous nous lavons
  tu te laves   vous vous lavez
  il, elle se lave ils, elles se lavent

Je me lave les mains avant de manger.
I wash my hands before eating.

la machine à laver   **washing machine**
                                                     (See **machine**)

---

le [lé] article, masc.   **the**
l' (before a vowel)
la [LA] fem.
les [LEH] pl., masc. and fem.

Le chat, la souris, l'ours et l'éléphant sont des animaux.
The cat, the mouse, the bear, and the elephant are animals.

---

le [lé] pronoun, masc.   **it; him**
l' (before a vowel)
la [LA] fem.
les [LEH] pl., masc. and fem.   **them**

Je l'aime.
I like him (her) (it).

Je la vois.
I see her (it).

Je les vois.
I see them.

---

la leçon [lé-SOHഢ] noun, fem.   **lesson**

La leçon d'aujourd'hui est difficile, n'est-ce pas?
Today's lesson is difficult, isn't it?

---

le lecteur de CD [lehk-TഢR-dé-SAY-DAY]   **CD player**
noun, masc.

J'ai un nouveau lecteur de CD.
I have a new CD player.

---

léger [lay-ZHAY] adjective, masc.   **light**
légère [lay-ZHEHR] fem.

Cette boîte est légère.
This box is light.

---

le légume [lay-GഢWM] noun, masc.   **vegetable**

Les légumes sont délicieux avec la viande.
Vegetables are delicious with meat.

---

lentement [lahഢt-MAHഢ] adverb   **slowly**

Grand-père marche lentement.
Grandfather walks slowly.

---

le léopard [lay-oh-PAR] noun, masc.   **leopard**

Le léopard est dans la forêt.
The leopard is in the forest.

---

les   **the** (See **le**, article)
les   **them** (See **le**, pronoun)

---

la lettre [LEHTR] noun, fem.   **letter**

Je mets la lettre dans l'enveloppe.
I put the letter in the envelope.

la boîte aux lettres   **mailbox** (See **boîte**)

---

leur [LEUHR] adjective, masc. and fem.   **their**
leurs pl.

Mes cousins partent. Où sont leurs valises?
My cousins are leaving. Where are their valises?

---

leur [LEUHR] pronoun   **to them, them**

Je leur donne une carte.
I give them a card.

---

se lever [se-le-VAY] verb   **to get up, to stand up**

je me lève	nous nous levons
tu te lèves	vous vous levez
il, elle se lève	ils, elles se lèvent

Lève-toi, Edouard. Tu es en retard.
Get up, Edward. You're late.

---

lever [lé-VAY] verb   **to raise**

je lève	nous levons
tu lèves	vous levez
il, elle lève	ils, elles lèvent

L'agent de police lève la main droite.
The policeman raises his right hand.

---

la lèvre [LEHVR] noun, fem.   **lip**

Regarde! La poupée ouvre les lèvres.
Look! The doll is opening its lips.

---

la librairie [lee-bray-ree] noun, fem.   **bookstore**

Combien de livres y a-t-il dans la librairie?
How many books are there in the bookstore?

---

le lion [LYOHⁿ] noun, masc.   **lion**

Le lion n'est pas un animal doux.
The lion is not a gentle animal.

---

lire [LEER] verb   **to read**

je lis	nous lisons
tu lis	vous lisez
il, elle lit	ils, elles lisent

Nous allons lire dans la bibliothèque.
We are going to read in the library.

---

le lit [LEE] noun, masc.   **bed**

Le chat est dans mon lit.
The cat is in my bed.

---

le livre [LEEVR] noun, masc.   **book**

Nous cherchons des livres intéressants.
We are looking for some interesting books.

---

loin (de) [LWAIⁿ] adverb   **far (from),**
                                                          distant (from)
Est-ce que Paris est loin de Washington?
Is Paris far from Washington?

---

long [LOHN] adjective, masc.
longue [LOHNG] fem.

long

Le pantalon du garçon est long.
The boy's pants are long.

le loup [LOO] noun, masc.   **wolf**

Qui a peur du méchant loup?
Who is afraid of the bad wolf?

lourd [LOOR] adjective, masc.   **heavy**
lourde [LOORD] fem.

La valise est très lourde.
The valise is very heavy.

> The Louvre is a great museum located in Paris.
>
> La Musée du Louvre est un grand musée qui se trouve à Paris.

la luge [LEWZH] noun, fem.   **sled**

Je m'amuse avec la luge.
I have a good time with the sled.

lui [LEW/EE] pronoun   **to him, to her; him, her**
Elle lui donne un café.
She is giving him a cup of coffee.

---

la lumière [lew-MYEHR] noun, fem.   **light**
*La lune ne donne pas beaucoup
de lumière.*
The moon does not give much light.

---

lundi [luhñ-DEE] noun, masc.   **Monday**
Que faites-vous le lundi?
What do you do on Mondays?

---

la lune [LEWN] noun, fem.   **moon**
L'astronaute marche sur la lune.
The astronaut walks on the moon.

---

les lunettes [lew-NEHT] noun, fem., pl.   **glasses**
Attention! Tu vas casser tes lunettes.
Be careful! You are going to break your glasses.

M

ma [MA]   **my** (See **mon**)

---

la machine [ma-SHEEN] noun, fem.   **machine**
la machine à laver [ma-shee-na-la-VAY]   **washing machine**
noun, fem.

Maman désire une machine à laver.
Mother wants a washing machine.

---

madame [ma-DAM] noun, fem.   **Mrs.**
mesdames [meh-DAM] pl.   **ladies**

Dis "Bonjour, Madame" à ta maîtresse.
Say "Good morning" to your teacher.

mademoiselle [ma-dm<u>wa</u>-ZEHL] noun, fem.   **Miss**
mesdemoiselles [meh-dm<u>wa</u>-ZEHL] pl.   **young ladies**

Mademoiselle Duval? Elle est un bon professeur.
Miss Duval? She is a good teacher.

---

le magasin [ma-ga-ZAI<u>N</u>] noun, masc.   **store**

Je vais au magasin avec mon amie.
I'm going to the store with my friend.

---

le magnétophone [ma-nay-tuh-FUHN]   **tape recorder**
noun, masc.

Le professeur emploie un magnétophone dans la classe.
The teacher uses a tape recorder in class.

---

mai [MAY] noun, masc.   **May**

Il y a trente et un jours au mois de mai.
There are thirty-one days in May.

---

maigre [MEHGR] adjective   **thin, skinny**

Vous êtes trop maigre. Il faut manger.
You are too thin. You must eat.

---

le maillot [ma-YOH] noun, masc.   **bathing suit**

Tu aimes mon nouveau maillot?
Do you like my new bathing suit?

---

la main [MAI<u>N</u>] noun, fem.   **hand**

J'ai les mains sales!
My hands are dirty!

---

la main droite [mai<u>n</u>-DR<u>W</u>AT]   **right hand** (See **droit**)
la main gauche [mai<u>n</u>-GOHSH]   **left hand** (See **gauche**)

---

maintenant [maiń-TNAHX] adverb   **now**

Tu dois prendre un bain maintenant!
You have to take a bath now!

---

mais [MEH] conjunction   **but**

Je veux aller au parc mais Papa dit "non."
I want to go to the park but Daddy says "no."

---

le maïs [ma-EES] noun, masc.   **corn**

Mmm, le maïs est bon!
Mmm, the corn is good!

---

la maison [meh-ZOHX] noun, fem.   **house, home**

Voici la maison de mon oncle.
Here is my uncle's house.

la maison de poupée   **dollhouse**
[meh-zohń-dé-poo-PAY]   (See **poupée**)

---

la maîtresse [meh-TREHS] noun, fem.   **teacher**
le maître [MEHTR] noun, masc.

La maîtresse est gentille.
The teacher is kind.

---

le mal [MAL] noun, masc.   **sore, evil, harm**
avoir mal à [a-vwar-mal-la]   **to have a sore ...;**
idiomatic expression   **to have a pain in the ...;**
                                                    to hurt ... (See **avoir**)

Je suis malade. J'ai mal à la tête.
I am sick. I have a headache.

Pierre a mal au pied.
Peter has a sore foot.

---

malade [ma-LAD] adjective   **sick**

Qu'as-tu? Je suis malade.
What's the matter? I am sick.

---

malheureux [ma-luh-REOH] adjective, masc.   **unhappy, sad**
malheureuse [ma-luh-REOHZ] fem.
*Il est malheureux parce qu'il ne peut pas
jouer à la balle.*
He is unhappy because he can't play ball.

---

la malle [MAL] noun, fem.   **trunk, suitcase**
Il est difficile de porter cette malle.
It is difficult to carry this trunk.

---

maman [ma-MAHN] noun, fem.   **Mother, Mom, Mama,
                                                       Mommy**
Maman, où sont mes chaussettes?
Mom, where are my socks?

---

le manège [ma-NEZH] noun, masc.   **merry-go-round**

Regarde les chevaux du manège!
Look at the horses on the merry-go-round!

124

manger [mahñ-ZHAY] verb   **to eat**

je mange	nous mangeons
tu manges	vous mangez
il, elle mange	ils, elles mangent

Le dimanche nous mangeons la dinde.
On Sundays we eat turkey.

---

le manteau [mahñ-TOH] noun, masc.   **coat**

Elle porte un manteau chaud en hiver.
She wears a warm coat in winter.

---

la marche [MARSH] noun, fem.   **step**

Il y a beaucoup de marches devant ce bâtiment.
There are many steps in front of this building.

---

le marché [mar-SHAY] noun, masc.   **market, store**

Qu'est-ce qu'on vend au marché?
What do they sell at the market?

le supermarché [sew-pehr-mar-SHAY]   **supermarket**
noun, masc.

Le supermarché est un grand marché.
The supermarket is a large market.

---

marcher [mar-SHAY] verb
   je marche   nous marchons
   tu marches   vous marchez
   il, elle marche   ils, elles marchent

to walk, to work (things), to operate

Nous marchons dans la rue.
We are walking on the street.

Cette lampe ne marche pas.
This lamp is not working.

---

mardi [mar-DEE] noun, masc.   **Tuesday**

Est-ce que mardi est un jour de congé?
Is Tuesday a day off?

---

la marelle [ma-REHL] noun, fem.   **hopscotch**
jouer à la marelle   **to play hopscotch**
[zhoo-ay-a-la-ma-REHL] idiomatic expression (See **jouer**)

Je ne sais pas jouer à la marelle.
I don't know how to play hopscotch.

---

le mari [ma-REE] noun, masc.   **husband**

Le mari de ma tante est mon oncle.
My aunt's husband is my uncle.

---

la marionnette [ma-ryoh-NEHT] noun, fem. **marionette**

Les marionnettes sont drôles.
The marionettes are amusing.

---

marron [ma-ROHN] adjective   **brown**

Le tapis est marron.
The rug is brown.

---

mars [MARS] noun, masc.   **March**

Il fait du vent en mars.
It is windy in March.

---

le marteau [mar-TOH] noun, masc.   **hammer**

Albert travaille avec un marteau.
Albert is working with a hammer.

---

le matin [ma-TAIN] noun, masc.   **morning**
Que mangez-vous le matin?
What do you eat in the morning?

---

mauvais [moh-VEH] adjective, masc.   **bad**
mauvaise [moh-VEHZ] fem.
Il fait mauvais aujourd'hui.
The weather is bad today.

---

me [mé] pronoun   **me; to me; myself**
Je m'habille le matin.
I get dressed in the morning.

Il me donne du pain.
He gives me some bread.

---

le mécanicien [may-ka-nee-SYAIN]   **mechanic**
noun, masc.
Je voudrais devenir mécanicien.
I would like to become a mechanic.

---

méchant [may-SHAHN] adjective, masc.   **naughty**
méchante [may-SHAHNT] fem.
Robert ne peut pas sortir. Il est méchant.
Robert cannot go out. He is naughty.

le médecin [may-TSAIN] noun, masc.   **doctor**

Le médecin entre dans l'hôpital.
The doctor enters the hospital.

---

le médicament [may-dee-ka-MAHN]   **medicine**
noun, masc.

Je n'aime pas ce médicament!
I don't like this medicine!

---

meilleur [may-YEUHR] adjective, masc.   **better**
meilleure fem.

Je pense que les cerises sont meilleures que les fraises.
I think that cherries are better than strawberries.

---

mélanger [may-lahn-ZHAY] verb   **to mix**
   je mélange   nous mélangeons
   tu mélagnes   vous mélangez
   il, elle mélange   ils, elles mélangent

Quand on joue aux dominos, on mélange les dominos.
When you play dominoes, you mix the dominoes.

---

le membre [MAHNBR] noun, masc.   **member**

Il est membre de notre équipe.
He is a member of our team.

---

même [MEHM] adjective, adverb   **same; even**

Mon amie et moi, nous portons la même robe.
My friend and I are wearing the same dress.

Elle pleure même quand elle est heureuse.
She cries even when she is happy.

moi-même [mwa-MEHM] pronoun   **myself**

Je veux faire le gâteau moi-même!
I want to make the cake myself!

mener [mé-NAY] verb   **to lead**

je mène	nous menons
tu mènes	vous menez
il, elle mène	ils, elles mènent

Il mène son chien dehors.
He leads his dog outside.

---

le mensonge [mahń-SOHŃ̄ZH] noun, masc.   **lie**

Il dit des mensonges!
He tells lies!

---

le menton [mahń-TOHŃ] noun, masc.   **chin**

Voici le menton de la poupée.
Here is the doll's chin.

---

la mer [MEHR] noun, fem.   **sea**

Est-ce qu'il y a beaucoup de poissons dans la mer?
Are there many fish in the sea?

---

merci [mehr-SEE] noun, masc.   **thank you**

*Quand ma grand-mère me donne un petit
gâteau je dis: "Merci."*
When my grandmother gives me a cookie I say,
"Thank you."

---

mercredi [mehr-kré-DEE] noun, masc.   **Wednesday**

C'est aujourd'hui mercredi—on sert du poulet.
Today is Wednesday—they are serving chicken.

la mère [MEHR] noun, fem.   **mother**

C'est l'anniversaire de ma mère aujourd'hui.
Today is my mother's birthday.

---

mes (See **mon**)

---

mesdames (See **madame**)

---

mesdemoiselles (See **mademoiselle**)

---

messieurs (See **monsieur**)

---

le métro [may-TROH] noun, masc.   **subway**

Pour aller au musée nous prenons le métro.
We take the subway to go to the museum.

---

mettre [MEHTR] verb   **to put, to put on;**
  je mets   nous mettons   **to set**
  tu mets   vous mettez
  il, elle met   ils, elles mettent

Ma soeur met ses gants.
My sister puts on her gloves.

Ma mère met le couvert.
My mother sets the table.

---

mettre une lettre à la poste   **to mail**
[meh-trewn-le-tra-la-PUHST] idiomatic expression

Mon frère met une lettre à la poste.
My brother mails a letter.

---

midi [mee-DEE] noun, masc.   **noon**

Il est midi. C'est l'heure du déjeuner.
It is noon. It's time for lunch.

---

mignon [mee-NYOHṄ] adjective, masc.   **cute, darling**
mignonne [mee-NYUHṄ] fem.

Le bébé est mignon.
The baby is cute.

---

le milieu [mee-LYEOH] noun, masc.   **middle**
au milieu de [oh-mee-LYEOH-dé]   **in the middle of**
preposition

Maman met les bonbons au milieu de la table.
Mom puts the candy in the middle of the table.

---

mille [MEEL] adjective   **thousand**

Combien coûte une auto? Mille francs?
How much does a car cost? A thousand francs?

---

le mille [MEEL] noun, masc.   **mile**

Mon ami demeure à un mille d'ici.
My friend lives one mile from here.

---

le million [mee-LYOHṄ] noun, masc.   **million**

Combien de livres as-tu? Un million!
How many books do you have? A million!

---

minuit [mee-NEW/EE] noun, masc.   **midnight**

Il est minuit. Pourquoi ne dors-tu pas?
It is midnight. Why aren't you sleeping?

---

la minute [mee-NEWT] noun, fem.   **minute**

Combien de minutes y a-t-il dans une heure?
How many minutes are there in an hour?

---

le miroir [mee-RWAR] noun, masc.   **mirror**

La petite fille se regarde dans le miroir.
The little girl is looking at herself in the mirror.

---

moi [MWAH] pronoun   **me, to me**

Qui frappe à la porte? C'est moi, Michel.
Who is knocking at the door? It's me, Michael.

moi-même [mwa-MEHM]   **myself** (See **même**)

---

moins [MWAIN] adverb   **less; to (in time**
                                              expressions)
Nous partons à deux heures moins vingt.
We are leaving at twenty minutes to two.

---

le mois [MWA] noun, masc.   **month**

Nous avons deux mois de vacances.
We have two months of vacation.

---

la moitié [mwa-TYAY] noun, fem.   **half**

Donnez-moi la moitié de la poire, s'il vous plait.
Give me half of the pear, please.

---

le moment [muh-MAHN] noun, masc.   **moment**

J'entre dans la poste pour un moment.
I am going into the post office for a moment.

mon [MOHN] adjective, masc.   **my**
ma [MA] fem.
mes [MEH] masc., fem., pl.

Mon frère est beau.
My brother is handsome.

Ma soeur est jolie.
My sister is pretty.

Mes cousins sont toujours gais.
My cousins are always cheerful.

---

le monde [MOHND] noun, masc.   **world**

Combien de nations y a-t-il dans le monde?
How many nations are there in the world?

tout le monde   **everyone, everybody**
                                                      (See **tout**)

---

la monnaie [muh-NAY] noun, fem.   **change (money)**
Le boucher dit: "Voici la monnaie de trente francs."
The butcher says, "Here is the change from 30 francs."

---

monsieur [muh-SYE] noun, masc.   **Mr., sir, gentleman**
messieurs [meh-SYEOH] pl.   **gentlemen**

L'épicier s'appelle monsieur Montand.
The grocer's name is Mr. Montand.

---

la montagne [mohn-TAN] noun, fem.   **mountain**
Les montagnes près de l'Espagne sont les Pyrénées.
The mountains near Spain are the Pyrenees.

---

monter [mohń-TAY] verb   **to go up; to ride**

Le cerf-volant monte dans le ciel.
The kite goes up into the sky.

Il monte à cheval.
He rides a horse.

Je monte à bicyclette.
I go bicycle riding.

la montre [MOHŃTR] noun, fem.   **watch**

Hélas, ma montre ne marche pas.
What a shame, my watch doesn't work.

montrer [mohń-TRAY] verb   **to show**
  je montre   nous montrons
  tu montres   vous montrez
  il, elle montre   ils, elles montrent

Montre-moi ton nouveau stylo.
Show me your new pen.

le morceau [muhr-SOH] noun, masc.   **piece**

Je désire un morceau de fromage.
I want a piece of cheese.

mordre [MUHRDR] verb   **to bite**
  je mords   nous mordons
  tu mords   vous mordez
  il, elle mord   ils, elles mordent

Les chats ne mordent pas.
Cats do not bite.

mort [MUHR] adjective, masc.   **dead**
morte [MUHRT] fem.

Tu pleures? Oui, ma tortue est morte.
You're crying? Yes, my turtle is dead.

le mot [MOH] noun, masc.   **word**

Je pense à un mot qui commence avec la lettre "a."
I'm thinking of a word that begins with the letter "a."

la mouche [MOOSH] noun, fem.   **fly**

Il y a des mouches dans la cuisine!
There are flies in the kitchen!

le mouchoir [moo-SHWAR] noun, masc.   **handkerchief**

J'emploie un mouchoir quand j'eternue.
I use a handkerchief when I sneeze.

mouillé [moo-YAY] adjective, masc.   **wet**
mouillée fem.

Mon cahier tombe dans l'eau. Oh, il est mouillé!
My notebook is falling into the water. Oh, it is wet!

le moustique [moos-TEEK] noun, masc.   **mosquito**

Papa, attrape le moustique! Il va me piquer.
Daddy, catch the mosquito! It's going to bite me.

le mouton [MOO-TOHN] noun, masc.   **sheep**

Le mouton est dans le champ.
The sheep is in the field.

le mur [MEWR] noun, masc.   **wall**
Il y a une image d'une fusée au mur de ma chambre.
There is a picture of a spaceship on my bedroom wall.

mûr [MEWR] adjective, masc.   **ripe**
mûre fem.
Quand la banane est jaune, elle est mûre.
When the banana is yellow, it is ripe.

le musée [mew-ZAY] noun, masc.   **museum**
Le musée est ouvert de deux heures jusqu'à cinq heures.
The museum is open from two to five o'clock.

le musicien [mew-zee-SYAIN] noun, masc.   **musician**
Le garçon désire devenir musicien.
The boy wants to become a musician.

la musique [mew-ZEEK] noun, fem.   **music**
Est-ce que vous savez lire les notes de musique?
Do you know how to read musical notes?

Claude Debussy was a famous French composer
of the nineteenth to twentieth century.

Claude Debussy était un célèbre compositeur
français du 19ème–20ème siècle.

N

nager [na-ZHAY] verb   **to swim**

je nage	nous nageons
tu nages	vous nagez
il, elle nage	ils, elles nagent

Je vais nager en été.
I go swimming in summer.

---

la nappe [NAP] noun, fem.   **tablecloth**

Ma tante met la nappe sur la table.
My aunt puts the tablecloth on the table.

---

la nation [na-SYOHพ] noun, fem.   **nation**

Il y a beaucoup de nations dans le monde.
There are many nations in the world.

les Nations Unies [na-syohพ-zew-NEE]   **United Nations**
noun, fem., pl.

Le bâtiment des Nations Unies est intéressant.
The United Nations building is interesting.

---

national [na-syoh-NAL] adjective, masc.   **national**
nationale fem.

Le quatre juillet est la fête nationale des Etats-Unis.
The Fourth of July is the national holiday of the United
States.

> July 14 is the French national holiday.
>
> Le quatorze juillet est la fête nationale française.

ne ... jamais [né ... zha-MEH] adverb   **never**
Je vais à l'école. Ma soeur ne va jamais   *(See jamais)*
à l'école.
I go to school. My sister never goes to school.

---

ne ... pas [né ... pa] adverb   **not**
Je vais à l'école. Mon grand-père ne va pas à l'école.
I go to school. My grandfather does not go to school.

---

ne ... plus [né .... plew] adverb   **no longer**
Je vais à l'école. Mon frère ne va plus à l'école.
I go to school. My brother no longer goes to school.

---

né [NAY] adjective, masc.   **born**
née fem.

Je suis né le deux mars.
I was born on March 2nd.

---

la neige [NEHZH] noun, fem.   **snow**
J'aime jouer dans la neige.
I like to play in the snow.

le bonhomme de neige   **snowman** (See **bonhomme**)

neiger [neh-ZHAY] verb   **to snow**
Il va neiger demain?
Is it going to snow tomorrow?

Il neige. [eel-NEHZH] idiomatic expression   **It is snowing.**
Regardez par la fenêtre. Il neige!
Look out the window. It's snowing!

---

n'est-ce pas? [nehs-PA]
idiomatic expression

Isn't that true?
Isn't that so?
Don't you agree?
Aren't you? (etc.)

Il fait mauvais, n'est-ce pas?
The weather is bad, isn't it?

Mon professeur est beau, n'est-ce pas?
My teacher is handsome, don't you agree?

---

nettoyer [neh-t<u>wa</u>-YAY] verb　　　　　　　**to clean**
  je nettoie　　　　nous nettoyons
  tu nettoies　　　　vous nettoyez
  il, elle nettoie　　ils, elles nettoient

Tu aides ta mère à nettoyer la maison?
Do you help your mother clean the house?

---

neuf [NEUHF, NEUHV] adjective　　　　　　　**nine**

Combien font neuf et deux? [NEUHF]
How much are nine and two?

J'ai neuf ans. [NEUHV]
I am nine years old.

---

neuf [NEUHF] adjective, masc.　　　　　　　**new**
neuve [NEUHV] fem.

Ma bicyclette est neuve.
My bicycle is new.

---

le neveu [né-VEOH] noun, masc.　　　　　　**nephew**

Il est le neveu de monsieur Duval.
He is Mr. Duval's nephew.

---

le nez [NAY] noun, masc.　　　　　　　　**nose**

Le nez de ma poupée est mignon.
My doll's nose is cute.

---

le nid [NEE] noun, masc. **nest**

Combien d'oeufs vois-tu dans le nid?
How many eggs do you see in the nest?

---

la nièce [NYEHS] noun, fem. **niece**

Elle est la nièce de l'avocat.
She is the lawyer's niece.

N'importe! [nain-PUHRT] **No matter!**
idiomatic expression

Vous n'avez pas de stylo? N'importe. Voici un crayon.
You don't have a pen? No matter! Here is a pencil.

Noël [no-ehl] noun, masc. **Christmas**

Le lumières de Noël sont belles.
Christmas lights are beautiful.

---

noir [NWAR] adjective, masc. **black**
noire fem.

Je porte mes souliers noirs.
I am wearing my black shoes.

le tableau noir chalkboard, blackboard
(See **tableau**)

---

le nom [NOHN] noun, masc. **name**

Quel est le nom de ce bâtiment?
What is the name of this building?

le nom (de famille) [nohn-dé-fa-MEEY] **surname**
noun, masc.

---

le nombre [NOHXBR] noun, masc.   **number (quantity)**

Tu as un grand nombre de livres!
You have a great number of books!
(See **numéro**)

---

non [NOHX] adverb   **no**

Lève-toi! Non, je ne veux pas me lever!
Get up! No, I don't want to get up!

---

le nord [NUHR] noun, masc.   **north**

Quand je vais de Marseille à Paris, je vais vers le nord.
When I go from Marseilles to Paris, I go toward the north.

---

la note [NUHT] noun, fem.   **mark (in school);**
                                         musical note

Tu as de bonnes notes?
Do you have good marks?

---

notre [NUHTR] adjective   **our**
nos [NOH] masc., fem., pl.

Notre maîtresse nous gronde aujourd'hui.
Our teacher is scolding us today.

---

nous [NOO] pronoun, pl.   **we; us, to us**

Nous allons à la plage.
We are going to the beach.

---

nouveau [noo-VOH] adjective, masc.   **new**
nouveaux masc., pl.
nouvel [noo-VEHL] masc. (before a vowel)
nouvelle [noo-VEHL] fem.

Regarde ma nouvelle tortue!
Look at my new turtle!

---

novembre [nuh-VAHXBR] noun, masc.   **November**

Novembre n'est pas le dernier mois de l'année.
November is not the last month of the year.

---

le nuage [NEWAZH] noun, masc.   **cloud**

Le soleil est derrière un nuage.
The sun is behind a cloud.

Il est couvert.
It is cloudy.

---

la nuit [NEW/EE] noun, fem.   **night, at night**

La nuit on peut voir de étoiles.
At night you can see the stars.

---

numérique [noo-may-REEK] adjective   **digital**

Avez-vous un appareil photo numérique?
Do you have a digital camera?

---

le numéro [new-may-ROH] noun, masc.   **number**

Quel est votre numéro de téléphone?
What is your telephone number? (See **nombre**)

O

obéir [oh-bay-EER] verb   **to obey**
  j'obéis   nous obéissons
  tu obéis   vous obéissez
  il, elle obéit   ils, elles obéissent

Quand je suis sage, j'obéis à mes parents.
When I am well behaved, I obey my parents.

---

occupé [uh-kew-PAY] adjective, masc.   **busy, occupied**
occupée fem.

Mon frère est occupé maintenant; il fait ses devoirs.
My brother is busy now; he is doing his homework.

---

l'océan [un-say-AHN] noun, masc.   **ocean**

L'océan Atlantique est à l'ouest de la France?
Is the Atlantic Ocean to the west of France?

---

octobre [uhk-TUHBR] noun, masc.   **October**

Il fait frais en octobre.
It is cool in October.

---

l'oeil [EUHY] noun, masc.   **eye**
les yeux [leh-ZYEOH] pl.

De quelle couleur sont vos yeux?
What color are your eyes?

---

l'oeuf [UHF] noun, masc.   **egg**
les oeufs [les-ZEOH] pl.

Maman demande: "Tu veux un oeuf ce matin?"
Mother asks, "Do you want an egg this morning?"

---

l'oignon [uhn-NYOHN] noun, masc.   **onion**

Je vais au marché pour acheter des oignons.
I am going to the store to buy some onions.

l'oiseau [wah-ZOH] noun, masc.   **bird**

L'oiseau chante très bien.
The bird sings very well.

---

l'ombre [OHⓍBR] noun, fem.   **shadow**

L'ombre danse avec moi.
My shadow dances with me.

---

on [OHⓍ] pronoun   **one; people; you; we;**
they; somebody

Quand on regarde par la fenêtre, on voit la Tour Eiffel.
When you look out of the window, you see the Eiffel Tower.

---

l'oncle [OHⓍKL] noun, masc.   **uncle**

Mon oncle est le frère de ma mère.
My uncle is my mother's brother.

---

l'ongle [OHⓍGL] noun, masc.   **fingernail**

J'ai honte. Mes ongles sont sales.
I am ashamed. My fingernails are dirty.

---

onze [OHⓍZ] adjective   **eleven**

Le fermier a onze poulets.
The farmer has eleven chickens.

---

l'or [UHR] noun, masc.   **gold**
en or [ahⓍ-NUHR]   **made of gold**

Je voudrais avoir une bague en or.
I would like to have a gold ring.

---

l'orage [un-RAZH] noun, masc.   **storm**

Il n'y a pas de classes à cause de l'orage.
There are no classes because of the storm.

---

orange [un-RAHZH] adjective   **orange**

J'ai besoin d'une jupe orange.
I need an orange skirt.

---

l'orange [uh-RAHZH] noun, fem.   **orange**

De quelle couleur est l'orange?
What color is the orange?

---

l'ordinateur [uhr-dee-na-TEUHR] noun, masc.   **computer**

As tu un ordinateur?
Do you have a computer?

le disque [DEESK] noun, masc.   **(computer) disk**

un écran [ay-KRAN] noun, masc.   **screen**

en ligne [AN-leeny]   **on line**
le technicien [TEK-nee-SYAIN] noun, masc.   **(computer)**
                                      technician

la technicienne [tek-nee-SYEHN] fem.

---

l'oreille [uh-RAY] noun, fem.   **ear**

Les oreilles du loup sont longues.
The wolf's ears are long.

---

l'oreiller [uh-ray-YAY] noun, masc.   **pillow**

Où est l'oreiller de Raoul?
Where is Ralph's pillow?

---

l'orteil [uhr-TEHY] noun, masc.   **toe**

Le bébé regarde ses orteils.
The baby looks at his toes.

---

oser [oh-ZAY] verb   **to dare (to)**
  j'ose   nous osons
  tu oses   vous osez
  il, elle ose   ils, elles osent

Tu oses me battre?
You dare to hit me?

ôter [oh-TAY] verb   **to take off, to remove**
  j'ôte   nous ôtons
  tu ôtes   vous ôtez
  il, elle ôte   ils, elles ôtent

Ôte le chapeau dans la maison.
Take off your hat in the house.

---

ou [oo] conjunction   **or**

Que désirez-vous, des pêches ou des pommes?
What would you like, peaches or apples?

---

où [oo] adverb   **where**

Où sont mes lunettes?
Where are my glasses?

---

oublier [oo-BLYAY] verb   **to forget**
  j'oublie   nous oublions
  tu oublies   vous oubliez
  il, elle oublie   ils, elles oublient

Elle oublie toujours son billet.
She always forgets her ticket.

---

l'ouest [WEHST] noun, masc.   **west**

Quand je vais de Lyon à Bordeaux, je vais vers l'ouest.
When I go from Lyons to Bordeaux, I go toward the west.

oui [WEE] adverb   **yes**

Veux-tu des bonbons? Oui, bien sûr!
Do you want some candy? Yes, of course!

l'ours [OORS] noun, masc.   **bear**

Les ours jouent dans l'eau.
The bears are playing in the water.

ouvert [oo-VEHR] adjective, masc.   **open**
ouverte [oo-VEHRT] fem.

La fenêtre est ouverte.
The window is open.

ouvrir [oo-VREER] verb   **to open**

j'ouvre	nous ouvrons
tu ouvres	vous ouvrez
il, elle ouvre	ils, elles ouvrent

J'ouvre mon pupitre pour chercher une gomme.
I open my desk to look for an eraser.

P

la page [PAHZH] noun, fem.   **page**

La carte de la France est à la page dix.
The map of France is on page ten.

le pain [PAIN] noun, masc.   **(loaf of) bread**

On voit beaucoup de pain dans la boulangerie.
You see a lot of bread in the bakery.

le petit pain [ptee-PAIN] noun, masc.   **roll**

Un petit pain, s'il vous plaît.
A roll, please.

le pain grillé [pain-gree-YAY] noun, masc. **toast**

Ma soeur préfère le pain grillé.
My sister prefers toast.

---

la paire [PEHR] noun, fem. **pair**

Je voudrais acheter une paire de gants.
I would like to buy a pair of gloves.

---

le palais [pa-LEH] noun, masc. **palace**

Le roi arrive au palais.
The king arrives at the palace.

---

le pamplemousse [pahn-plé-MOOS] noun, masc. **grapefruit**

Le pamplemousse n'est pas doux.
The grapefruit is not sweet.

---

le panier [pa-NYAY] noun, masc. **basket**

Il y a des pommes dans le panier.
There are apples in the basket.

---

le pantalon [pahn-ta-LOHN] noun, masc. **pants, trousers**

Le pantalon du garçon est sale.
The boy's pants are dirty.

---

papa [pa-PA] noun, masc. **Father, Dad, Papa, Daddy**

Papa, j'ai peur!
Daddy, I'm afraid!

---

le papier [pa-PYAY] noun, masc. **paper**

Il y a du papier dans mon cahier.
There is some paper in my notebook.

---

le paquebot [pak-BOH] noun, masc.   **steamship,**
ocean liner

Le paquebot traverse l'océan Atlantique.
The steamship crosses the Atlantic Ocean.

---

le paquet [pa-KEH] noun, masc.   **package**

Qu'est-ce qu'il y a dans le paquet?
What's in the package?

---

par [PAR] preposition   **by, through, out of**

Mon grand-père regarde par la fenêtre.
My grandfather looks out of the window.

---

le parachute [pa-ra-SHEWT] noun, masc.   **parachute**

Est-ce qu'il est dangereux de sauter en parachute?
Is it dangerous to jump with a parachute?

---

le parapluie [pa-ra-PLEW/EE] noun, masc.   **umbrella**

N'oublie pas ton parapluie.
Don't forget your umbrella.

---

le parc [PARK] noun, masc.   **park**

Le parc est tout près d'ici.
The park is near here.

---

parce que [pars-ké] conjunction   **because**

*Je ne vais pas au cinéma parce que je n'ai
pas d'argent.*
I am not going to the movies because I don't have
any money.

---

pardon [par-DOHN]   **I beg your pardon,**
idiomatic expression   **pardon me, excuse**
                             me, forgive me
Pardon! C'est votre sac, n'est-ce pas?
Excuse me! It's your pocketbook, isn't it?

---

pareil [pa-RAY] adjective, masc.   **similar, alike**
pareille fem.

Nos cravates sont pareilles.
Our ties are similar.

---

les parents [pa-RAHN] noun, masc., pl.   **parents, relatives**

Mes parents vont au travail le matin.
My parents go to work in the morning.

---

paresseux [pa-reh-SEOH] adjective, masc.   **lazy**
paresseuse [pa-reh-SEOHZ] fem.

Ma maîtresse dit que je suis paresseuse.
My teacher says I am lazy.

---

parler [par-LAY] verb   **to speak, to talk**
  je parle   nous parlons
  tu parles   vous parlez
  il, elle parle   ils, elles parlent

Nous parlons du film à la télévision.
We are talking about the movie on television.

---

partager [par-ta-ZHAY] verb   **to share**
  je partage   nous partageons
  tu partages   vous partagez
  il, elle partage   ils, elles partagent

Partageons le gâteau.
Let's share the cake!

---

partir [par-TEER] verb   **to leave, to go**
  je pars   nous partons
  tu pars   vous partez
  il, elle part   ils, elles partent

Ma tante part à cinq heures.
My aunt is leaving at five o'clock.

See also: laisser, quitter, sortir

---

partout [par-TOO] adverb   **all over, everywhere**

Je cherche ma montre partout.
I look everywhere for my watch.

---

le passager [pa-sa-ZHAY] noun, masc.   **passenger**
la passagère [pa-sa-ZHEHR] fem.

Il y a quatre passagers dans la voiture.
There are four passengers in the car.

passer [pa-SAY] verb   **to pass, to spend (time)**
  je passe   nous passons
  tu passes   vous passez
  il, elle passe   ils, elles passent

Elle passe deux semaines à la campagne.
She spends two weeks in the country.

---

la pastèque [pas-TEHK] noun, fem.   **watermelon**

La pastèque est un fruit délicieux.
Watermelon is a delicious fruit.

---

le patin [pa-TAIN] noun, masc.   **skate**
le patin (à glace) [pa-tain-(a-GLAS)] noun, masc. **ice skate**
le patin à roulettes [pa-tain-a-roo-LEHT]   **roller skate**
noun, masc.

Avez-vous des patins à glace ou des patins à roulettes?
Do you have ice skates or roller skates?

---

patiner [pa-tee-NAY] verb   **to skate**
  je patine   nous patinons
  tu patines   vous patinez
  il, elle patine   ils, elles patinent

Allons patiner!
Let's go skating!

---

la patte [PAT] noun, fem.   **paw**

Le chien a quatre pattes.
The dog has four paws.

---

pauvre [POHVR] adjective   **poor**

Ce garçon pauvre n'a pas beaucoup d'argent.
This poor boy does not have much money.

---

payer [pay-YAY] verb   **to pay, to pay for**

je paye	nous payons
tu payes	vous payez
il, elle paye	ils, elles payent

Maman paye la viande au boucher.
Mother pays the butcher for the meat.

---

le pays [pay-EE] noun, masc.   **country**

Quel est le nom du pays à l'est de la France?
What is the name of the country to the east of France?
(See **campagne**)

---

la peau [POH] noun, fem.   **skin**

*Le soleil me brûle la peau quand je prends
un bain de soleil.*
The sun burns my skin when I take a sunbath.

---

la pêche [PEHSH] noun, fem.   **peach; fishing**

On mange des pêches en été.
People eat peaches in summer.

aller à la pêche [a-lay-a-la-PEHSH]   **to go fishing**
idiomatic expression

Nous allons à la pêche.
We are going fishing. (See **aller**)

---

le peigne [PEHN] noun, masc.   **comb**

Où est mon peigne?
Where is my comb?

---

se peigner [sé-peh-NAY] verb   **to comb (one's hair)**
  je me peigne   nous nous peignons
  tu te peignes   vous vous peignez
  il, elle se peigne   ils, elles se peignent

Avant de sortir de la maison, je me peigne.
Before leaving the house, I comb my hair.

---

peindre [PAINDR] verb   **to paint**
  je peins   nous peignons
  tu peins   vous peignez
  il, elle peint   ils, elles peignent

Ma soeur est une artiste. Elle aime peindre.
My sister is an artist. She likes to paint.

---

la pelle [PEHL] noun, fem.   **shovel**

Mon frère joue avec une pelle.
My brother plays with a shovel.

---

pendant [pahn-DAHN] preposition   **during**

Je dors pendant la nuit.
I sleep during the night.

penser [pahń-SAY] verb | **to think**

je pense	nous pensons
tu penses	vous pensez
il, elle pense	ils, elles pensent

Je pense que je vais chez mon ami. D'accord?
I think I'll go to my friend's house. All right?

---

perdre [PEHRDR] verb | **to lose**

je perds	nous perdons
tu perds	vous perdez
il, elle perd	ils, elles perdent

Jacques perd toujours son chapeau.
Jack always loses his hat.

---

le père [PEHR] noun, masc. | **father**

Mon père est facteur.
My father is a mail carrier.

> Proverb: Like father, like son.
>
> Un proverbe: Tel père, tel fils.

---

la permission [pehr-mee-SYOHŃ] noun, fem. | **permission**

Tu as la permission d'aller à la campagne?
Do you have permission to go to the country?

---

le perroquet [peh-ruh-KAY] noun, masc. | **parrot**

Un perroquet est mon animal favori.
A parrot is my pet.

la perruche [peh-REWSH] noun, fem.   **parakeet**

Nous avons deux jolies perruches.
We have two pretty parakeets.

---

la personne [pehr-SUHN] noun, fem.   **person**
les personnes fem., pl.   **people**

Il y a sept personnes dans ma famille.
There are seven people in my family.

---

petit [PTEE] adjective, masc.   **small, little; short**
petite [PTEET] fem.

L'oiseau est petit.
The bird is small.

le petit déjeuner   **breakfast** (See **déjeuner**)
la petite-fille [pteet-FEEY] noun, fem.   **granddaughter**

Je suis la petite-fille de l'ingénieur.
I am the engineer's granddaughter.

le petit-fils [ptee-FEES] noun, masc.   **grandson**

Je suis le petit-fils du boucher.
I am the butcher's grandson.

le petit pain   **roll** (See **pain**)
les petits pois noun, masc., pl.   **peas**

---

un peu [PEOH] adverb   **a little**

Voulez-vous de la soupe? Un peu, s'il vous plaît.
Do you want any soup? A little, please.

---

la peur [PEUHR] noun, fem.   **fear**

avoir peur [PEUHR]   **to be afraid, to be**
idiomatic expression   **frightened, to fear**
                   (See **avoir**)

Avez-vous peur de l'orage?
Are you afraid of the storm?

---

peut-être [peoh-TEHTR] adverb   **maybe, perhaps**
Nous montons à cheval ce matin? Peut-être.
Are we going horseback riding this morning? Maybe.

---

la pharmacie [far-ma-SEE] noun, fem.   **pharmacy,**
La pharmacie se trouve près du parc.   **drugstore**
The pharmacy is located close to the park.

---

la photo [fuh-TOH] noun, fem.   **photograph, picture**
Regarde ma photo! Elle est drôle, n'est-ce pas?
Look at my picture. It's funny, isn't it?

---

la photocopieuse [foh-toh-koh-pee-uhz] noun, fem.   **copier**
J'aime ma photocopieuse.
I like my copier.

---

la phrase [FRAZ] noun, fem.   **sentence**
J'écris une phrase dans mon cahier.
I am writing a sentence in my notebook.

---

le piano [pya-NOH] noun, masc.   **piano**
jouer du piano idiomatic expression   **to play the piano**
Qui joue du piano dans votre famille?
Who plays the piano in your family?

---

la pièce [PYEHS] noun, fem.   **room**
Il y a deux pièces dans notre appartement.
There are two rooms in our apartment.

---

le pied [PYAY] noun, masc.   **foot**
aller à pied [a-lay-a-PYAY] verb   **to walk, to go on foot**
Nous allons au musée à pied.
We walk to the museum.

avoir mal au pied   **to have a sore foot**
[a-vwar-ma-loh-PYAY] verb   (See **avoir**)

---

la pierre [PYEHR] noun, fem.   **stone**

Il y a beaucoup de pierres dans le terrain de jeux.
There are many stones in the playground.

---

le pilote (d'avion) [pee-luht-da-VYOHN]   **(airplane) pilot**
noun, masc.

Mon cousin est pilote d'avion.
My cousin is an airplane pilot.

---

le pique-nique [peek-NEEK] noun, masc.   **picnic**
faire un pique-nique [feh-ruhn-peek-NEEK]   (See **faire**)

Nous faisons un pique-nique à la campagne.
We have a picnic in the country.

---

piquer [pee-KAY] verb   **to bite (insect); to sting**
   il, elle pique   ils, elles piquent

Les moustiques aiment me piquer.
The mosquitoes like to bite me.

---

la piscine [pee-SEEN] noun, fem.   **swimming pool**

J'ai la permission d'aller à la piscine avec vous.
I have permission to go to the pool with you.

le placard [pla-KAR] noun, masc.   **closet, poster**

Le placard est fermé.
The closet is closed.

---

la place [PLAS] noun, fem.   **place; seat; setting (table)**

Ma cousine met un couteau à chaque place.
My cousin puts a knife at each setting.

Je vais au tableau nor et je retourne à ma place.
I go to the blackboard and I return to my seat.

---

le plafond [pla-FOHM] noun, masc.   **ceiling**

Le plafond du château est très intéressant.
The ceiling of the chateau is very interesting.

---

la plage [PLAZH] noun, fem.   **beach**

Noun allons à la plage en été.
We go to the beach in summer.

---

se plaindre [sé-PLAIMDR] verb   **to complain**
  je me plains   nous nous plaignons
  tu te plains   vous vous plaignez
  il, elle se plaint   ils, elles se plaignent

Mon amie dit que je me plains toujours!
My friend says that I always complain!

---

le plaisir [pleh-ZEER] noun, masc.   **pleasure**

Tu viens avec nous? Avec plaisir!
Are you coming with us? With pleasure!

---

le plancher [plahñ-SHAY] noun, masc.   **floor**

Le stylo tombe sur le plancher.
The pen falls to the floor.

la planète [pla-NEHT] noun, fem.   **planet**

Savez-vous les noms de toutes les planètes?
Do you know the names of all the planets?

la plante [PLAHÑT] noun, fem.   **plant**

Il y a cinq plantes dans la salle de classe.
There are five plants in the classroom.

plat [PLA] adjective, masc.   **flat**
plate [PLAT] fem.

Le champ est plat.
The field is flat.

plein [PLAIÑ] adjective, masc.   **full**
pleine [PLEHN] fem.

La valise est pleine de vêtements.
The valise is full of clothes.

pleurer [pleuh-RAY] verb   **to cry, to weep**
   je pleure   nous pleurons
   tu pleures   vous pleurez
   il, elle pleure   ils, elles pleurent

Je pleure quand on me taquine.
I cry when somebody teases me.

pleuvoir [pleuh-vwar] verb   **to rain**

Vous pensez qu'il va pleuvoir?
Do you think it's going to rain?

Il pleut. [eel-pleuh]   **It is raining. It rains.**

idiomatic expression

Il pleut beaucoup au mois d'avril.
It rains a lot in the month of April.

---

plus [plew] adverb   **more, ...er**
                                                 (comparative of
Mon amie est plus grande que moi.   adjectives)
My friend is taller than I.

ne...plus   **no longer** (See **ne...plus**)
plus tard   **later** (See **tard**)
plusieurs [plew-zyeuhr] adjective   **several**

Il y a plusieurs autos sur la route.
There are several cars on the road.

---

la poche [puhsh] noun, fem.   **pocket**

J'ai des billes dans la poche.
I have some marbles in my pocket.

---

la poire [pwar] noun, fem.   **pear**

Est-ce que la poire est mûre?
Is the pear ripe?

---

le pois [PWA] noun, masc.   **pea**
les petits pois [ptee-PWA] noun, masc., pl.   **peas**

J'aime bien manger les petits pois.
I like to eat peas.

---

le poisson [pwah-SOHᴺ] noun, masc.   **fish**

Il y a beaucoup de poissons dans ce lac.
There are many fish in this lake.

le poisson rouge [pwah-sohᴺ-ROOZH] noun, masc.   **goldfish**

J'ai cinq poissons rouges.
I have five goldfish.

---

poli [puh-LEE] adjective   **polite**

Maman dit: "L'enfant poli ne parle pas la bouche pleine."
Mother says, "A polite child does not speak with
a full mouth."

---

la police [puh-LEES] noun, fem.   **police**
l'agent de police   **police officer** (See **agent...**)

---

la pomme [PUHM] noun, fem.   **apple**

Je mange une pomme tous les jours.
I eat an apple every day.

---

la pomme de terre [puhm-dé-TEHR] noun, fem.   **potato**

Aimez-vous les pommes de terre?
Do you like potatoes?

---

la pompe à incendie   **fire truck**
[pohᴺ-pa-aiᴺ-sahᴺ-DEE] noun, fem.

La pompe à incendie fait beaucoup de bruit.
The fire truck makes a lot of noise.

---

le pompier [pohń-PYAY] noun, masc.   **fireman**

Le pompier est très fort.
The fireman is very strong.

le pont [POHИ] noun, masc.   **bridge**

Où est le pont d'Avignon?
Where is the Avignon bridge?

la porte [PUHRT] noun, fem.   **door**

Fermez la porte, s'il vous plaît.
Please close the door.

porter [puhr-TAY] verb   **to carry; to wear**

je porte	nous portons
tu portes	vous portez
il, elle porte	ils, elles portent

Il porte ses livres.
He is carrying his books.

Elle porte un chapeau.
She is wearing a hat.

se porter [sé-puhr-TAY]   **to be (state of health),**
idiomatic expression   **to feel**

Comment vous portez-vous?
How are you?

la poste	post office (See **le bureau de poste**)
le bureau de poste	post office (See **le bureau**)
mettre une lettre à la poste	to mail a letter (See **mettre**)

---

le poulet [poo-LAY] noun, masc.   **chicken**

Qu'est-ce qu'on mange ce soir? Du poulet.
What are we eating this evening? Chicken.

---

la poupée [poo-PAY] noun, fem.   **doll**

Ma poupée s'appelle Sylvie.
My doll's name is Sylvia.

la maison de poupée   **dollhouse**
[meh-sohn-dé-poo-PAY] noun, fem.

---

pour [POOR] preposition   **for, in order to, to**

Elle va au magasin pour acheter des chemises.
She is going to the store to buy shirts.

---

le pourboire [poor-BWAR] noun, masc.   **tip**

L'homme laisse un pourboire pour le garçon.
The man leaves a tip for the waiter.

---

pourquoi [poor-KWAH] adverb   **why?**

Pourquoi êtes-vous en retard?
Why are you late?

---

pousser [poo-SAY] verb   **to push, to grow**
  je pousse   nous poussons
  tu pousses   vous poussez
  il, elle pousse   ils, elles poussent

Il me pousse!
He's pushing me!

Les fleurs poussent dans le jardin.
Flowers are growing in the garden.

---

pouvoir [poo-VWAR] verb   **to be able, (can, may)**
  je peux   nous pouvons
  tu peux   vous pouvez
  il, elle peut   ils, elles pouvent

Je ne peux pas faire mes devoirs. Les leçons sont trop difficiles.
I can't do my homework. The lessons are too difficult.

Puis-je aller à la pêche?
May I go fishing?

---

préférer [pray-fay-RAY] verb   **to prefer**
  je préfère   nous préférons
  tu préfères   vous préférez
  il, elle préfère   ils, elles préfèrent

Préfères-tu la ville ou la campagne?
Do you prefer the city or the country?

---

premier [pré-MYAY] adjective, masc.   **first**
première [pré-MYEHR] fem.

Le petit déjeuner est le premier repas de la journée.
Breakfast is the first meal of the day.

---

prendre [PRAHⁿDR] verb   **to take; to have (food)**
  je prends   nous prenons
  tu prends   vous prenez
  il, elle prend   ils, elles prennent

Nous prenons un bain de soleil à la plage.
We take a sunbath at the beach.

Maman prend un croissant pour le petit déjeuner.
Mom has a croissant for breakfast.

---

préparer [pray-pa-RAY] verb   **to prepare**
  je prépare   nous préparons
  tu prépares   vous préparez
  il, elle prépare   ils, elles préparent

Ma soeur prépare la salade.
My sister prepares the salad.

---

près de [PREH] preposition   **near, close to**

Bordeaux est près de l'océan Atlantique.
Bordeaux is near the Atlantic Ocean.

---

présent [pray-ZAHⁿ] adjective, masc.   **present, here**
présente [pray-ZAHⁿT] fem.

Mon amie Jeanne est présente; mon amie Suzanne est absente.
My friend Joan is present; my friend Susan is absent.

---

présenter [pray-sahⁿ-TAY] verb   **to introduce**
  je présente   nous présentons
  tu présentes   vous présentez
  il, elle présente   ils, elles présentent

Je vous présente mon petit-fils.
I would like to introduce my grandson to you.

---

le président [pray-zee-DAHN] noun, masc.   **president**

Qui est le président de la France?
Who is the president of France?

---

presque [PREHSK] adverb   **almost**

Il est presque six heures.
It is almost six o'clock.

---

prêt [PREH] adjective, masc.   **ready**
prête [PREHT] fem.

Es-tu prêt? Nous sommes en retard.
Are you ready? We are late.

---

prêter [preh-TAY] verb   **to lend**

je prête	nous prêtons
tu prêtes	vous prêtez
il, elle prête	ils, elles prêtent

Peux-tu me prêter ta bicyclette?
Can you lend me your bicycle?

---

je vous en prie [zhé-vóo-zahn-PREE]   **you're welcome**
idiomatic expression

Merci, mademoiselle.
Thank you, miss.

Je vous en prie, monsieur.
You're welcome, sir.

---

le prince [PRAINS] noun, masc.   **prince**
la princesse [PRAIN-SEHS] fem.

Le prince joue dans le jardin.
The prince is playing in the garden.

---

le printemps [prain-TAHN] noun, masc.   **spring**

Au printemps on voit beaucoup de fleurs.
You see a lot of flowers in the spring.

le prix [PREE] noun, masc.   **price**

Quel est le prix de ce livre?
What is the price of this book?

---

prochain [pro-SHAIN] noun, masc.   **next**
prochaine [proh-SHEHN] fem.

*Le professeur dit: "La semaine prochaine nous
avons un examen."*
The teacher says, "Next week we will have an examination."

---

le professeur [pruh-feh-SUHR] noun, masc.   **teacher**

Le professeur est dans la salle de classe.
The teacher is in the classroom.

---

profond [pruh-FOHN] adjective, masc.   **deep**
profonde [pruh-FOHND] fem.

Est-ce que la piscine est profonde?
Is the pool deep?

---

se promener [sé-pruhm-NAY]   **to walk**
verb, idiomatic expression

je me promène	nous nous promenons
tu te promènes	vous vous promenez
il, elle se promène	ils, elles se promènent

Elles se promènent dans le parc.
They are walking in the park.

faire une promenade   **to take a walk**
[feh-rewn-pruhm-NAD]
idiomatic expression

Ils vont faire une promenade.
They are going to take a walk.

---

promettre [pruh-MEHTR] verb   **to promise**

je promets	nous promettons
tu promets	vous promettez
il, elle promet	ils, elles promettent

Je promets de faire mes devoirs.
I promise to do my homework.

---

propre [PRUHPR] adjective   **clean; own**

Mes mains sont propres.
My hands are clean.

Ce n'est pas le livre de ma soeur; c'est mon propre livre.
It is not my sister's book; it is my own book.

---

puis [PEW-EE] adverb   **then**

J'écris une lettre; puis, je vais chez mon ami.
I write a letter; then I go to my friend's house.

---

punir [pew-NEER] verb   **to punish**

je punis	nous punissons
tu punis	vous punissez
il, elle punit	ils, elles punissent

Quand je suis méchant, maman me punit.
When I am naughty, Mom punishes me.

---

le pupitre [pew-PEETR] noun, masc.   **desk (pupil's)**

Son pupitre est trop petit.
His desk is too small.

---

le pyjama [pee-zha-MA] noun, masc.   **pajamas**

Je mets le pyjama à dix heures du soir.
I put on my pajamas at ten o'clock at night.

Q

quand [KAHN] adverb   **when**

Je lis un livre quand il pleut.
I read a book when it rains.

---

quarante [ka-RAHNT] adjective   **forty**

Connaissez-vous l'histoire des quarante voleurs?
Do you know the story of the forty thieves?

---

le quart [KAR] noun, masc.   **quarter**

Il est sept heures et quart.
It is a quarter after seven.

---

quatorze [ka-TUHRZ] adjective   **fourteen**

Le quatorze juillet est la fête nationale française.
July 14th is the French national holiday.

---

quatre [KATR] adjective   **four**

Il y a quatre personnes dans ma famille.
There are four people in my family.

---

quatre-vingt-dix [ka-tré-vain-DEES] adjective   **ninety**

Quelqu'un a quatre-vingt-dix ans?
Somebody is ninety years old?

---

quatre-vingts [ka-tré-VAIN] adjective   **eighty**

J'ai quatre-vingts billes!
I have eighty marbles!

---

que [ké] pronoun   **that; which; what; whom**
qu' (before a vowel)

Voici la lettre que j'écris.
Here is the letter that I am writing.

La femme que je vois est ma tante.
The woman whom I see is my aunt.

Qu'as-tu? [ka-TEW], **Qu'avez-vous?**   **What's the matter?**
[ka-vay-VOO] interjection

quel [KEHL] adjective, pronoun, masc.   **what, which;**
quelle fem.   **what a ...!**

Quel drapeau est le drapeau français?
Which flag is the French flag?

Quelle belle robe!
What a beautiful dress!

---

quelque [KEHL-ké] adjective   **any; some; several**

Il y a quelques chaises dans le salon.
There are several chairs in the living room.

---

quelque chose [kehl-ké-SHOHZ]   **something, anything**
pronoun

Est-ce qu'il y a quelque chose dans ce tiroir?
Is there something in this drawer?

---

quelquefois [kehl-ké-FWA] adverb   **sometimes**

Quelquefois je ne suis pas sage.
Sometimes I am not well-behaved.

---

quelqu'un [kehl-KUHN] pronoun, masc.   **someone,**
quelqu'une [kehl-KEWN] fem.   **somebody**

Quelqu'un est dans le restaurant.
Somebody is in the restaurant.

---

la querelle [ké-REHL] noun, fem.   **quarrel**

Quelquefois, mon père se querelle avec ma mère.
My father sometimes has a quarrel with my mother.

---

la question [kehs-TYOHɴ] noun, fem.   **question**

Le professeur demande: "Est-ce qu'il y a des questions?"
The teacher asks, "Are there any questions?"

---

la queue [KEOH] noun, fem.   **tail**

Mon chien remue la queue quand je rentre à la maison.
My dog wags his tail when I return home.

---

qui [KEE] pronoun   **who, which, that**

Qui vient chez nous?
Who is coming to visit us?

Je cherche mon stylo qui est sur le tapis.
I am looking for my pen, which is on the rug.

---

quinze [KAIɴZ] adjective   **fifteen**

*C'est aujourd'hui le quinze janvier, l'anniversaire de
Martin Luther King.*
Today is January 15th, the birthday of Martin Luther King.

---

quitter [kee-TAY] verb   **to leave, to take off**
   je quitte   nous quittons
   tu quittes   vous quittez
   il, elle quitte   ils, elles quittent

Nous quittons le musée à cinq heures.
We leave the museum at five o'clock.

See also: laisser, partir, sortir

---

quoi [KWA] interjection   **what**

Quoi? Tu n'as pas la monnaie pour l'autobus?
What? You don't have the change for the bus?

il n'y a pas de quoi.   **You're welcome.**
[eel-nee-a-pa-dé-KWA] idiomatic expression   **(polite)**
or
Je vous en prie. [zhé-voo-zahɴ-PREE] idiomatic expression

172

R

raconter [ra-kohń-TAY] verb   **to tell**
  je raconte   nous racontons
  tu racontes   vous racontez
  il, elle raconte   ils, elles racontent

Raconte-moi une histoire, maman.
Tell me a story, Mom.

---

la radio [ra-DYOH] noun, fem.   **radio**
La radio ne marche pas.
The radio is not working.

---

le raisin [reh-ZAIŃ] noun, masc.   **grape**
Mmm, nous avons des raisins!
Mmm, we have grapes!

> La Fontaine was a French author who wrote
> fables such as "The Fox and the Grapes."
>
> La Fontaine était un écrivain français qui a écris
> des fables comme "Le renard et les raisins."

---

la raison [reh-ZOHŃ] noun, fem.   **reason, right**
avoir raison [reh-ZOHŃ] idiomatic expression   **to be right**
(See **avoir**)

Grand-mère a toujours raison.
Grandmother is always right.

---

le rang [RAHŃ] noun, masc.   **row**
La maîtress dit: "Les enfants du premier rang,
levez-vous."
The teacher says, "Children in the first row, stand."

---

rapide [ra-PEED] adjective   **rapid, fast**

Le chien est rapide quand il court après un chat.
The dog is fast when he runs after a cat.

---

se rappeler [sé-ra-PLAY] verb   **to remember**
  je me rappelle   nous nous rappelons
  tu te rappelles   vous vous rappelez
  il, elle se rappelle   ils, elles se rappellent

Je ne peux pas me rappeller le nom de ce bâtiment.
I cannot remember the name of this building.

---

le rat [RA] noun, masc.   **rat**

J'ai peur des rats!
I am afraid of rats!

---

recevoir [ré-sé-VWAR] verb   **to receive, to get**
  je reçois   nous recevons
  tu reçois   vous recevez
  il, elle reçoit   ils, elles reçoivent

*Je reçois une carte postale de ma soeur toutes
les semaines.*
I receive a postcard from my sister every week.

---

le réfrigérateur [ray-free-zhay-ra-TUHR]   **refrigerator**
noun, masc.

Le réfrigérateur est dans la cuisine.
The refrigerator is in the kitchen.

---

regarder [ré-gar-DAY] verb   **to look at, to watch**
  je regarde   nous regardons
  tu regardes   vous regardez
  il, elle regarde   ils, elles regardent

J'aime regarder la télévision.
I like to watch television.

se regarder [sé-ré-gar-DAY]   **to look at oneself**
idiomatic expression
 je me regarde   nous nous regardons
 tu te regardes   vous vous regardez
 il, elle se regarde ils, elles regardent
Le singe se regarde dans la glace.
The monkey looks at itself in the mirror.

---

la règle [REHGL] noun, fem.   **ruler; rule**
La règle est longue.
The ruler is long.

Il faut obéir aux règles à l'école et à la maison.
We have to obey the rules at school and at home.

---

la reine [REHN] noun, fem.   **queen**
La reine est assise près du roi.
The queen is seated near the king.

---

remplir [rahń-PLEER] verb   **to fill**
 je remplis   nous remplissons
 tu remplis   vous remplissez
 il, elle remplit   ils, elles remplissent
Etienne remplit la boîte de papier.
Stephen fills the box with paper.

---

remuer [ré-mew-AY] verb   **to move, to shake,**
 je remue   nous remuons   **to wag**
 tu remues   vous remuez
 il, elle remue   ils, elles remuent
Elle remue vite ses doigts quand elle joue du piano.
She moves her fingers quickly when she plays the piano.

---

le renard [ré-NAR] noun, masc.   **fox**
Le renard court très vite.
The fox runs very fast.

---

rencontrer [rahn-kohn-TRAY] verb   **to meet**
   je rencontre   nous rencontrons
   tu rencontres   vous rencontrez
   il, elle rencontre   ils, elles rencontrent

Qui rencontre Le Petit Chaperon Rouge dans la forêt?
Who meets Little Red Riding Hood in the forest?

---

le rendez-vous [rahn-day-VOO] noun, masc.   **appointment**

A quelle heure est votre rendez-vous avec le médecin?
What time is your appointment with the doctor?

---

rendre [RAHNDR] verb   **to give back, to return**
   je rends   nous rendons
   tu rends   vous rendez
   il, elle rend   ils, elles rendent

Il me rend mes patins à roulettes.
He returns my roller skates.

---

rentrer [rahn-tray] verb   **to return**
   je rentre   nous rentrons
   tu rentres   vous rentrez
   il, elle rentre   ils, elles rentrent

Je rentre chez moi.
I return home.

---

renverser [rahn-vehr-SAY] verb   **to spill, to overturn**
   je renverse   nous renversons
   tu renverses   vous renversez
   il, elle renverse ils, elles renversent

Le bébé renverse l'assiette.
The baby overturns the plate.

réparer [ray-pa-RAY] verb   **to repair, to fix**
   je répare   nous réparons
   tu répares   vous réparez
   il, elle répare   ils, elles réparent

Mon frère répare la machine.
My brother is fixing the machine.

le repas [ré-PA] noun, masc.   **meal**

Quel repas préférez-vous?
Which meal do you prefer?

repasser [ré-pa-SAY] verb   **to iron**
   je repasse   nous repassons
   tu repasses   vous repassez
   il, elle repasse   ils, elles repassent

Ma mère repasse la chemise de Papa avec un fer.
My mother irons Dad's shirt with an iron.

répéter [ray-pay-TAY] verb   **to repeat**
   je répète   nous répétons
   tu répètes   vous répétez
   il, elle répète   ils, elles répètent

Le maître dit: "Répétez après moi."
The teacher says, "Repeat after me."

répondre [ray-POHNDR] verb   **to answer, to reply**
   je réponds   nous répondons
   tu réponds   vous répondez
   il, elle répond   ils, elles répondent

La petite fille ne peut pas répondre à la question.
The little girl cannot answer the question.

la réponse [ray-POHNS] noun, fem.   **answer**

J'écris la réponse correcte dans mon cahier.
I write the correct answer in my notebook.

se reposer [sé-ré-poh-SAY] verb   **to rest**

je me repose	nous nous reposons
tu te reposes	vous vous reposez
il, elle se repose	ils, elles se reposent

L'enfant court. Il ne veut pas se reposer.
The child runs. He does not want to rest.

---

le restaurant [rehs-tuh-RAHN] noun, masc.   **restaurant**

Le garçon travaille dans ce restaurant.
The waiter works in this restaurant.

---

rester [rehs-TAY] verb   **to stay, to remain**

je reste	nous restons
tu restes	vous restez
il, elle reste	ils, elles restent

Je voudrais rester chez ma grand-mère.
I would like to stay at my grandmother's house.

---

retard [ré-TAR] noun, masc.   **delay**
en retard [ahn-ré-TAR] adverb   **late**

François arrive en retard à l'école.
Frank comes late to school.

---

retourner [ré-toor-NAY] verb   **to return, to go back**

je retourne	nous retournons
tu retournes	vous retournez
il, elle retourne	ils, elles retournent

Il va au tableau noir et puis il retourne à sa place.
He goes to the blackboard and then he returns to his seat.

---

réussir [ray-~~ew~~-SEER] verb   **to succeed, to be successful**
je réussis   nous réussissons
tu réussis   vous réussissez
il, elle réussit   ils, elles réussissent

Il réussit à attraper un poisson.
He succeeds in catching a fish.

---

le réveille-matin [ray-vay-ma-TAIN]   **alarm clock**
noun, masc.

Le réveille-matin sonne trop fort.
The alarm clock rings too loudly.

---

se réveiller [sé-ray-vay-YAY] verb   **to wake up**
je me réveille   nous nous réveillons
tu te réveilles   vous vous réveillez
il, elle se réveille   ils, elles se réveillent

Nous nous réveillons de bonne heure.
We wake up early.

---

rêver [reh-VAY] verb   **to dream**
je rêve   nous rêvons
tu rêves   vous rêvez
il, elle rêve   ils, elles rêvent

Je rêve d'aller sur la lune!
I dream of going to the moon!

le rêve [REHV] noun, masc.   **dream**

---

revoir [ré-VWAR] verb   **to see again**
je revois   nous revoyons
tu revois   vous revoyez
il, elle revoit   ils, elles revoient

Je vais revoir le film.
I am going to see the film again.

au revoir   **good-bye** (See **au revoir**)

---

le rez-de-chaussée   **ground floor**
[rayd-shoh-SAY] noun, masc.

Notre appartement est au rez-de-chaussée.
Our apartment is on the ground floor.

---

le rhume [REWM] noun, masc.   **cold (illness)**

Tu ne peux pas sortir. Tu as un rhume.
You cannot go out. You have a cold.

---

riche [REESH] adjective   **rich, wealthy**

La femme riche porte des bijoux.
The rich lady wears jewels.

---

le rideau [ree-DOH] noun, masc.   **curtain**
les rideaux pl.

Les rideaux dans ma chambre sont trop longs.
The curtains in my room are too long.

---

rien [RYAIN] pronoun   **nothing, none**

Qu'est-ce que tu as dans la poche? Rien!
What do you have in your pocket? Nothing!

De rien. [dé-RYAIN] idiomatic expression   **You're welcome.**

Je lui donne une banane. Il dit: "Merci."
Je réponds: "De rien."
I give him a banana. He says, "Thanks."
I answer, "You're welcome."

---

rire [REER] verb   **to laugh**

je ris	nous rions
tu ris	vous riez
il, elle rit	ils, elles rient

Il rit quand il regarde les ours.
He laughs when he looks at the bears.

---

rivaliser [ree-va-lee-zay] verb   **to compete**
Nous rivalisons dans le concours.
We compete in the contest.

---

la rivière [ree-VYEHR] noun, fem.   **river**
Comment peut-on traverser la rivière?
How can we cross the river?

---

le riz [REE] noun, masc.   **rice**
Le riz est délicieux.
The rice is delicious.

---

la robe [RUHB] noun, fem.   **dress**
La robe de ma poupée est sale.
My doll's dress is dirty.

---

le rocher [ruh-SHAY] noun, masc.   **rock**
Quel grand rocher là-bas!
What a large rock over there!

---

le roi [RWA] noun, masc.   **king**
*Est-ce qu'il y a un roi en France? Non, il y a un
président.*
Is there a king in France? No, there is a president.

---

le rôle [ROHL] noun, masc.   **role, part**
Je veux jouer le rôle du prince.
I want to play the part of the prince.

---

rond [ROHN] adjective, masc.   **round**
ronde [ROHND] fem.
L'assiette est ronde.
The plate is round.

---

le rosbif [ruhz-BEEF] noun, masc.   **roast beef**

Je voudrais un sandwich de rosbif, s'il vous plaît.
I would like a roast beef sandwich, please.

---

rose [ROHZ] adjective   **pink**

J'aime porter mon ruban rose dans les cheveux.
I like to wear my pink ribbon in my hair.

---

la roue [ROO] noun, fem.   **wheel**

Mon oncle répare la roue de ma bicyclette.
My uncle fixes the wheel of my bicycle.

---

rouge [ROOZH] adjective   **red**

Les voitures s'arrêtent quand le feu est rouge.
The cars stop when the light is red.

---

rouler [roo-LAY] verb   **to roll, to go**

je roule	nous roulons
tu roules	vous roulez
il, elle roule	ils, elles roulent

Le patin à roulettes roule dans la rue.
The roller skate is rolling into the street.

---

la route [ROOT] noun, fem.   **road, route, highway**

Quel est le nom de cette route?
What's the name of this road?

---

le ruban [rew-BAHN] noun, masc.   **ribbon**

Elle porte un joli ruban.
She is wearing a pretty ribbon.

---

la rue [REW] noun, fem.   **street**

Il est dangereux de jouer à la balle dans la rue.
It is dangerous to play ball in the street.

rusé [rew-ZAY] adjective, masc.   **clever, cunning**
rusée fem.

Le voleur est rusé; il grimpe sur un arbre.
The thief is clever; he climbs a tree.

S

sa   (See **son**)

---

le sable [SABL] noun, masc.   **sand**

A la plage, je m'assieds sur le sable.
At the beach I sit on the sand.

---

le sac [SAK] noun, masc.   **bag, sack, purse**
le sac à main [sa-ka-MAIN] noun, masc.   **handbag,**
                                                       pocketbook
J'achète un sac à main pour ma mère.
I am buying a handbag for my mother.

---

sage [SAZH] adjective, noun, masc.   **well-behaved;**
                                                 wise, wise person
Les petites filles sont plus sages
que les petits garçons.
Little girls are better behaved than little boys.

Grand-père est un sage.
Grandfather is wise.

---

sain et sauf [sain-ay-SOHF]   **safe and sound**
idiomatic expression

Je retourne à la maison sain et sauf.
I come home safe and sound.

---

la saison [seh-ZOHN] noun, fem.   **season**

Combien de saisons y a-t-il?
How many seasons are there?

---

la salade [sa-LAD] noun, fem. | **salad**

Ma cousine met la salade au milieu de la table.
My cousin puts the salad in the middle of the table.

---

sale [SAL] adjective | **dirty**

Ma chemise est sale!
My shirt is dirty!

---

la salle [SAL] noun, fem. | **room**
la salle de classe [sal-dé-KLAS] noun, fem. | **classroom**

La salle de classe est vide.
The classroom is empty.

---

la salle à manger [sa-la-mahń-ZHAY] | **dining room**
noun, fem.

Maman entre dans la salle à manger.
Mother enters the dining room.

---

la salle de bain [sal-dé-BAIŃ] noun, fem. | **bathroom**

La salle de bain est petite.
The bathroom is small.

---

le salon [sa-LOHŃ] noun, masc. | **living room**

Qui est dans le salon?
Who is in the living room?

---

samedi [sam-DEE] noun, masc.   **Saturday**

Faisons un pique-nique samedi.
Let's have a picnic Saturday.

---

le sandwich [sahń-DWEESH] noun, masc.   **sandwich**

Tu veux un sandwich ou une salade?
Do you want a sandwich or a salad?

---

le sang [SAHŃ] noun, masc.   **blood**

J'ai mal au genou. Regarde le sang!
My knee hurts. Look at the blood!

---

sans [SAHŃ] preposition   **without**

Je vais en classes sans mon ami. Il est malade.
I'm going to class without my friend. He is sick.

---

la santé [sahń-TAY] noun, fem.   **health**

*Maman dit: "Les bonbons ne sont pas bons pour la
santé."*
Mother says, "Candy is not good for your health."

---

le saute-mouton [soht-moo-TON] noun, masc.   **leapfrog**
jouer à saute-mouton   **to play leapfrog**
[zhoo-ay-ah-soht-moo-TON]
idiomatic expression

Nous jouons à saute-mouton.
We play leapfrog.

---

sauter [soh-TAY] verb   **to jump, to leap**
  je saute   nous sautons
  tu sautes   vous sautez
  il, elle saute   ils, elles sautent

Le garçon saute de l'escalier.
The boy jumps from the stairs.

sauter à la corde [soh-tay-a-la-KUHRD]   **jump rope**
                                         (See **la corde**)

---

la sauterelle [soh-TREHL] noun, fem.   **grasshopper**

Le garçon essaye d'attraper la sauterelle.
The boy tries to catch the grasshopper.

---

sauvage [soh-VAZH] adjective   **wild**

Les animaux sauvages habitent la forêt.
Wild animals live in the forest.

---

sauver [soh-VAY] verb   **to save, to rescue**

je sauve	nous sauvons
tu sauves	vous sauvez
il, elle sauve	ils, elles sauvent

Mon oncle me sauve quand je tombe dans l'eau.
My uncle saves me when I fall into the water.

---

le savant [sa-VAHN] noun, masc.   **scientist**
la savante [sa-VAHNT] fem.

Je voudrais devenir savant.
I would like to become a scientist.

> Pierre and Marie Curie were French scientists
> who discovered radium.
>
> Pierre et Marie Curie étaient savants français qui
> ont découvert le radium.

savoir [sa-VWAR] verb **to know (people), to know how to**
je sais	nous savons
tu sais	vous savez
il, elle sait	ils, elles savent

Je sais monter à bicyclette.
I know how to ride a bicycle.

See also: connaitre

---

le savon [sa-VOHN] noun, masc. **soap**

N'oublie pas d'employer le savon!
Don't forget to use soap!

---

la science [SYAHNS] noun, fem. **science**

J'aime aller en classe de science.
I like to go to my science class.

---

se [sé] pronoun **himself, herself, themselves**

Il se lave.
He washes himself.

Elle se peigne.
She combs her hair.

Elles se lèvent à sept heures.
They get up at seven o'clock.

---

le seau [SOH] noun, masc. **pail, bucket**
les seaux pl.

Le fermier remplit le seau de lait.
The farmer fills the pail with milk.

---

sec [SEHK] adjective, masc. **dry**
sèche [SEHSH] fem.

Est-ce que le plancher est sec, Maman?
Is the floor dry, Mom?

---

le secours [SKOOR] noun, masc.   **help**
Au secours! [oh-SKOOR] interjection   **Help!**
Quand je tombe je crie: "Au secours!"
When I fall I cry, "Help!"

---

le secret [sé-KREH] noun, masc.   **secret**
Dis-moi le secret!
Tell me the secret!

---

seize [SEHZ] adjective   **sixteen**
Je dois lire seize pages ce soir!
I have to read sixteen pages this evening!

---

le sel [SEHL] noun, masc.   **salt**
Passez-moi le sel, s'il vous plaît.
Pass me the salt, please.

---

selon [SLOHṊ] preposition   **according to**
Selon mon frère, il va neiger demain.
According to my brother, it is going to snow tomorrow.

---

la semaine [SMEHN] noun, fem.   **week**
Le calendrier nous montre les sept jours de la semaine.
The calendar shows us the seven days of the week.

---

sensationnel [sahṊ-sa-syohṊ-NEHL] interjection   **great, sensational, marvelous, wonderful**
Tu vas au théâtre? Sensationnel!
You're going to the theater? Marvelous!

---

le sentier [sahṊ-TYAY] noun, masc.   **path**
Ce sentier mène au pont.
This path leads to the bridge.

sentir [sahń-TEER] verb   **to smell; to feel**
  je sens   nous sentons
  tu sens   vous sentez
  il, elle sent   ils, elles sentent

Le gâteau sent bon.
The cake smells good.

---

sept [SEHT] adjective   **seven**
Voilà sept pommes.
There are seven apples.

---

septembre [sehp-TAHŃBR] noun, masc.   **September**
Est-ce qu'on retourne à l'école le premier septembre?
Do we go back to school on the first of September?

---

sérieux [say-RYEOH] adjective, masc.   **serious**
sérieuse [say-RYEOHZ] fem.

On joue un film sérieux au cinéma.
They are playing a serious film at the movies.

---

le serpent [sehr-PAHŃ] noun, masc.   **snake**

Est-ce qu'il y a des serpents en France?
Are there any snakes in France?

---

serrer la main à [seh-RAY]　　　　　　**to shake hands**
idiomatic expression
   je serre la main　　　　nous serrons la main
   tu serres la main　　　　vous serrez la main
   il, elle serre la main　ils, elles serrent la main

Alain, serre la main à ton voisin.
Alan, shake hands with your neighbor.

---

la serveuse [sehr-VEOHZ] noun, fem.　　**server, waitress**
le serveur [sehr-VEUHR] noun, masc.　　**waiter, server**

La serveuse est dans le restaurant.
The waitress is in the restaurant.

---

la serviette [sehr-VYEHT] noun, fem.　　**napkin; towel;**
　　　　　　　　　　　　　　　　　　　briefcase
Il y a quatre serviettes sur la table.
There are four napkins on the table.

Ma serviette est dans la salle de bain.
My towel is in the bathroom.

Laurent, n'oublie pas ta serviette.
Lawrence, don't forget your briefcase.

---

servir [sehr-VEER] verb　　　　　　　　**to serve**
   je sers　　　　　　　nous servons
   tu sers　　　　　　　vous servez
   il, elle sert　　　　ils, elles servent

Je sers le dîner à mon chien.
I serve my dog his dinner.

---

seul [SEUHL] adjective, masc.　　　　　**only; alone**
seule fem.

C'est la seule fleur dans le jardin.
It is the only flower in the garden.

Je suis seul dans le salon.
I am alone in the living room.

seulement [seuhl-MAHN̈] adverb   **only**

J'ai seulement un poisson rouge.
I have only one goldfish.

---

si [SEE] adverb   **so**

Le bébé mange si lentement!
The baby eats so slowly!

---

si [SEE] conjunction   **if, whether**
s' (before il)

Je vais à la fenêtre pour voir s'il pleut.
I am going to the window to see if it is raining.

S'il pleut, je ne peux pas sortir.
If it is raining, I cannot go out.

---

siffler [see-FLAY] verb   **to whistle**
  je siffle   nous sifflons
  tu siffles   vous sifflez
  il, elle siffle   ils, elles sifflent

Quand je siffle, mon ami sait que je suis à la porte.
When I whistle, my friend knows that I'm at the door.

---

silencieux [see-lahn̈-SYEOH] adjective, masc.   **quiet, silent**
silencieuse [see-lahn̈-SYEOHZ] fem.

La rue dans la ville n'est jamais silencieuse.
The city street is never quiet.

---

s'il vous plaît [seel-VOO-PLEH] idiomatic expression   **please**
s'il te plaît (familiar)

Donnez-moi un crayon, s'il vous plaît, monsieur Duval.
Please give me a pencil, Mr. Duval.

Donne-moi un crayon, s'il te plaît, Pierrot.
Please give me a pencil, Pete.

le singe [SAINZH] noun, masc.　　　　　　　　**monkey**

Le singe mange une banane.
The monkey is eating a banana.

---

six [SEES, SEEZ, SEE] adjective　　　　　　　　**six**

Combien de crayons avez-vous? Six. [SEES]
How many pencils do you have? Six.

Il a six amis. [SEEZ] *(before a vowel)*
He has six friends.

Il a six clous. [SEE] *(before a consonant)*
He has six nails. (metal)

---

le soda [soh-DA] noun, masc.　　　　　　　　**soda**

Je bois du soda.
I am drinking soda.

---

la soeur [SEUHR] noun, fem.　　　　　　　　**sister**

Ma tante est la soeur de ma mère.
My aunt is my mother's sister.

---

la soif [SWAF] noun, fem.　　　　　　　　　　**thirst**
avoir soif [a-vwar-SWAF] idiomatic expression　**to be thirsty**

Avez-vous soif? Oui, j'ai soif.
Are you thirsty? Yes, I'm thirsty. (See **avoir**)

---

le soin [SWAIN] noun, masc.　　　　　　　　　**care**
avec soin [a-vehk-SWAIN] adverb　　**with care, carefully**

Paul verse l'eau dans le verre avec soin.
Paul pours water into the glass carefully.

---

le soir [SWAR] noun, masc.　　　　　**evening, night**

Le soir je regarde la télé.
I watch television in the evening.

soixante [swa-SAHN/T] adjective   **sixty**

Il y a soixante minutes dans une heure.
There are sixty minutes in an hour.

---

soixante-dix [swa-sahn/t-DEES] adjective   **seventy**

La grand-mère de Nanette a soixante-dix ans.
Nancy's grandmother is seventy years old.

---

le soldat [suhl-DA] noun, masc.   **soldier**

Mon cousin est soldat.
My cousin is a soldier.

---

le soleil [suh-LAY] noun, masc.   **sun**

A quelle heure est-ce que le soleil se lève?
What time does the sun rise?

---

le bain de soleil [bain-dé-suh-LAY] noun, masc.   **sunbath**

Je prends un bain de soleil sur l'herbe.
I take a sunbath on the grass.

---

le sommeil [suh-MAY] noun, masc.   **sleep**
avoir sommeil [a-vwar-suh-MAY]   **to be sleepy**
idiomatic expression

Qui a sommeil?
Who is sleepy? (See **avoir**)

---

son [SOHN] adjective   **his; her; its; one's**
sa [SA] fem.
ses [SEH] masc., fem., pl.

Il mène son chien dans la rue.
He is leading his dog into the street.

Regardez sa jolie robe!
Look at her pretty dress!

Ses livres sont lourds.
Her books are heavy.

---

sonner [suh-NAY] verb   **to ring; to strike (clock)**
  je sonne   nous sonnons
  tu sonnes   vous sonnez
  il, elle sonne   ils, elles sonnent

Le téléphone sonne.
The telephone is ringing.

---

la sorte [SUHRT] noun, fem.   **sort, kind, type**

Quelle sorte de viande est-ce?
What kind of meat is this?

---

sortir [suhr-TEER] verb   **to go out, to leave**
  je sors   nous sortons
  tu sors   vous sortez
  il, elle sort   ils, elles sortent

L'infirmière sort de l'hôpital.
The nurse leaves the hospital.

See also: laisser, partir, quitter

---

la soucoupe [soo-KOOP] noun, fem.   **saucer**

La femme met la tasse sur la soucoupe.
The woman puts the cup on the saucer.

---

le souhait [soo-EH] noun, masc.   **wish**

Quand je me couche je fais un souhait.
When I go to bed I make a wish.

---

le soulier [soo-LYAY] noun, masc.   **shoe**

Mes souliers sont mouillés.
My shoes are wet.

---

la soupe [SOOP] noun, fem.   **soup**

Ma soeur sert la soupe à mon frère.
My sister serves soup to my brother.

---

sourd [SOOR] adjective, masc.   **deaf**
sourde [SOORD] fem.

Tu ne m'entends pas? Tu es sourd?
You don't hear me? You're deaf?

---

sourire [soo-REER] verb   **to smile**
  je souris   nous sourions
  tu souris   vous souriez
  il, elle sourit   ils, elles sourient

Tu souris toujours quand je te donne un petit gâteau.
You always smile when I give you a cookie.

---

la souris [soo-REE] noun, fem.   **mouse**

Il y a des souris dans ce champ.
There are mice in this field.

---

sous [soo] preposition   **under**

La carotte pousse sous la terre.
The carrot grows under the ground.

---

souvent [soo-VAHN] adverb   **often**

Je prends souvent l'autobus.
I often go by bus.

---

le sport [SPUHR] noun, masc.   **sport**

Quel est votre sport favori?
What is your favorite sport?

> Soccer is the national sport of France.
>
> Le football est le sport national de la France.

---

la station-service [sta-syohn-sehr-VEES]   **gas station**
noun, fem.

Enfin! Violà une station-service!
Finally! There is a gas station!

---

la stéréo [STAY-ray-oh] noun, fem.   **stereo**

Regardez la stéréo!
Look at the stereo!

---

stupide [stew-PEED] adjective   **stupid, foolish**

Est-ce que l'éléphant est intelligent ou stupide?
Is the elephant intelligent or stupid?

---

le stylo [stee-LOH] noun, masc.   **pen**

Je laisse toujours mon stylo à la maison.
I always leave my pen at home.

le stylo à bille [stee-loh-a-BEEY] noun, masc.   **ballpoint pen**
J'écris avec un stylo à bille.
I am writing with a ballpoint pen.

---

la sucette [sew-SEHT] noun, fem.   **lollipop**
Mmm, j'aime la sucette.
Mmm, I like the lollipop.

---

le sucre [sewKR] noun, masc.   **sugar**
Maman sert le sucre avec le thé.
Mother serves sugar with tea.

---

le sud [sewD] noun, masc.   **south**
Marseille est au sud de la France.
Marseilles is in the south of France.

---

suivre [sew-/-EEVR] verb   **to follow**
   je suis   nous suivons
   tu suis   vous suivez
   il, elle suit   ils, elles suivent
Les élèves de la classe suivent la maîtresse.
The pupils in the class follow the teacher.

---

le supermarché (See **marché**)

---

sur [sewR] preposition   **on**
La règle est sur le pupitre.
The ruler is on the desk.

---

sûr [sewR] adjective, masc.   **sure, certain**
sûre fem.
Je suis sûr que le train arrive bientôt.
I am sure that the train will come soon.
bien sûr (See **bien**)

---

la surprise [sewr-PREEZ] noun, fem.   **surprise**

Une surprise pour moi?
A surprise for me?

---

surtout [sewr-TOO] adverb   **above all, especially**

J'aime regarder la télévision, surtout le samedi matin.
I like to watch television, especially Saturday mornings.

---

surveiller [sewr-vay-YAY] verb   **to watch over,**
                                        to look after

je surveille	nous surveillons
tu surveilles	vous surveillez
il, elle surveille	ils, elles surveillent

La chatte surveille ses petits (chats).
The cat looks after her kittens.

T

ta (See **ton**)

---

la table [TABL] noun, fem.   **table**

La brosse est sur la table.
The brush is on the table.

---

le tableau [ta-BLOH] noun, masc.   **chalkboard, picture**
le tableau noir [ta-bloh-NWAR]   **blackboard**
noun, masc.

L'élève écrit au tableau noir.
The pupil writes on the blackboard.

---

le tablier [ta-BLYAY] noun, masc.   **apron**

Marthe porte un tablier à l'école.
Martha wears an apron at school.

---

la tache [TASH] noun, fem.   **spot, stain**

Il y a une tache sur le tapis.
There is a stain on the rug.

---

tacheté [tash-TAY] adjective, masc.   **spotted**
tachetée fem.

Ma tortue est tachetée.
My turtle is spotted.

---

la taille [TAHY] noun, fem.   **size; waist**

Dans un magasin on me demande:
"Quelle est votre taille?"
In a store they ask me, "What is your size?"

---

le tailleur [tah-YEUHR] noun, masc.   **tailor**

Mon voisin est tailleur.
My neighbor is a tailor.

---

se taire [sé-TEHR] idiomatic expression   **to be quiet**
   je me tais   nous nous taisons
   tu te tais   vous vous taisez
   il, elle se tait   ils, elles se taisent

On me dit toujours: "Tais-toi!"
They always tell me, "Be quiet!"

---

le tambour [tahⁿ-<u>boor</u>] noun, masc.   **drum**

Je fais du bruit quand je joue du tambour.
I make noise when I play the drum.

---

tant [TAHⁿ] adverb   **so much, so many**

Tant de raisins!
So many grapes!

---

la tante [TAHⁿT] noun, fem.   **aunt**

Ma tante est vendeuse.
My aunt is a salesperson.

---

le tapis [ta-PEE] noun, masc.   **rug**

Le tapis est sur le plancher.
The rug is on the floor.

---

taquiner [ta-kee-NAY] verb   **to tease**

  je taquine   nous taquinons
  tu taquines   vous taquinez
  il, elle taquine   ils, elles taquinent

Mon frère me taquine toujours!
My brother always teases me!

---

tard [TAR] adverb   **late**

Il est tard. Dépêchons-nous.
It is late. Let's hurry.

> Proverb: Better late than never.
>
> Un proverbe: Mieux vaut tard que jamais.

plus tard [plew-TAR] adverb   **later**

Il est huit heures maintenant. Le facteur arrive plus tard.
It is eight o'clock now. The mailman comes later.

---

la tarte [TART] noun, fem.   **pie**

Aimez-vous la tarte aux pommes?
Do you like apple pie?

---

la tartine [tar-TEEN] noun, fem.   **bread and butter (jam) snack**

Je prends une tartine quand je rentre à la maison.
I have a snack (of bread and jam) when I come home.

---

la tasse [TAS] noun, fem.   **cup**

Je mets la tasse sur la soucoupe.
I put the cup on the saucer.

---

le taxi [ta-KSEE] noun, masc.   **taxi**

Mon frère conduit un taxi.
My brother drives a taxi.

---

te [té] pronoun   **you, to you; yourself**

Je te donne du lait.
I give you some milk.

Tu te lèves trop tard!
You get up too late!

---

le technicien (See **l'ordinateur**)

---

la télé (See **télévision**)

---

le téléphone [tay-lay-FUHN] noun, masc.   **telephone**

J'aime parler au téléphone.
I like to talk on the telephone.

le portable [pr-TAH-bl] noun, masc.   **cell phone**

le téléviseur [tay-lay-vee-ZEUHR] noun, masc.   **television set**
Le téléviseur ne marche pas.
The television set is not working.

la télévision [tay-lay-vee-ZYOHM]   **television**
la télé [tay-LAY] noun, fem.
Mon frère et moi, nous regardons la télévision.
My brother and I watch television.
l'antenne de télévision (See **antenne**)
le cable [KAHBL] noun, masc.   **cable television (TV)**

le temps [TAHM] noun, masc.   **weather**
Quel temps fait-il? Il fait du soleil.
What is the weather? The sun is shining. (See **faire**)

la tente [TAHMT] noun, fem.   **tent**
*Quand je suis à la colonie de vacances je dors
dans une tente.*
When I am at camp I sleep in a tent.

le terrain de jeux [teh-raiṅ-dé-ZHEOH]   **playground**
noun, masc.
Nous jouons à la balle au terrain de jeux.
We play ball in the playground.

la terre [TEHR] noun, fem.   **earth; ground**
Quand l'astronaute est sur la lune, il voit la terre.
When the astronaut is on the moon, he sees the earth.
le tremblement de terre   **earthquake**
[trahm-blé-mahn-dé-tehr] noun, masc.

terrible! [teh-REEBL] adjective   **dreadful!**

J'ai une mauvaise note. Terrible!
I have a bad mark. Dreadful!

---

la tête [TEHT] noun, fem.   **head**

Le soldat tourne la tête.
The soldier turns his head.

---

le texto [TEHX-toh] noun, masc.   **text message**

Oh! J'ai un texto!
Oh! I have a text message!

envoyer par texto verb   **to send a text message**

---

le thé [TAY] noun, masc.   **tea**

Tu veux du thé ou du café?
Do you want tea or coffee?

---

le théâtre [tay-AHTR] noun, masc.   **theater**

Qu'est-ce qu'on joue au théâtre?
What are they performing at the theater?

Tiens! [TYAIN] interjection   **Say! Well!**

Tiens! Il commence à neiger.
Say! It's beginning to snow.

---

le tigre [TEEGR] noun, masc.   **tiger**

Le tigre est un grand chat sauvage.
The tiger is a big, wild cat.

---

le timbre [TAINBR] noun, masc.   **stamp (postage)**

Je mets un timbre sur l'enveloppe.
I put a stamp on the envelope.

---

la tirelire [teer-LEER] noun, fem.   **money box, piggy bank**
Je n'ai pas beaucoup d'argent dans ma tirelire.
I do not have much money in my piggy bank.

---

tirer [tee-RAY] verb   **to pull, to drag**
  je tire   nous tirons
  tu tires   vous tirez
  il, elle tire   ils, elles tirent
Il tire le chien qui ne veut pas avancer.
He is pulling the dog that does not want to go on.

---

le tiroir [tee-RWAR] noun, masc.   **drawer**
Je mets l'appareil dans un tiroir.
I put the camera in a drawer.

---

toi [TWA] pronoun   **you, to you**
C'est toi, Jacques, qui as mon bâton?
Do you have my stick, Jack?

---

les toilettes [twa-LEHT] noun, fem., pl.   **restroom(s)**
Les toilettes se trouvent là-bas.
The restrooms are over there.

---

le toit [TWA] noun, masc.   **roof**
Je regarde la ville du toit de la maison.
I look at the city from the roof of the house.

---

la tomate [tuh-MAT] noun, fem.   **tomato**
La tomate est rouge quand elle est mûre.
The tomato is red when it is ripe.

---

tomber [tohń-BAY] verb   **to fall**
  je tombe   nous tombons
  tu tombes   vous tombez
  il, elle tombe   ils, elles tombent

Le cerf-volant tombe par terre.
The kite falls to the ground.

---

ton [TOHŃ] adjective, masc.   **your**
ta [TA] fem.
tes [TEH] masc., fem., pl.

Ton cousin est beau.
Your cousin is handsome.

Ta voisine est gentille.
Your neighbor is kind.

Tes parents sont grands.
Your parents are tall.

---

le tonnerre [tuh-NEHR] noun, masc.   **thunder**

Après l'éclair on entend le tonnerre.
After the lightning you hear the thunder.

---

le tort [TUHR] noun, masc.   **wrong, injustice, harm**
avoir tort [a-vwar-TUHR]   **to be wrong**
idiomatic expression

Vous dites qu'il fait beau? Vous avez tort; il pleut.
You say that it is good weather? You are wrong; it is
raining. (See **avoir**)

---

la tortue [tuhr-TEW] noun, fem.   **turtle, tortoise**

La tortue marche lentement.
The turtle walks slowly.

---

tôt [TOH] adverb   **early**

Nous nous levons tôt pour aller en ville.
We get up early to go to the city.

---

toucher [too-SHAY] verb   **to touch**

je touche	nous touchons
tu touches	vous touchez
il, elle touche	ils, elles touchent

"Défense de toucher aux fleurs."
"Do not touch the flowers."

---

toujours [too-ZHOOR] adverb   **always, forever**

Les feuilles tombent toujours en automne.
The leaves always fall in autumn.

---

la toupie [too-PEE] noun, fem.   **top (toy)**

As-tu une toupie?
Do you have a top?

---

la tour [TOOR] noun, fem.   **tower**

La Tour Eiffel est très haute.
The Eiffel Tower is very tall.

---

le tour [TOOR] noun, masc.   **turn; trip**

Je voudrais faire le tour du monde.
I would like to take a trip around the world.

> The "Tour de France" is an international bicycle
> race around France.
>
> Le Tour de France est un concours de bicyclettes
> autour de la France.

tourner [toor-NAY] verb   **to turn**

je tourne	nous tournons
tu tournes	vous tournez
il, elle tourne	ils, elles tournent

Je tourne la page du dictionnaire.
I turn the page of the dictionary.

---

tousser [too-SAY] verb   **to cough**

je tousse	nous toussons
tu tousses	vous toussez
il, elle tousse	ils, elles toussent

Le bébé tousse. Il a un rhume.
The baby is coughing. He has a cold.

---

tout [TOO] adjective, masc.   **all, every**
tous masc., pl.
toute [TOOT] fem.

Je mets toutes mes lettres dans un tiroir.
I put all my letters in a drawer.

tout à coup [too-ta-KOO] adverb   **suddenly**

Tout à coup le médecin entre.
Suddenly the doctor enters.

tout à fait [too-ta-FEH] adverb   **completely**

Mon maillot n'est pas tout à fait sec.
My bathing suit is not completely dry.

tout à l'heure [too-ta-LEUHR] adverb   **in a little while**

Je vais à la plage tout à l'heure.
I am going to the beach in a little while.

tous les jours   **every day** (See **jour**)
tout le monde [tool-MUHND] pronoun   **everybody,**
                                                               everyone

Tout le monde aime le samedi soir.
Everyone likes Saturday night.

tout de suite [too-dsew/EET] adverb   **immediately, right away**

J'appelle le chien et il vient tout de suite.
I call the dog and he comes immediately.

le train [TRAIN̄] noun, masc.   **train**

Allons jouer avec mon train électrique.
Let's play with my electric train.

le traîneau [treh-NOH] noun, masc.   **sled**
les traîneaux pl.

Mon chien tire le traîneau.
My dog pulls the sled.

tranquille [trahn̄-KEEL] adjective   **quiet, calm**

J'aime aller à la pêche quand l'eau est tranquille.
I like to go fishing when the water is calm.

le travail [tra-VAHY] noun, masc.   **work**

Maman a beaucoup de travail à faire.
Mother has a lot of work to do.

travailler [tra-vah-YAY] verb   **to work**

je travaille	nous travaillons
tu travailles	vous travaillez
il, elle travaille	ils, elles travaillent

Le fermier travaille dehors.
The farmer works outside.

traverser [tra-vehr-SAY] verb   **to cross**

je traverse	nous traversons
tu traverses	vous traversez
il, elle traverse	ils, elles traversent

On peut traverser le lac?
Can we cross the lake?

treize [TREHZ] adjective   **thirteen**

L'escalier a treize marches.
The staircase has thirteen steps.

---

trente [TRAHNT] adjective   **thirty**

Quels mois ont trente jours?
Which months have thirty days?

---

très [TREH] adverb   **very**

Le château est très grand.
The castle is very big.

---

tricoter [tree-kuh-TAY] verb   **to knit**

je tricote	nous tricotons
tu tricotes	vous tricotez
il, elle tricote	ils, elles tricotent

J'apprends à tricoter.
I am learning how to knit.

---

triste [TREEST] adjective   **sad**

Pourquoi es-tu triste?
Why are you sad?

C'est triste   **That's too bad!**
(See **dommage**)

---

trois [TRWA] adjective   **three**

Il y a trois verres sur la table.
There are three glasses on the table.

---

tromper [trohn-PAY] verb   **to deceive; to cheat**

je trompe	nous trompons
tu trompes	vous trompez
il, elle trompe	ils, elles trompent

Dans le film, le voleur trompe l'agent de police.
In the film, the robber deceives the policeman.

---

trop [TROH] adverb   **too (much),**
                                                too (many),
La petite fille dit: "Cette cuiller est   **too (___)**
trop grande pour moi!"
The little girl says, "This spoon is too big for me!"

---

le trottoir [truh-TWAR] noun, masc.   **sidewalk**

Le trottoir est très étroit.
The sidewalk is very narrow.

---

le trou [TROO] noun, masc.   **hole**

J'ai un trou dans ma chaussette.
I have a hole in my sock.

---

trouver [troo-VAY] verb   **to find; to think**
  je trouve   nous trouvons
  tu trouves   vous trouvez
  il, elle trouve   ils, elles trouvent

Où est mon autre gant? Je ne peux pas le trouver.
Where is my other glove? I can't find it.

Tu trouves que l'examen est difficile?
Do you think the examination is difficult?

---

il, elle se trouve [sé-TROOV]   **is located**
idiomatic expression
ils, elles se trouvent pl.

Le bureau de poste se trouve là-bas.
The post office is located over there.

---

tu [TEW] pronoun

you (familiar)

Comment vas-tu?
How are you?

> When you say "you" in French, it can be "vous" or "tu." "Vous" is used in formal situations; "tu" is used with members of the family or friends.
>
> Quand on dit "you" en français, on emploie "vous" ou "tu." On emploie "vous" dans les situations formalles, "tu" avec membres de la famille ou des amis.

---

tuer [tew-AY] verb

to kill

je tue	nous tuons
tu tues	vous tuez
il, elle tue	ils, elles tuent

Maman tue la mouche.
Mother kills the fly.

U

---

un [UHN] article, masc.
une [EWN] fem.

a, an; one
a, an; one

Un singe est dans l'arbre.
A monkey is in the tree.

Je porte une cravate.
I am wearing a tie.

---

uni [ew-NEE] adjective, masc.   **united**
unie fem.

Le garçon habite les Etats Unis.
The boy lives in the United States.

*Le bâtiment des Nations Unies se trouve dans
la ville de New York.*
The United Nations building is located in New York City.

---

l'université [ew-nee-vehr-see-TAY] noun, fem.   **university**

L'université se trouve dans la vallée.
The university is located in the valley.

---

l'usine [ew-ZEEN] noun, fem.   **factory**

Mon père travaille à l'usine.
My father works in the factory.

---

utile [ew-TEEL] adjective   **useful**

Quelques insectes sont utiles.
Some insects are useful.

V

les vacances [va-KAHNS] noun, fem., pl.   **vacation**
les grandes vacances   **summer vacation**
[grahnd-va-KAHNS] noun, fem., pl.

Où allez-vous pendant les grandes vacances?
Where are you going during the summer vacation?

---

vacciner [va-ksee-NAY] verb   **to vaccinate**
  je vaccine   nous vaccinons
  tu vaccines   vous vaccinez
  il, elle vaccine   ils, elles vaccinent

J'ai peur quand le médecin me vaccine.
I am afraid when the doctor vaccinates me.

---

la vache [VASH] noun, fem.   **cow**

La vache est dans le champ.
The cow is in the field.

---

la vague [VAG] noun, fem.   **wave**

Je vois des vagues à la plage.
I see waves at the beach.

---

la vaisselle [veh-SEHL] noun, fem.   **the dishes**

Est-ce que vous lavez la vaisselle chez vous?
Do you wash the dishes at your house?

---

la valise [va-LEEZ] noun, fem.   **valise, suitcase**

Je mets mes vêtements dans la valise.
I put my clothes in the valise.

---

la vallée [va-LAY] noun, fem.   **valley**

Il y a beaucoup de fleurs dans la vallée.
There are many flowers in the valley.

---

la vanille [va-NEEY] noun, fem.   **vanilla**

J'aime la glace à la vanille.
I like vanilla ice cream.

---

le vélo (See **bicyclette**)   **bicycle**

---

le vendeur [vahń-DEUHR] noun, masc.   **salesman, salesperson**

la vendeuse [vahń-DEUHZ] fem.   **saleswoman, salesperson**

Le vendeur nous montre des chaussures.
The salesman shows us some shoes.

---

vendre [VAHNDR] verb   **to sell**

je vends	nous vendons
tu vends	vous vendez
il, elle vend	ils, elles vendent

On vend des médicaments dans ce magasin.
They sell medicine in this store.

---

vendredi [vahn-dré-DEE] noun, masc.   **Friday**

Qu'est-ce qu'on mange le vendredi? Du poisson!
What do we eat on Friday? Fish!

---

venir [vé-NEER] verb   **to come, to arrive**

je viens	nous venons
tu viens	vous venez
il, elle vient	ils, elles viennent

Ma tante vient nous voir.
My aunt comes to see us.

---

venir de [vé-NEER-dé] idiomatic expression   **to have just**

Je viens de faire un voyage en avion.
I have just taken an airplane trip.

---

le vent [VAHN] noun, masc.   **wind**

Quand il fait du vent je perds mon chapeau.
When it is windy, I lose my hat. (See **faire**)

---

le ventilateur [vahn-tee-la-TEUHR] noun, masc.   **fan**

Nous employons le ventilateur quand il fait chaud.
We use the fan when it is hot.

le ventre [VAHⱯTR] noun, masc.   **stomach, abdomen**
avoir mal au ventre   **to have a**
[a-vwar-ma-loh-VAHⱯTR]   **stomachache**
idiomatic expression

As-tu mal au ventre?
Do you have a stomachache? (See **avoir**)

---

le ver [VEHR] noun, masc.   **worm**

Il y a un ver dans la pomme.
There's a worm in the apple.

---

la vérité [vay-ree-TAY] noun, fem.   **truth**

C'est la vérité!
That's the truth!

---

le verre [VEHR] noun, masc.   **glass**

Je mets le verre sur la table avec soin.
I put the glass on the table carefully.

---

en verre [ahⱯ-VEHR]   **made of glass**

Mes lunettes sont en verre.
My glasses are made of glass.

---

vers [VEHR] preposition   **toward**

Nous allons ver l'hôtel.
We are going toward the hotel.

---

verser [vehr-SAY] verb   **to pour**

je verse	nous versons
tu verses	vous versez
il, elle verse	ils, elles versent

Marguerite verse le café dans une tasse.
Margaret pours coffee into a cup.

---

vert [VEHR] adjective, masc.   **green**
verte [VEHRT] fem.

Quand la banane n'est pas mûre, elle est verte.
When the banana is not ripe, it is green.

---

la veste [VEHST] noun, fem.   **jacket**

Mon grand-père porte un pantalon et une veste.
My grandfather wears pants and a jacket.

---

les vêtements [veht-MAHN] noun, masc., pl.   **clothes, clothing**

Mes vêtements sont sur le lit.
My clothes are on the bed.

---

la viande [VYAHND] noun, fem.   **meat**

La femme va à la boucherie pour acheter de la viande.
The woman goes to the butcher shop to buy meat.

---

vide [VEED] adjective   **empty**

Le tiroir est vide.
The drawer is empty.

---

vieux [VYEOH] adjective, masc.   **old**
vieille [VYAY] fem.
vieil [VYAY] masc., before a vowel

Le livre est vieux et la montre est vieille.
The book is old and the watch is old.

---

le village [vee-LAZH] noun, masc.   **village**

Mon cousin habite un village à la campagne.
My cousin lives in a village in the country.

la ville [VEEL] noun, fem.   **city**

La ville de New York est grande.
The city of New York is big.

le vin [VAIN] noun, masc.   **wine**

Le garçon apporte le vin.
The waiter brings the wine.

vingt [VAIN] adjective   **twenty**

Dix et dix font vingt.
Ten and ten are twenty.

violet [vyoh-LEH] adjective, masc.   **violet, purple**
violette [vyoh-LEHT] fem.

Est-ce qu'il y a des fleurs violettes?
Are there any purple flowers?

le violon [vyoh-LOHN] noun, masc.   **violin**

Le musicien joue du violon.
The musician plays the violin.

visiter [vee-zee-TAY] verb   **to visit**

je visite	nous visitons
tu visites	vous visitez
il, elle visite	ils, elles visitent

Mes parents visitent ma colonie de vacances.
My parents visit my camp.

---

vite [VEET] adverb   **fast, quickly**

Mon frère marche trop vite.
My brother walks too fast.

---

la vitrine [vee-TREEN] noun, fem.   **store window**

Nous allons regarder les choses dans les vitrines.
We are going to look at the things in the store windows.

---

vivre [VEEVR] verb   **to live**

je vis	nous vivons
tu vis	vous vivez
il, elle vit	ils, elles vivent

Est-ce que des animaux sauvages vivent dans cette forêt?
Do any wild animals live in this forest?

See also: demeurer, habiter

---

voici [vwa-SEE] adverb   **here is, here are**

Voici ma toupie.
Here is my top. (toy)

---

voilà [vwa-LA] adverb   **there is, there are**

Voilà le poisson dans l'eau.
There is the fish in the water.

voir [VWAR] verb   **to see**

je vois	nous voyons
tu vois	vous voyez
il, elle voit	ils, elles voient

Je vois l'avion dans le ciel.
I see the airplane in the sky.

---

le voisin [vwa-ZAIN] noun, masc.   **neighbor**
la voisine [vwa-ZEEN] fem.

Mon voisin Bernard demeure près de chez moi.
My neighbor Bernard lives near me.

---

la voiture [vwa-TEWR] noun, fem.   **car, automobile;**
                                       baby carriage
La voiture est dans le garage.
The car is in the garage.

---

la voix [VWA] noun, fem.   **voice**

La voix de ma tante est douce.
My aunt's voice is sweet.

à haute voix   **in a loud voice, aloud** (See **haut**)
à voix basse   **in a low voice** (See **bas**)

---

voler [vuh-LAY] verb   **to fly; to steal**

je vole	nous volons
tu voles	vous volez
il, elle vole	ils, elles volent

Le pilote d'avion vole dans l'avion.
The airplane pilot flies in the airplane.

Qui vient de voler ma cuiller?
Who has just stolen my spoon?

---

le voleur [vuh-LEUHR] noun, masc.   **thief, robber, burglar**

On cherche le voleur de la banque.
They are looking for the bank thief.

---

votre [VUHTR] pronoun   **your**
vos [VOH] pl.

Où est votre magnétophone?
Where is your tape recorder?

Où sont vos timbres?
Where are your stamps?

---

je voudrais [voo-DREH]   **I would like ...**
il, elle voudrait [voo-DREH]   **He would like,**
                            She would like ...
ils, elles voudraient   **They would like ...**

Je voudrais faire une promenade.
I would like to take a walk.

Elle voudrait faire des emplettes.
She would like to go shopping.

---

vouloir [voo-LWAR] verb   **to want, to wish**
   je veux   nous voulons
   tu veux   vous voulez
   il, elle veut   ils, elles veulent

Le bébé pleure parce qu'il veut son jouet.
The baby is crying because he wants his toy.

vouloir dire (See **dire**)   **to mean**

---

vous [voo] pronoun   **you, to you; yourself**

Comment allez-vous?
How are you?

Je vous donne un billet.
I am giving you a ticket.

---

le voyage [vwa-YAZH] noun, masc.   **trip**
faire un voyage [feh-ruhń-vwa-YAZH]   **to take a trip**
idiomatic expression

Nous faisons un voyage au château.
We are taking a trip to the castle. (See **faire**)

voyager [vwa-ya-ZHAY] verb   **to travel**
  je voyage   nous voyageons
  tu voyages   vous voyagez
  il, elle voyage   ils, elles voyagent

Jacques voyage en bicyclette.
Jack travels by bicycle.

le voyageur [vwa-ya-ZHEUHR] noun, masc.   **traveler**

Le voyageur est fatigué.
The traveler is tired.

vrai [VREH] adjective, masc.   **true**
vraie fem.

C'est une histoire vraie!
It's a true story!

vraiment [vreh-MAHŃ] adverb   **really**

Tu sais que je voudrais devenir astronaute? Vraiment!
Do you know that I would like to become an astronaut?
Really!

W

le wagon [va-GOHᴺ] noun, masc.   **car (railroad)**
Ce train a cinq wagons.
This train has five cars.

Y

les yeux [leh-ZYEOH] masc., pl.   **eyes** (See **oeil**)

Z

le zèbre [ZEHBR] noun, masc.   **zebra**
Est-ce un zèbre ou un cheval?
Is it a zebra or a horse?

le zéro [zay-ROH] noun, masc.   **zero**
Il y a un zéro dans le numéro dix.
There is a zero in the number ten.

le zoo [ZOH] noun, masc.   **zoo**
J'aime regarder les tigres au zoo.
I like to watch the tigers at the zoo.

zoologique [zuh-uh-luh-ZHEEK] adjective
le jardin zoologique (See **jardin**)   **zoo**

French Verb Supplement
Les Verbes Français

Verbes Réguliers
Regular Verbs

Présent (Present)	Imparfait (Imperfect)	Passé Composé (Past Indefinite)	Futur (Future)

CHANTER (to sing)

Présent	Imparfait	Passé Composé	Futur
Je chante	chantais	j'ai chanté	chanterai
tu chantes	chantais	tu as chanté	chanteras
il, elle chante	chantait	il, elle a chanté	chantera
nous chantons	chantions	nous avons chanté	chanterons
vous chantez	chantiez	vous avez chanté	chanterez
ils, elles chantent	chantaient	ils, elles ont chanté	chanteront

FINIR (to finish, to end)

Présent	Imparfait	Passé Composé	Futur
Je finis	finissais	j'ai fini	finirai
tu finis	finissais	tu as fini	finiras
il, elle finit	finissait	il, elle a fini	finira
nous finissons	finissions	nous avons fini	finirons
vous finissez	finissiez	vous avez fini	finirez
ils, elles finissent	finissaient	ils, elles ont fini	finiront

RENDRE (to give back, to return)

Présent	Imparfait	Passé Composé	Futur
Je rends	rendais	j'ai rendu	rendrai
tu rends	rendais	tu as rendu	rendras
il, elle rend	rendait	il, elle a rendu	rendra
nous rendons	rendions	nous avons rendu	rendrons
vous rendez	rendiez	vous avez rendu	rendrez
ils, elles rendent	rendaient	ils, elles ont rendu	rendront

Verbes Irréguliers
Irregular Verbs

ALLER (to go)

Je vais	allais	je suis allé(e)	irai
tu vas	allais	tu es allé(e)	iras
il, elle va	allait	il, elle est allé(e)	ira
nous allons	allions	nous sommes allé(e)s	irons
vous allez	alliez	vous êtes allé(e)s	irez
il, elles vont	allaient	ils, elles sont allé(e)s	iront

AVOIR (to have)

J'ai	avais	j'ai eu	aurai
tu as	avais	tu as eu	auras
il, elle a	avait	il, elle a eu	aura
nous avons	avions	nous avons eu	aurons
vous avez	aviez	vous avez eu	aurez
ils, elles ont	avaient	ils, elles ont eu	auront

DIRE (to say, to tell)

Je dis	disais	j'ai dit	dirai
tu dis	disais	tu as dit	diras
il, elle dit	disait	il, elle a dit	dira
nous disons	disions	nous avons dit	dirons
vous dites	disiez	vous avez dit	direz
ils, elles disent	disaient	ils, elles ont dit	diront

ETRE (to be)

Je suis	étais	j'ai été	serai
tu es	étais	tu as été	seras
il, elle est	était	il, elle a été	sera
nous sommes	étions	nous avons été	serons
vous êtes	étiez	vous avez été	serez
ils, elles sont	étaient	ils, elles ont été	seront

FAIRE (to do, to make)

Je fais	faisais	j'ai fait	ferai
tu fais	faisais	tu as fait	feras
il, elle fait	faisait	il, elle a fait	fera
nous faisons	faisions	nous avons fait	ferons
vous faites	faisiez	vous avez fait	ferez
ils, elles font	faisaient	ils, elles ont fait	feront

METTRE (to put, to place)

Je mets	mettais	j'ai mis	mettrai
tu mets	mettais	tu as mis	mettras
il, elle met	mettait	il, elle a mis	mettra
nous mettons	mettions	nous avons mis	mettrons
vous mettez	mettiez	vous avez mis	mettrez
ils, elles mettent	mettaient	ils, elles ont mis	mettront

POUVOIR (to be able, can)

Je peux or puis	pouvais	j'ai pu	pourrai
tu peux	pouvais	tu as pu	pourras
il, elle peut	pouvait	il, elle a pu	pourra
nous pouvons	pouvions	nous avons pu	pourrons
vous pouvez	pouviez	vous avez pu	pourrez
ils, elles peuvent	pouvaient	ils, elles ont pu	pourront

PRENDRE (to take)

Je prends	prenais	j'ai pris	prendrai
tu prends	prenais	tu as pris	prendras
il, elle prend	prenait	il, elle a pris	prendra
nous prenons	prenions	nous avons pris	prendrons
vous prenez	preniez	vous avez pris	prendrez
ils, elles prennent	prenaient	ils, elles ont pris	prendront

SAVOIR (to know)

Je sais	savais	j'ai su	saurai
tu sais	savais	tu as su	sauras
il, elle sait	savait	il, elle a su	saura
nous savons	savions	nous avons su	saurons
vous savez	saviez	vous avez su	saurez
ils, elles savent	savaient	ils, elles ont su	sauront

VENIR (to come)

Je viens	venais	je suis venu(e)	viendrai
tu viens	venais	tu es venu(e)	viendras
il, elle vient	venait	il, elle est venu(e)	viendra
nous venons	venions	nous sommes venu(e)s	viendrons
vous venez	veniez	vous êtes venu(e)s	viendrez
ils, elles viennent	venaient	ils, elles sont venu(e)s	viendront

VOIR (to see)

Je vois	voyais	j'ai vu	verrai
tu vois	voyais	tu as vu	verras
il, elle voit	voyait	il, elle a vu	verra
nous voyons	voyions	nous avons vu	verrons
vous voyez	voyiez	vous avez vu	verrez
ils, elles voient	voyaient	ils, elles ont vu	verront

VOULOIR (to want)

Je veux	voulais	j'ai voulu	voudrai
tu veux	voulais	tu as voulu	voudras
il, elle veut	voulait	il, elle a voulu	voudra
nous voulons	voulions	nous avons voulu	voudrons
vous voulez	vouliez	vous avez voulu	voudrez
ils, elles veulent	voulaient	ils, elles ont voulu	voudront

Anglais-Français

(English-French)

La Clef de la Prononciation Anglaise

(English Pronunciation Key)

Les Notes

1. Il y a des sons en anglais qui n'existent pas en français.

2. En général, les voyelles en anglais sont courtes.

3. Les sons des exemples en français ne sont pas exacts. Ils sont seulement approximatifs.

LES CONSONNES

L'ortographe anglaise	Le symbole phonémique
b	b
c	k
ç	s
ch, tch	ch
d	d
f	f
g	g
j	zh
h, wh	h
dg	dj
k	k
l	l
m	m
n	n
ng	ng
p	p
qu	kw
r	r
s	s
sh, tion	sh
t	t
v	v
w	w
wh	wh, h
x	ks, gs
y	y
z, s	z
th	th
th (voiced)	<u>th</u>

LES VOYELLES

L'ortographe anglaise	Exemple en anglais	Symbole phonémique	Exemples en français: à peu près pareil au mot français
a e u	but	é	le rocher
a	cat	a	la balle
a o	cot	a̱	mal
é, a ez, ay	play	ei	le bébé
a ah	father	ah	la page
ai, ais	air	eh	l'aéroport
è, ê, e	gel	e	
ee ea	feet	i	le fils
i	hit	i̱	—
i uy	buy	a̱i	la taille
o oa ow	boat	o̱h	beau
oo u ou	boot	u	trouver
oy	boy	o̱i	—
au, ough o, augh	order	a̱w	le bord
ur	curtain	u̱r, euh	l'heure
ow, ou, ough	how	o̱w	—
u, oo	book	auh	le feu

A

a [ɇ] article   **un,** masc.

A monkey is in the tree.   **une,** fém.
Un singe est dans l'arbre.

I am wearing a tie.
Je porte une cravate.

---

above all [e-bev A̲W̲L̲] adverbe   **surtout**

I like to watch television, Saturday mornings above all.
J'aime regarder la television, surtout le samedi matin.

---

absent [AB-sɇnt] adjectif   **absent,** masc.

George is absent today.   **absente,** fém.
Georges est absent aujourd'hui.

---

according to [ɇ-k̲A̲W̲R̲-ding tɇ] préposition   **selon**

According to my brother, it is going to snow tomorrow.
Selon mon frère, il va neiger demain.

---

actor [AK-tɇr] nom   **l'acteur,** masc.
actress [AK-tres]   **l'actrice,** fém.

The actor is handsome.
L'acteur est beau.

---

addition (See **check**)   **l'addition**

---

address [é-DREHS] nom   **l'adresse,** fém.

What is your address?
Quelle est votre adresse?

---

adventure [ad-VEN-chér] nom   **l'aventure,** fém.

I like to read the adventures of Astérix.
J'aime lire les aventures d'Astérix.

---

to be afraid of [BE-FREID]   **avoir peur**
expression idiomatique

Are you afraid of the lion?
As-tu peur du lion?

---

after [AF-tér] préposition   **après**

September is the month after August.
Septembre est le mois après août.

---

afternoon [af-tér-NUN] nom   **l'après-midi,** masc.

It is two o'clock in the afternoon.
Il est deux heures de l'après-midi.

---

again [é-GEN] adverbe   **encore**

Read the letter once again.
Lisez la lettre encore une fois.

---

against [é-GENST] préposition   **contre**

Henry puts the mirror against the wall.
Henri met le miroir contre le mur.

---

age (used in exp. with "How old...?") [EIDJ] nom   **l'âge,** masc.

How old are you? I am eight (years old).
Quel âge as-tu? J'ai huit ans.

---

agreed! [é-GRID]   **accord: d'accord!**
expression idiomatique

Do you want to play with me? O.K.!
Veux-tu jouer avec moi? D'accord!

---

to aid (help) [EID] verbe   **aider**

I aid	we aid
you aid	you aid
he, she, it aids	they aid

John helps his sister carry the books.
Jean aide sa soeur à porter les livres.

---

air (look) [EHR] nom   **l'air,** masc.

The tiger has a ferocious look.
Le tigre a l'air féroce.

This young man is ill. He needs air.
Ce jeune homme est malade. Il a besoin de l'air.

---

airplane [EHR-plein] nom   **l'avion,** fém.
by airplane   **en avion**
(airplane) pilot [EHR-plein PAI-lét] nom   **le pilote (d'avion)**

My cousin is an airplane pilot.
Mon cousin est pilote (d'avion).

jet airplane nom   **l'avion à réaction**

airport [ehr-P<u>AWR</u>T] nom   **l'aéroport,** masc.

My uncle works at the airport.
Mon oncle travaille à l'aéroport.

---

alarm clock [é-LAHRM K<u>LA</u>K] nom   **le réveille-matin**

The alarm clock rings too loudly.
Le réveille-matin sonne trop fort.

Alas! (What a pity!) [é-LAS] interjection   **Hélas!**

What a pity! You can't come with me.
Hélas! Tu ne peux pas venir avec moi.

---

alike (similar) [é-L<u>AI</u>K] adjectif   **pareil**

Our ties are similar.
Nos cravates sont pareilles.

---

all [<u>AWL</u>] adjectif   **tout**

all over (everywhere) adverbe   **partout**

I look everywhere for my watch.
Je cherche ma montre partout.

all right (okay) expression idiomatique   **d'accord!**

Do you want to play with me? O.K.!
Veux-tu jouer avec moi? D'accord!

---

almost [<u>aw</u>l-M<u>OH</u>ST] adverbe   **presque**

It is almost six o'clock.
Il est presque six heures.

---

alone [é-L<u>OH</u>N] adjectif   **seul**

I am alone in the living room.
Je suis seul dans le salon.

---

aloud [é-L<u>OW</u>D] adverbe   **à haute voix**

---

alphabet [AL-fa-bet] nom   **l'alphabet,** masc.

There are twenty-six letters in the French alphabet?
Il y vingt-six lettres dans l'alphabet français?

already [awl-RE-di] adverbe   **déjà**

It is already time to leave?
Il est déjà l'heure de partir?

also (too) [AWL-soh] adverbe   **aussi**

I want some candy too!
Moi aussi, je veux des bonbons!

always (forever) [AWL-weiz] adverbe   **toujours**

The leaves always fall in autumn.
Les feuilles tombent toujours en automne.

ambulance [AM-byu-lans] nom   **l'ambulance,** fém.

The ambulance is going to the hospital.
L'ambulance va à l'hôpital.

American [é-MER-i-kén] nom; adjectif   **américain,** masc.
                                                  américaine, fém.
It's an American airplane.
C'est un avion américain.

amusing [é-MYUZ-ing] adjectif   **amusant,** masc.
                                           amusante, fém.
The bear is amusing.
L'ours est amusant.

an [AN] article   **un,** masc.
                                                       une, fém.
I am wearing a tie.
Je porte une cravate.

---

and [AND] conjonction   **et**

Andrew and his friend are playing together.
André et son ami jouent ensemble.

---

angry [AN-gri] adjectif   **fâché,** masc.
                                                       fâchée, fém.
When I tease my sister, Mom is angry.
Quand je taquine ma soeur, Maman est fâchée.

---

animal [AN-i̱-mél] nom   **la bête**

The lion is a wild animal.
Le lion est une bête sauvage.

animal   **l'animal,** masc.
                                                   les animaux, pl.
The animals are in the forest.
Les animaux sont dans la forêt.

pet [pet] nom   **l'animal favori,** masc.

My dog is my pet.
Mon chien est mon animal favori.

---

anniversary (birthday) [an-i̱-<u>vur</u>-sér-i] nom   **l'anniversaire,**
                                                              masc.
Happy Birthday! How old are you?
Joyeux anniversaire! Quel âge as-tu?

---

annoyed [é-N<u>oi</u>D] adjectif   **ennuyé,** masc.
                                                       ennuyée, fém.

Mother is annoyed when I make too much noise.
Maman est ennuyée quand je fais trop de bruit.

---

another [é-NÉTH-ér] adjectif   **autre**
Here is another pencil.
Voici un autre crayon.

other [ÉTH-ér] adjectif   **l'autre**
Here is my handkerchief. The others are on the bed.
Voici mon mouchoir. Les autres sont sur le lit.

---

answer [AN-sér] nom   **la réponse**
I write the correct answer in my notebook.
J'écris la réponse correcte dans mon cahier.

to answer verbe   **répondre**
   I answer   we answer
   you answer   you answer
   he, she, it answers they answer

The little girl cannot answer the question.
La petite fille ne peut pas répondre à la question.

---

ant [ANT] nom   **la fourmi**
The ant is very small.
La fourmi est très petite.

---

any [EN-i] adjectif   **quelque**
any (also shows possession)   **de**
         du, masc. (*contraction of* de + le)
                de la, fém.
      des, pl. (*contraction of* de + les)

anything [EN-i-thing] pronoun   **quelque chose**
Is there anything in this drawer?
Est-ce qu'il y a quelque chose dans ce tiroir?

---

apartment [é-PAHRT-mént] nom   **l'appartement,** masc.
My apartment is on the third floor.
Mon appartement est au deuxième étage.

---

appearance (look) [é-PIR-éns] nom **l'air,** masc.

The tiger has a ferocious appearance (look).
Le tigre a l'air féroce.

---

appetite [AP-é-tait] nom **l'appétit,** masc.

Hearty appetite! (Enjoy your meal!)
Bon appétit!

---

apple [AP-él] nom **la pomme**

I eat an apple every day.
Je mange une pomme tous les jours.

---

appointment [é-POINT-mént] nom **le rendez-vous**

What time is your appointment with the counselor?
A quelle heure est votre rendez-vous avec le conseiller?

---

apricot [A-pri-kat] nom **l'abricot**

The apricot is delicious.
L'abricot est délicieux.

April [EI-prél] nom **avril**

It rains a lot in April.
Il pleut beaucoup en avril.

---

apron [EI-prén] nom   **le tablier**

Martha wears an apron at school.
Marthe porte un tablier à l'école.

---

aquarium (fish tank) [é-KWEHR-yém] nom   **l'aquarium,**

There are some goldfish in the fish tank.   masc.
Il y a des poissons rouges dans l'aquarium.

---

architect [ahr-ki-TEKT] nom   **l'architecte**

Frank Lloyd Wright was a famous American architect.
Frank Lloyd Wright était un architecte célèbre des Etats-
Unis.

---

arm [AHRM] nom   **le bras**

The man has a sore arm.
L'homme a mal au bras.

---

armchair [AHRM-chehr] nom   **le fauteuil**

I like to sit in the armchair.
J'aime m'asseoir dans le fauteuil.

---

army [AHR-mi] nom   **l'armée,** fém.

Soldiers are in the army.
Les soldats sont dans l'armée.

---

around [é-ROWND] adverbe   **autour de**

I would like to take a trip around the world.
Je voudrais faire un voyage autour du monde.

---

to arrange [é-REINDJ] verbe   **arranger**

   I arrange   we arrange
   you arrange   you arrange
   he, she, it arranges   they arrange

The teacher arranges his papers.
Le professeur arrange ses papiers.

---

to arrest [é-REST] verbe   **arrêter**

I arrest	we arrest
you arrest	you arrest
he, she, it arrests	they arrest

The policeman arrests the man.
L'agent arrête l'homme.

---

to arrive [é-RAIV] verbe   **arriver**

I arrive	we arrive
you arrive	you arrive
he, she, it arrives	they arrive

The postman arrives at ten o'clock.
Le facteur arrive à dix heures.

---

artist [AHR-tist] nom   **l'artiste,** masc.

My brother is an artist.
Mon frère est artiste.

---

as [AZ] préposition   **comme**

As for dessert, she has chocolate ice cream.
Comme dessert elle prend une glace au chocolat.

---

to ask [ASK] verbe   **demander**

I ask	we ask
you ask	you ask
he, she, it asks	they ask

I ask Father, "May I go to the fair?"
Je demande à Papa: "Je peux aller à la foire?"

astronaut [AS-tré-n<u>aw</u>t] nom   **l'astronaute,** masc., fém.

The astronaut takes a trip in a spaceship.
L'astronaute fait un voyage en fusée.

---

at [AT] préposition   **à**
at night   **la nuit**

At night you can see the stars.
La nuit on peut voir des étoiles.

---

to attend [é-TEND] verbe   **assister**

I attend	we attend
you attend	you attend
he, she, it attends	they attend

We attend a soccer game.
Nous assistons à un jeu de football.

---

at the side of (next) [NEKST] préposition   **à côté de**

At the restaurant Peter is seated next to Carolyn.
Au restaurant Pierre est assis à côté de Caroline.

August [<u>AW</u>-gést] nom   **août,** masc.

In August it is hot.
En août il fait chaud.

---

aunt [ANT] nom   **la tante**

My aunt is a saleslady.
Ma tante est vendeuse.

---

automobile (car) [KAHR] nom   **la voiture**

The car is in the garage.
La voiture est dans le garage.

---

autumn [AW-tém] nom   **l'automne,** masc.

In autumn it is cool.
En automne il fait frais.

---

avenue [AV-é-nyu] nom   **l'avenue,** fém.

The Avenue des Champs-Elysées is in Paris.
L'Avenue des Champs-Elysées est à Paris.

B

baby [BEI-bi] nom   **le bébé**

Mary plays with the baby.
Marie joue avec le bébé.

baby carriage [BEI-bi KAR-idj]   **la voiture**

---

back [BAK] nom   **les dos**

Is it Robert? I don't know. I see only his back.
C'est Robert? Je ne sais pas. Je vois seulement le dos.

to give back   **rendre**

---

bad [BAD] adjectif   **mauvais,** masc.
                                         mauvaise, fém.
The weather is bad today.
Il fait mauvais aujourd'hui.

that's too bad   **c'est dommage!,**
expression idiomatique   **c'est triste!**

---

bag [BAG] nom   **le sac**

I carry a bag.
Je porte un sac.

---

baggage [BAG-idj] nom   **les bagages**
The baggage is ready for the trip.
Les bagages sont prêts pour le voyage.

baker [BEI-kér] nom   **le boulanger**

The baker makes bread.
Le boulanger fait le pain.

bakery [BEI-kér-i] nom   **la boulangerie**
The baker is in the bakery.
Le boulanger est dans la boulangerie.

ball [BAWL] nom   **la balle**
The ball is round.
La balle est ronde.

to play ball [PLEI BAWL]   **jouer à la balle**

balloon [bé-LUN] nom   **le ballon**
"Oh! I'm losing my balloon," cries the little girl.
"Oh! Je perds mon ballon," crie la petite fille.

ballpoint pen [BAWL-point PEN] nom   **le stylo à bille**
I like to write with a ballpoint pen.
J'aime écrire avec un stylo à bille.

banana [bé-NAN-é] nom   **la banane**
The banana is ripe when it is yellow.
La banane est mûre quand elle est jaune.

bank [BANGK] nom   **la banque**

Do you have any money in the bank?
Avez-vous de l'argent à la banque?

---

baseball [BEIS-b<u>aw</u>l] nom   **le base-ball**

My cousin plays baseball.
Mon cousin joue au base-ball.

> Le base-ball, le football américain, et le football
> sont très populaires aux Etats-Unis.
>
> Baseball, football, and soccer are very popular in
> the United States.

---

basement (cellar) [BEIS-mént] nom   **la cave**

There are several packages in the cellar.
Il y a plusieurs paquets dans la cave.

---

basket [BAS-k<u>i</u>t] nom   **le panier**

There are apples in the basket.
Il y a des pommes dans le panier.

---

basketball [BAS-k<u>i</u>t-b<u>aw</u>l] nom   **le basket-ball**

My friend plays basketball.
Mon camarade joue au basket-ball.

---

bath [BATH] nom   **le bain**

I take a bath at nine in the evening.
A neuf heures du soir, je prends un bain.

bathroom   **la salle de bain**
sunbath   **le bain de soleil**
bathing suit   **le maillot**

Do you like my new bathing suit?
Tu aimes mon nouveau maillot?

---

bathroom sink   **le lavabo**

The washstand is in the bathroom.
Le lavabo est dans la salle de bain.

---

to be [BI] verbe   **être**

I am	we are
you are	you are
he, she, it is	they are

Dad, where are we?
Papa, où sommes-nous?

---

to be able (can) [BI EI-bl] verbe   **pouvoir**

I can	we can
you can	you can
he, she, it can	they can

I can't do my homework. The lessons are too difficult.
Je ne peux pas faire mes devoirs. Les leçons sont trop difficiles.

---

beach [BICH] nom   **la plage**

We go to the beach in summer.
Nous allons à la plage en été.

---

to be acquainted with (know)   **connaître**
[BI é-KWEIN-téd with] verbe
   I am acquainted with   we are acquainted with
   you are acquainted with   you are acquainted with
   he, she is acquainted with they are acquainted with

Are you acquainted with my teacher?
Connais-tu mon maître?

---

to be afraid [BI é-FREID]   **avoir peur**
expression idiomatique

Are you afraid of the storm?
Avez-vous peur de l'orage?

---

beak [BIK] nom   **le bec**

The bird has a yellow beak.
L'oiseau a un bec jaune.

---

bear [BEHR] nom   **l'ours,** masc.

The bears are playing in the water.
Les ours jouent dans l'eau.

---

beard [BIRD] nom   **la barbe**

My brother, who is at the university, has a beard.
Mon frère, qui est à l'université, a une barbe.

---

to be ashamed [BI é-SHEIMD]   **avoir honte**
expression idiomatique

He is ashamed because he is naughty.
Il a honte parce qu'il est méchant.

beast (animal) [BIST] nom   **la bête**

The lion is a wild beast.
Le lion est une bête sauvage.

---

beautiful [BYU-té-fél] adjectif   **beau,** masc.
The sky is beautiful.   **belle,** fém.
Le ciel est beau.

---

to be named [BI NEImd] verbe   **s'appeler**

my name is	our name is
your name is	your name is
his, her, its name is	their name is

What is your name? My name is Henry.
Comment vous appelez-vous? Je m'appelle Henri.

---

be careful! [BI KEHR-fél] interjection   **attention!**

The teacher says, "Be careful!"
Le professeur dit: "Attention!"

Pay attention! expression idiomatique   **Faites attention!**

---

because [bi-KAWZ] conjonction   **parce que**

I am not going to the movies because I don't have any money.
Je ne vais pas au cinéma parce que je n'ai pas d'argent.

because of   **à cause de**

I have to stay home because of the snow.
Je dois rester à la maison à cause de la neige.

---

to become [bi-KÉM] verbe   **devenir**

I become	we become
you become	you become
he, she, it becomes	they become

He would like to become a doctor.
Il voudrait devenir médecin.

bed [BED] nom   **le lit**

The cat is in my bed.
Le chat est dans mon lit.

---

to go to bed expression idiomatique   **se coucher**
bedroom [bed-RUM] nom   **la chambre**

This apartment has three bedrooms.
Cet appartement a trois chambres.

---

bee [BI] nom   **l'abeille,** fém.

The bee is dangerous.
L'abeille est dangereuse.

---

beefsteak (steak) [BIF-steik] nom   **le bifteck**

The steak is good.
Le bifteck est bon.

---

before [bi-FAWR] préposition   **avant**

The teacher arrives before the students.
Le professeur arrive avant les étudiants.

---

to be frightened (afraid) [bi FRAI-ténd]   **avoir peur**
expression idiomatique

Are you afraid of the storm?
Avez-vous peur de l'orage?

---

to begin [bi-GIN] verbe   **commencer**

I begin	we begin
you begin	you begin
he, she, it begins	they begin

The French class begins at nine o'clock.
La classe de français commence à 9 heures.

---

to behave [bi-HEIV] verbe   **se conduire**

The children behave well at the table.
Les enfants se conduisent bien à table.

---

behind [bi-HAIND] préposition   **derrière; en arrière de**

One boy is behind the other.
Un garçon est en arrière des autres.

---

behind adverbe   **derrière**

Carolyn is behind the chair.
Caroline est derrière la chaise.

---

to be hungry [BI HÉN-gri]   **avoir faim**
expression idiomatique

Are you hungry? Yes, I'm hungry.
Avez-vous faim? Oui, j'ai faim.

---

to believe [bi-LIV] verbe   **croire**

I believe	we believe
you believe	you believe
he, she, it believes	they believe

I believe I can go to the movies.
Je crois que je peux aller au cinéma.

---

bell [BEL] nom   **la cloche**

The bell rings at noon.
A midi la cloche sonne.

doorbell [DAWR-bel] nom   **le bouton**

belt [BELT] nom   **la ceinture**

Well! You're wearing a new belt!
Tiens! Tu portes une nouvelle ceinture!

---

to be quiet [BI KW<u>AI</u>-ét] expression idiomatique   **se taire**
   I am quiet   we are quiet
   you are quiet   you are quiet
   he, she, it is quiet they are quiet

They always tell me, "Be quiet!"
On me dit toujours: "Tais-toi!"

---

to be right [BI R<u>AI</u>T] expression idiomatique   **avoir raison**

Grandmother is always right.
Grand-mère a toujours raison.

---

to be sleepy [BI SLI-pi]   **avoir sommeil**
expression idiomatique

Who is sleepy?
Qui a sommeil?

---

to be successful (succeed) [BI sék-SES-fél] verbe   **réussir**
   I succeed   we succeed
   you succeed   you succeed
   he, she, it succeeds they succeed

He succeeds in catching a fish.
Il réussit à attraper un poisson.

---

to be thirsty [BI TH<u>UR</u>-sti]   **avoir soif**
expression idiomatique

Are you thirsty? Yes, I'm thirsty.
Avez-vous soif? Oui, j'ai soif.

better [BET-ér] adjectif

*I think that cherries are better
than strawberries.*
Je pense que les cerises sont
meilleures que les fraises.

meilleur, masc.
meilleure, fém.

---

between [bi-TWIN] préposition

entre

What is the number between fourteen and sixteen?
Quel est le numéro entre quatorze et seize?

---

to be wrong [BI RAWNG]
expression idiomatique

avoir tort

*You say that it is good weather?
You are wrong; it is raining.*
Vous dites qu'il fait beau?
Vous avez tort; il pleut.

---

bicycle [BAI-sik-él] nom

la bicyclette

When the weather is good, Bernard rides his bicycle.
Quand il fait beau Bernard va à bicyclette.

bicycle (bike)

le vélo

Do you have a bike?
As-tu un vélo?

to ride a bicycle [RAID]
expression idiomatique

monter (aller) à bicyclette

---

big [BIG] adjectif   **grand,** masc.
big (obese)   **gros,** masc.
                                                          grosse, fém.

bigger   **plus grand que**

My brother is bigger than I.
Mon frère est plus grand que moi.

bill (money) [BIL] nom   **le billet**

I am rich! I have a ten-franc note!
Je suis riche! J'ai un billet de dix francs!

bird [BURD] nom   **l'oiseau,** masc.

The bird is on a branch of the tree.
L'oiseau est sur une branche de l'arbre.

birth [BURTH] nom   **la naissance**

He had lived in Paris from birth.
Depuis sa naissance il avait vécu à Paris.

birthday [BURTH-dei] nom   **l'anniversaire,** masc.

Happy birthday! How old are you?
Joyeux anniversaire! Quel âge as-tu?

to bite [BAIT] verbe   **mordre, piquer**
   I bite   we bite
   you bite   you bite
   he, she, it bites   they bite

Do cats bite?
Est-ce que les chats mordent?

black [BLAK] adjectif — **noir,** masc. **niore,** fém.

I am wearing my black shoes.
Je porte mes souliers noirs.

---

blackboard [BLAK-b<u>aw</u>rd] nom — **le tableau noir**

The pupil writes on the blackboard.
L'élève écrit au tableau noir.

---

blanket [BLANG-k<u>i</u>t] nom — **la couverture**

In winter I like a warm blanket on my bed.
En hiver j'aime une couverture chaude sur le lit.

---

blind [BL<u>AI</u>ND] adjectif — **aveugle**

This man is blind.
Cet homme est aveugle

---

blonde [BL<u>A</u>ND] adjectif — **blond,** masc. **blonde,** fém.

Do you have blond hair?
Avez-vous les cheveux blonds?

---

blood [BL<u>U</u>D] nom — **le sang**

My knee hurts. Look at the blood!
J'ai mal au genou. Regarde le sang!

---

blow [BL<u>OH</u>] nom (knock) — **le coup**

There are two blows on the door.
On frappe deux coups à la porte.

---

blue [BLU] adjectif — **bleu,** masc. **bleue,** fém.

The sky is blue, isn't it?
Le ciel est bleu, n'est-ce pas?

---

boat [B<u>OH</u>T] nom   **le bateau**

I see a boat in the water.
Je vois un bateau dans l'eau.

---

book [BAUHK] nom   **le livre**

We are looking for some interesting books.
Nous cherchons des livres intéressants.

---

bookstore [BAUHK-st<u>ow</u>r] nom   **la librairie**

There are so many books in the bookstore!
Il y a tant de livres dans la librairie!

---

boot [BUT] nom   **la botte**

When it snows I put on my boots.
Quand il neige je mets mes bottes.

---

born [B<u>AWR</u>N] adjectif   **né,** masc.
     née, fém.

I was born on March 2nd.
Je suis né le deux mars.

---

to borrow [BAR-<u>oh</u>] verbe   **emprunter**

I borrow   we borrow
you borrow   you borrow
he, she, it borrows   they borrow

May I borrow the eraser?
Je peux emprunter la gomme?

---

bottle [BA-tél] nom   **la bouteille**

Be careful! The bottle is made of glass.
Attention! La bouteille est en verre.

---

boulevard [bul-VAHRD] nom   **le boulevard**

Students walk on the Boulevard St. Michel in Paris.
Les étudiants se promènent sur le boulevard St-Michel à
Paris.

---

bouquet [bu-KEI] nom   **le bouquet**

"Here is a bouquet of flowers, Martha," says Frank.
"Voici un bouquet, Marthe," dit François.

---

box [BAKS] nom   **la boîte**

There is candy in the box.
Il y a des bonbons dans la boîte.

letter box (mailbox) [LET-er b<u>a</u>ks] nom   **la boîte**
                                                                      aux lettres
He puts the letter in the mailbox.
Il met la lettre dans la boîte aux lettres.

---

boy [BOI] nom   **le garçon**

The boy is playing with his sister.
Le garçon joue avec sa soeur.

---

branch [BRANCH] nom   **la branche**

The tree has many branches.
L'arbre a beaucoup de branches.

---

brave [BREIV] adjectif   **courageux,** masc.
    courageuse, fém.

The prince is brave when he saves the princess.
Le prince est courageux quand il sauve la princesse.

---

bread [BRED] nom   **le pain**

You see a lot of bread in the bakery.
On voit beaucoup de pain dans la boulangerie.

bread and butter (jam) snack   **la tartine**
expression idiomatique

(loaf of) bread [LOHF] nom   **le pain**

You see many loaves of bread in the bakery.
On voit beaucoup de pains dans la boulangerie.

roll nom   **le petit pain**

A roll, please.
Un petit pain, s'il vous plaît.

toast nom   **le pain grillé**

My sister prefers toast.
Ma soeur préfère le pain grillé.

---

to break [BREIK] verbe   **casser**
I break   we break
you break   you break
he, she, it breaks   they break

Be careful! Don't break the plate!
Attention! Ne casse pas l'assiette!

---

breakfast [BREK-fĕst] nom   **le petit déjeuner**

---

bridge [BRIDJ] nom   **le pont**
Where is the bridge of Avignon?
Où est le pont d'Avignon?

---

briefcase [BRIF-keis] nom   **la serviette**
Lawrence, don't forget your briefcase.
Laurent, n'oublie pas ta serviette.

---

to bring [BRING] verbe   **apporter**
I bring   we bring
you bring   you bring
he, she, it brings   they bring

They bring valises to camp.
Ils apportent des valises à la colonies de vacances.

---

to bring (people) verbe   **amener**
The boy brings his sister home.
Le garçon amène sa soeur à la maison.

---

broad (See **wide**)   **large**

broadcast [BRAWD-kast] nom   **l'émission, fém.**

What time is the broadcast on music from Montreal?
A quelle heure est l'émission de la musique de Montréal?

---

broom [BRUM] nom   **le balai**

Mary cleans the floor with a broom.
Marie nettoie le plancher avec un balai.

---

brother [BRÉ-thér] nom   **le frère**

I am little, but my brother is big.
Je suis petit, mais mon frère est grand.

---

brown (hair) [BROWN] adjectif   **brun, masc.**
                                                      brune, fém.
The boy has brown hair.
Le garçon a les cheveux bruns.

---

brown (things) adjectif   **marron**

The rug is brown.
Le tapis est marron.

---

brush [BRÉSH] nom   **la brosse**

The hairbrush is bigger than the toothbrush.
La brosse à cheveux est plus grande que la brosse à dents.

---

to brush (oneself) verbe   **se brosser**

  I brush   we brush
  you brush   you brush
  he, she, it brushes   they brush

Laura is brushing her hair.
Laure se brosse les cheveux.

bucket (pail) [BÉ-kĭt] nom   **le seau**
The farmer fills the bucket with milk.   **les seaux,** pl.
Le fermier remplit le seau de lait.

---

building [BĬL-dĭng] nom   **le bâtiment**
The buildings are very tall in the city.
Les bâtiments son très hauts dans la ville.

---

bunch of flowers [BAUHNCH] nom   **le bouquet**
"Here is a bunch of flowers, Martha," says Frank.
"Voici un bouquet, Marthe," dit François.

---

burglar [BUR-glér] nom   **le voleur**
They are looking for the burglar at the bank.
On cherche le voleur à la banque.

---

to burn [BURN] verbe   **brûler**

I burn	we burn
you burn	you burn
he, she, it burns	they burn

We burn wood in the fireplace.
On brûle du bois dans la cheminée.

---

bus [BÉS] nom   **l'autobus,** masc.
The children go to school by bus.
Les enfants vont à l'école en autobus.

---

but [BĖT] conjonction   **mais**

I want to go to the park but Daddy says "no."
Je veux aller au parc mais papa dit "non."

---

butcher [BAUHCH-ér] nom   **le boucher**

The butcher sells meat.
Le boucher vend de la viande.

butcher shop nom   **la boucherie**

You go to the butcher shop to buy meat.
On va à la boucherie pour acheter de la viande.

---

butter [BĖT-ér] nom   **le beurre**

Pass the butter, please.
Passez-moi le beurre, s'il vous plaît.

---

button [BĖT-én] nom   **le bouton**

This coat has only three buttons.
Ce manteau a seulement trois boutons.

---

to buy [BAI] verbe   **acheter**

I buy	we buy
you buy	you buy
he, she, it buys	they buy

I would like to buy an orange.
Je voudrais acheter une orange.

---

by [BAI] préposition	**par**
by air	**en avion**
by car	**en auto; en voiture**
by airmail	**par avion**

C

cabbage [KAB-idj] nom   **le chou**

Do you prefer cabbage or carrots?
Préférez-vous le chou ou les carottes?

café [ka-FEI] nom   **le café**

There is a café on the corner.
Il y a un café au coin de la rue.

cake [KEIK] nom   **le gâteau**

Mom makes a pretty cake for me.
Maman prépare un joli gâteau pour moi.

cookie   **le petit gâteau**

calendar [KAL-én-dér] nom   **le calendrier**

According to the calendar, today is May 12th.
Selon le calendrier c'est aujourd'hui le 12 mai.

to call [KAWL] verbe   **appeler**
  I call   we call
  you call   you call
  he, she, it calls they call

I call my friend.
J'appelle mon amie.

---

calm [KAHM] adjectif   **tranquille**

I like to go fishing when the water is calm.
J'aime aller à la pêche quand l'eau est tranquille.

---

camera [KAM-ré] nom   **l'appareil,** masc.

Look at my camera. It is new.
Regarde mon appareil. Il est nouveau.

digital camera nom **un appareil photo numérique,** masc.
or, **le caméscope,** masc.

---

camp [KAMP] nom   **la colonie de vacances**

My cousin spends eight weeks at camp.
Mon cousin passe huit semaines à la colonie de vacances.

---

can [KAN] verbe   **pouvoir**
  I can   we can
  you can   you can
  he, she, it can they can

I can't do my homework. The lessons are too difficult.
Je ne peux pas faire mes devoirs. Les leçons sont
trop difficiles.

---

candy [KAN-di] nom   **les bonbons**

Children like candy.
Les enfants aiment les bonbons.

---

capital [KAP-i-tél] nom   **la capitale**

Do you know the name of the capital of the United States?
Savez-vous le nom de la capitale des Etats-Unis?

> Washington, D.C. est la capitale des Etats-Unis.
>
> Washington, D.C. is the capital of the United
> States.

---

car [KAHR] nom   **l'auto,** fém.

The car goes along the road.
L'auto roule sur la route.

---

car (railroad) nom   **le wagon**

This train has five cars.
Ce train a cinq wagons.

---

card [KAHRD] nom   **la carte**

Do you know how to play cards?
Savez-vous jouer aux cartes?

---

carefully [KEHR-fé-li] adverbe   **avec soin**

Paul pours water into the glass carefully.
Paul verse l'eau dans le verre avec soin.

---

carrot [KAR-ét] nom   **la carotte**

Rabbits eat carrots.
Les lapins mangent des carottes.

---

to carry [KAR-i] verbe   **porter**

I carry	we carry
you carry	you carry
he, she, it carries	they carry

The dog is carrying a newspaper in its mouth.
Le chien porte un journal dans la bouche.

---

castle [KAS-él] nom   **le château**

The king lives in a large castle.
Le roi habite un grand château.

---

cat [KAT] nom   **le chat**

The cat is playing with the ball.
Le chat joue avec la balle.

---

to catch [KACH] verbe   **attraper**

I catch	we catch
you catch	you catch
he, she, it catches	they catch

Hurray! John catches the ball.
Bravo! Jean attrape la balle.

CD [SI-DI] nom   **le CD**

I love this new CD by Celine Dion!
J'adore ce nouveau CD de Céline Dion!

CD player nom   **le lecture CD,** masc.

---

ceiling [SI-ling] nom   **le plafond**

The ceiling of the chateau is very interesting.
Le plafond du château est très intéressant.

---

celery [SEL-ri] nom   **le céleri**

Mother makes a salad with celery.
Maman fait une salade avec du céleri.

---

cellar (basement) [SEL-ér] nom   **la cave**

There are several packages in the cellar.
Il y a plusieures paquets dans la cave.

---

certain, sure [SUR-tén] adjectif   **sûr,** masc.
                                       sûre, fém.
I am certain that the train will come soon.
Je suis sûr que le train arrive bientôt.

---

chair [CHEHR] nom   **la chaise**

This chair is too big for me.
Cette chaise est trop grande pour moi.

---

chalk [CHAWK] nom   **la craie**

The boy is writing on the blackboard with chalk.
Le garçon écrit au tableau noir avec la craie.

chalk board   **le tableau noir**

---

change (money) [CHEINDJ] nom   **la monnaie**

The butcher says, "Here is the change from 30 francs."
Le boucher dit: "Voici la monnaie de trente francs."

---

to change verbe   **changer**

I change	we change
you change	you change
he, she, it changes	they change

We have to change to another train.
Il faut changer de train.

---

cheap(ly) [CHIP-(li)] adverbe   **bon marché**

Bread is cheap; it is not expensive.
On vend le pain bon marché; il ne coûte pas cher.

---

to cheat (deceive) [CHIT] verbe   **tromper**

I cheat	we cheat
you cheat	you cheat
he, she, it cheats	they cheat

In the film, the robber deceives the policeman.
Dans le film, le voleur trompe l'agent de police.

---

check (in restaurant) [CHEK] nom   **l'addition**

After dinner, Dad asks for the check.
Apres le dîner, Papa demande l'addition.

(to play) checkers (See **to play**)   **jouer aux dames**

---

cheerful [CHIR-fél] adjectif   **gai,** masc.

My sister is always cheerful.   **gaie,** fém.
Ma soeur est toujours gaie.

---

cheese [CHIZ] nom   **le fromage**

My sister has cheese for dessert.
Ma soeur prend du fromage comme dessert.

---

cherry [CHER-i] nom   **la cerise**

I am going to pick cherries.
Je vais cueillir des cerises.

(to play) chess (See **to play**)   **jouer aux échecs**

---

chicken [CHIK-én] nom   **le poulet**

What are we eating this evening? Chicken.
Qu'est-ce qu'on mange ce soir? Du poulet.

---

child [CHAILD] nom   **l'enfant,** masc., fém.
children [CHIL-dren] pl.   **les enfants,** pl.

The children are playing on the playground.
Les enfants jouent au terrain de jeux.

---

chimney (fireplace) [CHIM-ni] nom   **la cheminée**

The shoes are near the fireplace.
Les chaussures sont près de la cheminée.

---

chin [CHIN] nom   **le menton**

Here is the doll's chin.
Voici le menton de la poupée.

---

chocolate [CHA-klit] nom   **le chocolat**

What? You don't like chocolates?
Comment? Tu n'aimes pas les chocolats?

---

to choose [CHUZ] verbe   **choisir**

I choose	we choose
you choose	you choose
he, she, it chooses	they choose

In the examination, choose the correct answer.
Dans l'examen, choisissez la réponse correcte.

---

chop [CHᴀP] nom   **la côtelette**

Do you prefer a veal cutlet or a lamb chop?
Préfères-tu une côtelette de veau ou de mouton?

Christmas [KRɪS-MES] nom   **Noël,** masc.

Christmas comes on December 25th.
Noël vient le vingt-cinq décembre.

church [CHUᴦCH] nom   **l'église,** fém.

There is a big church in the city.
Il y a une grande église dans la ville.

cigarette [sɪg-é-RET] nom   **la cigarette**

Does your uncle smoke cigarettes?
Est-ce que ton oncle fume des cigarettes?

circle [SUR-kél] nom   **le cercle**

The boys form a circle to play.
Les garçons forment un cercle pour jouer.

circus [SUᴦ-kés] nom   **le cirque**

There are many animals at the circus.
Il y a beaucoup d'animaux au cirque.

city [SɪT-i] nom   **la ville**

The city of Paris is big.
La ville de Paris est grande.

class [KLAS] nom   **la classe**
classroom [KLAS-rum]   **la salle de classe**

We are in the classroom.
Nous sommes dans la salle de classe.

---

clean [KLIN] adjectif   **propre**

My hands are clean.
Mes mains sont propres.

to clean verbe   **nettoyer**
  I clean   we clean
  you clean   you clean
  he, she, it cleans   they clean

Do you help your mother clean the house?
Tu aides ta mère à nettoyer la maison?

cleaning woman (maid) [KLIN-ing WÉ-mén] nom   **la bonne**

The maid cleans the house.
La bonne nettoie la maison.

street cleaner   **la balayeur des rues**

---

clear [KLIR] adjectif   **clair,** masc.
                                                              claire, fém.
What a beautiful, clear day!
Quelle belle journée claire!

---

clever (cunning) [KLEV-ér] adjectif   **rusé,** masc.
                                                        rusée, fém.

The cat is clever.
Le chat est rusé.

---

to climb [KLAIM] verbe   **grimper**
  I climb   we climb
  you climb   you climb
  he, she, it climbs   they climb

The cat climbs the tree.
Le chat grimpe sur l'arbre.

---

clock [KLAK] nom   **l'horloge,** fém.

The clock strikes twice. It is two o'clock.
L'horloge sonne deux fois. Il est deux heures.

---

to close [KLOHZ] verbe   **fermer**
  I close   we close
  you close   you close
  he, she, it closes   they close

Please close the window.
Fermez la fenêtre, s'il vous plaît.

---

close friend [klohs FREND] nom   **le camarade**

My friend and I are going to the park to play.
Mon camarade et moi, nous allons jouer au parc.

---

closet nom   **le placard**

The closet is closed.
Le placard est fermé.

---

closet (cupboard) [KLAHZ-it] nom   **l'armoire,** fém.

The cupboard is empty (bare).
L'armoire est vide.

---

close to, near préposition   **près de**

Bordeaux is near the Atlantic Ocean.
Bordeaux est près de l'océan Atlantique.

---

clothes (clothing) [KLOHZ] nom   **les vêtements**

My clothes are on the bed.
Mes vêtements sont sur le lit.

---

cloud [KLOWD] nom   **le nuage**

The sun is behind a cloud.
Le soleil est derrière un nuage.

cloudy [KLOWD-i] adjectif   **couvert**

---

clown [KLOWN] nom   **le clown**

When I am at the circus I say "Hello" to the clown.
Quand je suis au cirque je dis "Bonjour" au clown.

---

coat [KOHT] nom   **le manteau**

She wears a warm coat in winter.
Elle porte un manteau chaud en hiver.

coffee [KAF-i] nom   **le café**

Do you want some coffee?
Voulez-vous du café?

cold [KOHLD] nom   **le froid**

When it is cold in winter, I am cold.
Quand il fait froid en hiver, j'ai froid.

it is cold	**il fait froid**
be cold	**avoir froid**
cold (illness)	**le rhume**

color [KUL-ér] nom   **la couleur**

What color is the banana?
De quelle couleur est la banane?

to color verbe   **colorier**

I color	we color
you color	you color
he, she, it colors	they color

We color with crayons.
Nous colorions avec les crayons de couleur.

comb [KOHM] nom   **le peigne**

Where is my comb?
Où est mon peigne?

to comb (one's hair) verbe   **se peigner**
   I comb   we comb
   You comb   you comb
   he, she, it combs   they comb

I comb my hair before leaving the house.
Avant de sortir de la maison, je me peigne.

---

to come [KŬM] verbe   **venir**
   I come   we come
   you come   you come
   he, she, it comes   they come

My father comes from work at 6:00 o'clock.
Mon père vient du travail à six heures.

to come into verbe   **entrer**

They come into the house.
Ils entrent dans la maison.

---

comfortable [KŬM-fér-té-bél] adjectif   **comfortable**

The sofa is very comfortable.
Le canapé est très comfortable.

---

to command (order) [ké-MAND] verbe   **commander**

In the restaurant Father orders dinner.
Dans le restaurant Papa commande le dîner.

---

company [KÉM-pé-ni] nom   **la compagnie**

*The Bardot Company is located on the corner
(of the street).*
La Compagnie Bardot se trouve au coin de la rue.

---

to compete [kém-PIT] verbe   **rivaliser**

We compete for a prize.
Nous rivalisons pour un prix.

---

to complain [kém-PLEIN] verbe   **se plaindre**

   I complain   we complain
   you complain   you complain
   he, she, it complains they complain

My friend says that I always complain!
Mon amie dit que je me plains toujours!

---

completely [kem-PLIT-li] adverbe   **tout à fait**

My bathing suit is not completely dry.
Mon maillot n'est pas tout à fait sec.

---

computer [kém-PYU-tér] nom   **l'ordinateur,** masc.

My friend has a computer.
Mon amie a un ordinateur.

> Steven Jobs a rendu populaire l'ordinateur
> personnel dans les années 1970.
>
> Steven Jobs popularized the personal computer in
> the 1970s.

(computer) disk [disk] nom   **le disque**
(computer) technician   **technicien,** masc.
[TEK-ni-shén] nom   **technicienne,** fém.

printer [PRIN-tr] nom   **une imprimante,** fém.

screen [SKRIN] nom   **un écran,** masc.

contest [KAN-test] nom   **la compétition**
Who is going to win the contest?   **le concours**
Qui va gagner la compétition?

---

to continue [kén-TIN-yu] verbe   **continuer**
I continue	we continue
you continue	you continue
he, she, it continues	they continue

I will continue to play the piano until five o'clock.
Je continue à jouer du piano jusqu'à cinq heures.

---

to cook [KAUHK] verbe   **faire la cuisine**
Who's cooking?
Qui fait la cuisine?

---

cookie [KAUHK-i] nom   **le petit gâteau**

---

cool [KUL] adjectif   **frais,** masc.
It is cool   **fraîche,** fém.
Il fait frais.

---

to copy [KAP-i] verbe   **copier**
I copy	we copy
you copy	you copy
he, she, it copies	they copy

We have to copy the sentences that are on the blackboard.
Il faut copier les phrases qui sont au tableau noir.

copier [kah-pee-ehr] nom   **la photocopieuse,** fém.

---

corn [KAWRN] nom   **le maïs**
Mmm, the corn is good!
Mmm, les maïs est bon!

corner [K<u>AW</u>R-n*é*r] nom   **le coin**

You must cross the street at the corner.
Il faut traverser la rue au coin.

---

correct [k*é*-REKT] adjectif   **correct,** masc.
                                                          correcte, fém.
*The teacher says, "Write the correct
answer."*
Le professeur dit: "Ecrivez la réponse correcte."

correct (fair) adjectif   **juste**

But it's my turn. It isn't fair!
Mais c'est mon tour. Ce n'est pas juste!

---

to cost (See **price**) [K<u>A</u>ST] verbe   **coûter**
  it costs   they cost

How much does this comb cost?
Combien coûte ce peigne?

---

cotton [K<u>A</u>T-*é*n] nom   **le coton**
made of cotton   **en coton**

He is wearing a cotton shirt.
Il porte une chemise en coton.

---

to cough [K<u>A</u>F] verbe   **tousser**
  I cough   we cough
  you cough   you cough
  he, she, it coughs they cough

The baby is coughing. He has a cold.
Le bébé tousse. Il a un rhume.

---

counselor [KOWN-s*é*-l*é*r] nom   **le conseiller,** masc.
                                               la conseillère, fém.

What is the name of the counselor?
Comment s'appelle la conseillère?

---

to count [KOWNT] verbe   **compter**

I count	we count
you count	you count
he, she, it counts	they count

He knows how to count from five to one:
five, four, three, two, one.
Il sait compter de cinq à un: cinq, quatre, trois, deux, un.

---

country [KƏN-tri] nom   **le pays**

What is the name of the country to the east of France?
Quel est le nom du pays à l'est de la France?

country (opposite of city) nom   **la campagne**

It's nice weather. Let's go to the country!
Il fait beau. Allons à la compagne!

---

courageous [ké-REI-djés] adjectif   **courageux,** masc.
                                                courageuse, fém.
The prince is courageous when
he saves the princess.
Le prince est courageux quand il sauve la princesse.

---

cousin [KƏZ-én] nom   **le cousin**
                                                la cousine
My cousin Paul is ten years old and my
cousin Mary is eighteen.
Mon cousin Paul a dix ans et ma cousine
Marie a dix-huit ans.

---

cover (blanket) [KƏV-ér] nom   **la couverture**

In winter I like a warm blanket on my bed.
En hiver j'aime une couverture chaude sur le lit.

covered [KƏV-érd] adjectif   **couvert,** masc.
                                                couverte, fém.
The tree is covered with snow.
L'arbre est couvert de neige.

---

cow [KOW] nom   **la vache**

The cow is in the field.
La vache est dans le champ.

---

cradle nom   **le berceau**

---

crayon [KREI-én] nom   **le crayon de couleur**

I draw with a crayon.
Je dessine avec un crayon de couleur.

---

crazy (mad) [KREIZ-i] adjectif   **fou,** masc.
                              folle, fém.
The dog is mad.
Le chien est fou.

---

croissant nom   **le croissant**

Harriet has a croissant for breakfast.
Henriette prend un croissant pour le petit déjeuner.

---

to cross [KRAS] verbe   **traverser**

I cross	we cross
you cross	you cross
he, she, it crosses	they cross

Can we cross the lake?
On peut traverser le lac?

to cry [KRAI] verbe   **pleurer**

I cry	we cry
you cry	you cry
he, she, it cries	they cry

I cry when somebody teases me.
Je pleure quand on me taquine.

---

cunning (clever) [KØN-ing] adjectif   **rusé,** masc.
                                                   rusée, fém.
The thief is clever; he climbs a tree.
Le voleur est rusé; il grimpe sur un arbre.

---

cup [KØP] nom   **la tasse**

I put the cup on the saucer.
Je mets la tasse sur la soucoupe.

---

cupboard [KØB-érd] nom   **le buffet**

There are plates in the cupboard.
Il y a des assiettes dans le buffet.

---

curious [KYUR-yés] adjectif   **curieux,** masc.
                                                   curieuse, fém.
*She is curious. She would like to open
the package.*
Elle est curieuse. Elle voudrait ouvrir le paquet.

---

curtain [KØR-tén] nom   **le rideau**
                                                     les rideaux
The curtains in my room are too long.
Les rideaux dans ma chambre sont trop longs.

---

to cut [KɛT] verbe   **couper**

I cut	we cut
you cut	you cut
he, she, it cuts	they cut

Dad cuts the bread with a knife.
Papa coupe le pain avec un couteau.

---

cute [KYUT] adjectif   **mignon,** masc.
                                     mignonne, fém.

The baby is cute.
Le bébé est mignon.

---

cutlet [KɛT-lét] nom   **la côtelette**

Do you prefer a veal cutlet or a lamb chop?
Préfères-tu une côtelette de veau ou de mouton?

D

Dad (Daddy) [DAD] nom   **papa**

Daddy, I'm afraid!
Papa, j'ai peur!

---

damp [DAMP] adjectif   **humide**

My bathing suit is damp.
Mon maillot est humide.

to dance [DANS] verbe   **danser**

I dance	we dance
you dance	you dance
he, she, it dances	they dance

My sister likes to dance.
Ma soeur aime danser.

---

dangerous [DEIN-gjér-és] adjectif   **dangereux,** masc.
                                               dangereuse, fém.
It is dangerous to run into the street
to catch a ball.
Il est dangereux de courir dans la rue pour
attraper une balle.

---

to dare (to) [DEHR] verbe   **oser**

I dare	we dare
you dare	you dare
he, she, it dares	they dare

You dare to hit me?
Tu oses me battre?

---

dark [DAHRK] adjectif   **foncé,** masc.
                                                    foncée, fém.
She is wearing a dark blue dress.
Elle porte une robe bleu foncé.

---

date [DEIT] nom   **la date**

What is the date?
Quelle est la date?

---

daughter [DA-tér] nom   **la fille**

I should like to introduce my daughter, Amy.
Je vous présente ma fille, Aimée.

---

day [DEI] nom　　　　　　　　　　　**la journée**
le jour

I am going to spend the day at my cousin's house.
Je vais passer la journée chez ma cousine.

What day of the week is it?
Quel jour de la semaine est-ce?

---

day off nom　　　　　　　　　**le jour de congé**

Thursday is a day off for French students?
Le jeudi est un jour de congé pour les élèves français?

New Year's Day nom　　　　　　**le Jour de l'An**

January 1st is New Year's Day.
Le premier janvier est le Jour de l'An.

every day adverbe　　　　　　　**tous les jours**

I read every day.
Je lis tous les jours.

---

dead [DED] adjectif　　　　　　　**mort,** masc.
morte, fém.

You're crying? Yes, my turtle is dead.
Tu pleures? Oui, ma tortue est morte.

---

deaf [DEF] adjectif　　　　　　　**sourd,** masc.
sourde, fém.

You don't hear me? You're deaf?
Tu ne m'entends pas? Tu es sourd?

---

dear [DIR] adjectif　　　　　　　**cher,** masc.
chère, fém.

---

to deceive (cheat) [di-SIV] verbe　　　**tromper**
　　I deceive　　　　　we deceive
　　you deceive　　　　you deceive
　　he, she, it deceives　they deceive

In the film, the robber deceives the policeman.
Dans le film, le voleur trompe l'agent de police.

December [di-SEM-bér] nom **décembre,** masc.

It is cold in December.
Il fait froid en décembre.

---

to decorate [DEK-é-reit] verbe **décorer**
   I decorate   we decorate
   you decorate   you decorate
   he, she, it decorates   they decorate

He is decorating his bicycle.
Il décore sa bicyclette.

---

deep [DIP] adjectif **profond,** masc.
profonde, fém.
Is the pool deep?
Est-ce que la piscine est profonde?

---

delicious [di-LISH-és] adjectif **délicieux,** masc.
délicieuse, fém.
The cake is delicious.
Le gâteau est délicieux.

---

delighted, happy [di-LAI-téd] adjectif **heureux,** masc.
heureuse, fém.
Everyone is happy at a party.
A une fête tout le monde est heureux.

---

dentist [DEN-tist] nom **le dentiste**
The dentist says, "Open your mouth."
Le dentiste dit: "Ouvre la bouche."

---

desert [DEZ-ért] nom   **le désert**

The desert is very dry.
Le désert est très sec.

desk [DESK] nom   **le bureau**

The teacher's desk is big.
Le bureau du professeur est grand.

desk (pupil's) nom   **le pupitre**

dessert [di-ZURT] nom   **le dessert**

I would like to have a strawberry tart for dessert.
Comme dessert je désire une tarte aux fraises.

to detest (hate) [di-TEST] verbe   **détester**

I detest	we detest
you detest	you detest
he, she, it detests	they detest

He hates spinach.
Il déteste les épinards.

> Emily Dickinson était une poète américaine qui a écrit presque 2,000 poèmes.
>
> Emily Dickinson was an American poet who wrote almost 2,000 poems.

dictionary [DIK-shén-ehr-i] nom   **le dictionnaire**

How many words are there in the dictionary?
Combien de mots y a-t-il dans le dictionnaire?

different [DIF-rent] adjectif

These loaves of bread are different.
Ces pains sont différents.

différent, masc.
differente, fém.

---

difficult [DIF-é-kélt] adjectif

It is difficult to read this letter.
Il est difficile de lire cette lettre.

difficile

---

digital [DI-dgi-tel] adjectif

There is a digital sign.
Voilà une affiche numérique.

numérique

---

dining room (See **room**)

la salle à manger

---

dinner [DIN-ér] nom

We eat dinner at eight o'clock.
Nous prenons le dîner à huit heures.

le dîner

---

to direct [di-REKT] verbe

I direct	we direct
you direct	you direct
he, she, it directs	they direct

My brother is directing the game.
Mon frère dirige le jeu.

diriger

---

dirty [DUR-ti] adjectif

My shirt is dirty!
Ma chemise est sale!

sale

---

dishes [DISH-és] nom

Do you wash the dishes at your house?
Est-ce que vous lavez la vaisselle chez vous?

la vaisselle

---

displeased, angry [dis-PLIZD] adjectif   **fâché,** masc.
When I tease my sister, Mom is angry.   **fâchée,** fém.
Quand je taquine ma soeur, Maman est fâchée.

---

distant [DIS-tént] adjectif   **loin**
Robert is very distant.
Robert est très loin.

---

to do [DU] verbe   **faire**
  I do   we do
  you do   you do
  he, she, it does   they do

He does his homework.
Il fait ses devoirs.

---

doctor [DAK-tér] nom   **le docteur, le médecin**
Mother says, "You are sick. I am going to call the doctor."
Maman dit: "Tu es malade. Je vais appeler le docteur."

---

dog [DAG] nom   **le chien**
Do you have a dog?
As-tu un chien?

puppy   **le petit chien**

---

doll [DAL] nom   **la poupée**
My doll's name is Sylvia.
Ma poupée s'appelle Sylvie.

dollhouse   **la maison de poupée**

---

dollar [DAL-ér] nom   **le dollar**
Here is a dollar for you.
Voilà un dollar pour toi.

---

dominoes [DAM-é-nohz] nom　　　　　　　**les dominos**

My cousin plays dominoes well.
Mon cousin joue bien aux dominos.

---

donkey [DÉNG-ki] nom　　　　　　　　　**l'âne, masc.**

*The donkey does
not want to walk!*
L'âne ne veut pas
marcher!

---

door [DAWR] nom　　　　　　　　　　　　**la porte**

Please close the door.
Fermez la porte, s'il vous plaît.

---

doorbell [DAWR-bel] nom　　　　　　　　**le bouton**

*Here we are at Virginia's house.
Where is the doorbell?*
Nous voici à la porte de Virginie.
Où est le bouton?

---

doorknob [DAWR-nob] nom　　　　　　　**le bouton**

---

down there [DOWN -thehr] adverbe　　　　**là-bas**

Do you see your brother coming down there?
Tu vois ton frère qui arrive, là-bas?

---

dozen [DÉZ-én] adjectif　　　　　　　　**la douzaine**

She is buying a dozen pears.
Elle achète une douzaine de poires.

---

to drag (pull) [DRAG] verbe   **tirer**

I drag	we drag
You drag	you drag
he, she, it drags	they drag

He is pulling a bag of potatoes.
Il tire un sac de pommes de terre.

to draw [DRAW] verbe   **dessiner**

I draw	we draw
you draw	you draw
he, she, it draws	they draw

Go to the board and draw a house.
Va au tableau noir et dessine une maison.

drawer [DRAWR] nom   **le tiroir**

I put the camera in a drawer.
Je mets l'appareil dans un tiroir.

dreadful! [DRED-fél] interjection   **terrible!**

I have a bad mark. Dreadful!
J'ai une mauvaise note. Terrible!

dream [DRIM] nom   **le rêve**

Do you always have dreams?
Avez-vous toujours les rêves?

to dream verbe   **rêver**

I dream	we dream
you dream	you dream
he, she, it dreams	they dream

I dream of going to the moon!
Je rêve d'aller à la lune!

dress [DRES] nom   **la robe**

My doll's dress is dirty.
La robe de ma poupée est sale.

---

to dress verbe   **s'habiller**

I dress	we dress
you dress	you dress
he, she, it dresses	they dress

I get up, I get dressed, I go to school.
Je me lève, je m'habille, je vais à l'école.

---

drink [DRĪNGK] nom   **le boisson**

Do you want to order a drink?
Tu veux commander un boisson?

---

to drink verbe   **boire**

I drink	we drink
you drink	you drink
he, she, it drinks	they drink

The child is drinking milk.
L'enfant boit du lait.

---

to drive [DRĀĪV] verbe   **conduire**

I drive	we drive
you drive	you drive
he, she, it drives	they drive

Too bad! I am too young to drive the car.
Hélas! Je suis trop jeune pour conduire l'auto.

---

driver [DRĀĪV-ér] nom   **le chauffeur**

The driver stops when the light is red.
Le chauffeur s'arrête quand le feu est rouge.

---

drum [DRᴀ́M] nom   **le tambour**

I make noise when I play the drum.
Je fais du bruit quand je joue du tambour.

---

dry [DRᴀɪ] adjectif   **sec,** masc.
                                                                 sèche, fém.
Is the floor dry, Mom?
Est-ce que le plancher est sec, maman?

---

duck [Dᴀ́K] nom   **le canard**

There are some ducks on the lake.
Voilà des canards sur le lac.

---

during [Dᴜʀ-ɪng] préposition   **pendant**

I sleep during the night.
Je dors pendant la nuit.

DVD [DI-vi-di] nom   **le DVD,** masc.

Mary has a good DVD.
Marie a un bon DVD.

DVD player nom   **le lecteur DVD,** masc.

E

each [ICH] adjectif   **chaque**

I put a fork at each place.
Je mets une fourchette à chaque place.

each one pronoun   **chacun,** masc.

Here are five girls; each one has a flower.   **chacune,** fém.
Voilà cinq jeunes filles; chacune a une fleur.

---

ear [IR] nom   **l'oreille,** fém.

The wolf's ears are long.
Les oreilles du loup sont longues.

---

early [UR-li] adverbe   **tôt**

The rooster gets up early.
Le coq se lève tôt.

---

to earn (win) [URN] verbe   **gagner**

I earn	we earn
you earn	you earn
he, she, it earns	they earn

Our team wins!
C'est notre équipe qui gagne!

---

earth [URTH] nom   **la terre**

When the astronaut is on the moon, he sees the earth.
Quand l'astronaute est sur la lune, il voit la terre.

---

earthquake [URTH-kweik] nom   **le tremblement de terre**

I am afraid of earthquakes.
J'ai peur des tremblements de terre.

---

east [IST] nom   **l'est,** masc.

When I go from Paris to Strasbourg, I go toward the east.
Quand je vais de Paris à Strasbourg, je vais vers l'est.

---

easy [I-zi] adjectif   **facile**

It is easy to do my homework.
Il est facile de faire mes devoirs.

---

to eat [IT] verbe   **manger**

I eat	we eat
you eat	you eat
he, she, it eats	they eat

On Sundays we eat turkey.
Le dimanche nous mangeons la dinde.

---

edge (See **shore**)   **le bord**

---

egg [EG] nom   **l'oeuf,** masc.

Do you want an egg this morning?
Tu veux un oeuf ce matin?

---

eight [EIT] adjectif   **huit**

I have eight insects.
J'ai huit insectes.

---

eighteen [ei-TIN] adjectif   **dix-huit**

She is eighteen years old.
Elle a dix-huit ans.

---

eighty [EI-ti] adjectif   **quatre-vingts**

I have eighty marbles!
J'ai quatre-vingts billes!

---

electric [i-LEK-trik] adjectif   **électrique**

Look! They sell electric knives!
Regarde! On vend des couteaux électriques!

---

electric stove   **le fourneau électrique**

---

elephant [EL-é-fént] nom   **l'éléphant,** masc.

There is a big elephant in the zoo.
Il y a un grand éléphant dans le jardin zoologique.

eleven [i-LEV-én] adjectif   **onze**

The farmer has eleven chickens.
Le fermier a onze poulets.

e-mail [I-meyl] nom   **un email,** masc.

I e-mail my cousin.
J'envoie un message à ma cousine par email.

to e-mail verbe   **envoyer un message par email**

empty [EMP-ti] adjectif   **vide**

The drawer is empty.
Le tiroir est vide.

end [END] nom   **la fin**

It is the end of the lesson.
C'est la fin de la leçon.

Un proverbe: Tout est bien qui finit bien.

Proverb: All's well that ends well.

engineer [en-dji-NIR] nom   **l'ingénieur,** masc.

I would like to become an engineer.
Je voudrais devenir ingénieur.

English [ING-lish] nom, adjectif   **l'anglais,** masc.

They speak English in the United States.
On parle anglais aux Etats-Unis.

---

enough [i-NÉF] adverbe   **assez**

Do you have enough potatoes?
As-tu assez de pommes de terre?

---

to enter (go into) [EN-tér] verbe   **entrer**

I enter	we enter
you enter	you enter
he, she, it enters	they enter

They go into the house.
Ils entrent dans la maison.

---

entrance [EN-tréns] nom   **l'entrée,** fém.

We are looking for the entrance.
Nous cherchons l'entrée.

---

envelope [EN-vé-lohp] nom   **l'enveloppe,** fém.

The mailman gives me an envelope.
Le facteur me donne une enveloppe.

---

equal (same) [I-kwél] adjectif   **égal,** masc.
                                          égale, fém.

Do you want ice cream or cake?   **égaux,** pl.
(Oh, it doesn't make any difference.)
(Oh, it's all the same to me.)
Tu veux la glace ou le gâteau? Oh, cela m'est égal.

to erase [i-REIS] verbe   **effacer**

I erase	we erase
you erase	you erase
he, she, it erases	they erase

Oh, a mistake! I have to erase this word.
Oh, une faute! Je dois effacer ce mot.

eraser [i-REI-sér] nom   **la brosse, la gomme**

I have to erase this sentence with the eraser.
Je dois effacer cette phrase avec la brosse.

---

error (mistake) [ER-ér] nom   **la faute**

I make errors when I write in French.
Je fais des fautes quand j'écris en français.

---

especially [es-PESH-é-li] adverbe   **surtout**

I like to watch television, especially Saturday mornings.
J'aime regarder la télévision, surtout le samedi matin.

---

euro [YU-ro] nom   **l'euro**

How many euros do you have?
Combien d'euros avez-vous?

---

even [I-vén] adverbe   **même**

She cries even when she is happy.
Elle pleure même quand elle est heureuse.

---

evening [IV-ning] nom   **le soir**

I watch television in the evening.
Le soir je regarde la télé.

Good evening expression idiomatique   **Bonsoir**

---

every [EV-ri] adjectif   **tout**
                                              tous, masc., pl.
                                                  toute, fém.

every day   **tous les jours**
everybody (everyone) pronoun   **tout le monde**

Everybody likes Saturday night.
Tout le monde aime le samedi soir.

everywhere [ev-ri-WHEHR] adverbe   **partout**

I look everywhere for my watch.
Je cherche ma montre partout.

---

examination [eg-zam-i-NEI-shén] nom   **l'examen,** masc.

Do you have a good mark on the examination?
Tu as une bonne note à l'examen?

---

excellent [EK-sé-lént] adjectif   **excellent,** masc.
                                                excellente, fém.
The teacher says, "This work is
excellent."
Le professeur dit: "Ce travail est excellent."

---

excuse me [ek-SKYUZ MI]   **excusez-moi, pardon**
expression idiomatique

Excuse me. Here are your packages.
Excusez-moi. Voici vos paquets.

---

expensive [ek-SPEN-siv] adjectif   **cher,** masc.
                                                    chère, fém.
This bicycle is too expensive.
Cette bicyclette est trop chère.

---

to explain [ek-SPLEIN] verbe   **expliquer**
   I explain   we explain
   you explain   you explain
   he, she, it explains   they explain

Joan, can you explain this sentence to me?
Jeanne, tu peux m'expliquer cette phrase?

extraordinary (unusual)   **extraordinaire**
[ek-STRAWR-di-ner-i] adjectif

We are going to take an extraordinary trip
in a rocket ship.
Nous allons faire un voyage extraordinaire en fusée.

eye [AI] nom   **l'oeil,** masc.
What color are your eyes?   **les yeux,** pl.
De quelle couleur sont vos yeux?

F

face [FEIS] nom   **la figure**
She is washing her face.
Elle se lave la figure.

factory [FAK-té-ri] nom   **l'usine,** fém.
My father works in the factory.
Mon père travaille à l'usine.

fair [FEHR] nom   **la foire**

We are going to the fair to have a good time.
Nous allons à la foire pour nous amuser.

---

fair adjectif   **juste**

But it's my turn. It isn't fair!
Mais c'est mon tour. Ce n'est pas juste!

---

fairy [FEHR-i] nom   **la fée**
fairy tale   **le conte de fées**

Read this fairy tale to me.
Lisez-moi ce conte de fées.

---

fall (autumn) [FAL] nom   **l'automne,** masc.

In autumn it is cool.
En automne il fait frais.

---

to fall verbe   **tomber**

I fall	we fall
you fall	you fall
he, she, it falls	they fall

The kite falls to the ground.
Le cerf-volant tombe par terre.

---

false [FALS] adjectif   **faux,** masc.
                                 fausse, fém.

He is six years old, true or false?
Il a six ans, vrai ou faux?

---

family [FAM-é-li] nom   **la famille**

How many people are there in your family?
Combien de personnes y a-t-il dans votre famille?

---

famous [FEI-més] adjectif   **célèbre**

The president of France is famous.
Le président de la France est célèbre.

fan [FAN] nom   **le ventilateur**

We use the fan when it is hot.
Nous employons le ventilateur quand il fait chaud.

---

far [FAHR] adverbe   **loin (de)**

Is Paris far from Washington?
Est-ce que Paris est loin de Washington?

---

farm [FAHRM] nom   **la ferme**

There are cows and horses on the farm.
Il y a des vaches et des chevaux à la ferme.

chicken	le poulet	pig	le cochon
cow	la vache	rabbit	le lapin
donkey	l'âne	rooster	le coq
goat	la chèvre	turkey	la dinde
horse	le cheval	sheep	le mouton

---

farmer [FAHR-mér] nom   **le fermier**

My grandfather is a farmer.
Mon grand-père est fermier.

---

fast [FAST] adjectif   **rapide**

The dog is fast when he runs after a cat.
Le chien est rapide quand il court après un chat.

---

fast adverbe   **vite**

My brother walks too fast.
Mon frère marche trop vite.

---

fat [FAT] adjectif   **gros,** masc.
                                                       grosse, fém.
The elephant is fat.
L'éléphant est gros.

father [FAH-<u>th</u>ér] nom   **le père**

My father is a mailman.
Mon père est facteur.

Father (Daddy) nom   **Papa**

Daddy, I'm afraid!
Papa, j'ai peur!

---

favorite [FEI-vér-<u>i</u>t] adjectif   **favori,** masc.
                                                      favorite, fém.
What is your favorite toy?
Quel est ton jouet favori?

---

fax [FAKS] nom   **le fax,** masc.
to fax verbe   **faxer**

I am receiving a fax.
Je reçois un fax.

---

to fear (to be afraid of) [FIR]   **avoir peur**
expression idiomatique

Are you afraid of the storm?
Avez-vous peur de l'orage?

February [FEB-ru-er-i] nom   **février**

How many days are there in February?
Combien de jours y a-t-il en février?

---

to feel [FIL] verbe   **sentir**
  I feel   we feel
  you feel   you feel
  he, she, it feels   they feel
to feel like [FIL L<u>AI</u>K]   **avoir envie de**
expression idiomatique

I feel like taking a walk.
J'ai envie de faire une promenade.

---

feet [FIT] nom   **les pieds**

---

ferocious [fer-OH-shos], **fierce** [FIRS] adjectif   **féroce**
Who is afraid of a ferocious tiger?
Qui a peur d'un tigre féroce?

---

fever [FI-vér] nom   **la fièvre**
I have to stay in bed. I have a fever.
Je dois rester au lit. J'ai de la fièvre.

---

few [fiU] adjectif   **peu de**
Few people came to the meeting.
Peu de gens sont venus à la reunion.

---

field [FILD] nom   **le champ**

The sheep are in the field.
Les moutons sont dans le champ.

---

fifteen [fif-TIN] adjectif   **quinze**
Today is January 15th, the birthday of
Martin Luther King, Jr.
C'est aujourd'hui le quinze janvier, l'anniversaire
de Martin Luther King, Jr.

---

fifty [FIF-ti] adjectif   **cinquante**
There are fifty states in the United States.
Il y a cinquante états dans les Etats-Unis.

---

to fight [FAIT] verbe   **se battre**
Why are those children fighting?
Pourquoi se battent les enfants là-bas?

---

to fill [FIL] verbe   **remplir**

I fill	we fill
you fill	you fill
he, she, it fills	they fill

Stephen fills the box with paper.
Etienne remplit la boîte de papier.

---

film [FILM] nom   **le film**

Are they playing a good film at the movies?
On joue un bon film au cinéma?

> Les films de Hollywood offrent des distractions
> pour les gens en Amérique et à travers le monde,
> et ils reflètent une diversité de thèmes.
>
> Hollywood films provide entertainment in America
> and worldwide, and reflect a diversity of themes.

---

finally [FAI-nél-i] adverbe   **enfin**

It is good weather, finally!
Il fait beau, enfin!

---

to find [FAIND] verbe   **trouver**

I find	we find
you find	you find
he, she, it finds	they find

I like to find shells.
J'aime trouver des coquillages.

---

finger [FIN-gér] nom   **le doigt**

The baby has ten little fingers.
Le bébé a dix petits doigts.

---

fingernail nom   **l'ongle,** masc.

I am ashamed. My fingernails are dirty.
J'ai honte. Mes ongles sont sales.

---

to finish [FIN-ish] verbe   **finir**

I finish   we finish
you finish   you finish
he, she, it finishes   they finish

I am going to finish my work before going out.
Je vais finir mon travail avant de sortir.

---

fire [FAIR] nom   **le feu**

The fire is hot.
Le feu est chaud.

---

fireman nom   **le pompier**

The fireman is very strong.
Le pompier est très fort.

---

fireplace nom   **la cheminée**

We burn wood in the fireplace.
On brûle du bois dans la cheminée.

---

fire truck   **la pompe à incendie**

The fire truck makes a lot of noise.
La pompe à incendie fait beaucoup de bruit.

---

first [FURST] adjectif   **premier,** masc.
                                                              première, fém.
Breakfast is the first meal of the day.
Le petit déjeuner est le premier repas de la journée.

---

fish [FISH] nom   **le poisson**

There are many fish in this lake.
Il y a beaucoup de poissons dans ce lac.

fishing [FISH-ing] nom   **la pêche**
to go fishing expression idiomatique   **aller à la pêche**

We are going fishing.
Nous allons à la pêche.

fish tank nom   **l'aquarium,** masc.

There are some goldfish and plants in the fish tank.
Il y a des poissons rouges et des plantes dans l'aquarium.

five [FAIV] adjectif   **cinq**

The hand has five fingers.
La main a cinq doigts.

to fix [FIKS] verbe   **réparer**

I fix	we fix
you fix	you fix
he, she, it fixes	they fix

My brother is fixing the computer.
Mon frère répare l'ordinateur.

flag [FLAG] nom   **le drapeau,** masc.
                                             les drapeaux, pl.
There are two flags in the classroom.
Il y a deux drapeaux dans la salle de classe.

flat [FLAT] adjectif

plat, masc.
plate, fém.

The field is flat.
Le champ est plat.

---

flight attendant [flait é-tendént] nom

l'hôtesse de l'air

The flight attendant serves us a good meal.
L'hôtesse de l'air nous sert un bon repas.

---

floor [FLAWR] nom

le plancher

The pen falls to the floor.
Le stylo tombe sur le plancher.

floor (of a building)
ground floor

l'étage
le rez-de-chaussée

---

flower [FLOW-ér] nom

la fleur

We have many flowers in the garden.
Nous avons beaucoup de fleurs dans le jardin.

---

fly [FLAI] nom

la mouche

There are flies in the kitchen!
Il y a des mouches dans la cuisine!

---

to fly verbe

voler

I fly	we fly
you fly	you fly
he, she, it flies	they fly

The airplane pilot flies in the airplane.
Le pilote d'avion vole dans l'avion.

fog [FAG] nom   **le brouillard**

It is difficult to see because of the fog.
Il est difficile de voir à cause du brouillard.

---

to follow [FAL-<u>oh</u>] verbe   **suivre**

  I follow   we follow
  you follow   you follow
  he, she, it follows   they follow

The pupils in the class follow the teacher.
Les élèves de la classe suivent la maîtresse.

---

foolish (stupid) [FU-<u>li</u>sh] adjectif   **stupide**

Is the elephant intelligent or foolish?
Est-ce que l'éléphant est intelligent ou stupide?

---

foot [FAUHT] nom   **le pied,** nom.
feet [FIT] nom, pl.   **les pieds,** pl.
to walk, go on foot expression idiomatique   **aller à pied**

We walk to the museum.
Nous allons au musée à pied.

to have a sore foot   **avoir mal au pied**
expression idiomatique

---

for [fér] préposition   **comme**

For dessert she has chocolate ice cream.
Comme dessert elle prend de la glace au chocolat.

---

for préposition   **depuis**

She has been waiting for her aunt for an hour.
Elle attend sa tante depuis une heure.

---

for préposition   **pour**

She is going to the store to buy stockings.
Elle va au magasin pour acheter des bas.

foreign [FAHR-én] adjectif

étranger, masc.
étrangère, fém.

I would like to travel to foreign countries.
Je voudrais voyager aux pays étrangers.

forest [FAR-ist] nom

le bois, masc.
la forêt, fém.

There are a hundred trees in the forest!
Il y a cent arbres dans la forêt!

forever (always) [fawr-EV-ér] adverbe

toujours

The leaves always fall in autumn.
Les feuilles tombent toujours en automne.

to forget [fawr-GET] verbe

oublier

I forget	we forget
you forget	you forget
he, she, it forgets	they forget

She always forgets her ticket.
Elle oublie toujours son billet.

fork [FAWRK] nom

la fourchette

I eat meat with a fork.
Je mange la viande avec une fourchette.

to form (make) [FAWRM] verbe

former

I form	we form
you form	you form
he, she, it forms	they form

I make a snowball with the snow.
Je forme une balle avec la neige.

forty [FAWR-ti] adjectif   **quarante**

Do you know the story of the forty thieves?
Savez-vous l'histoire des quarante voleurs?

---

four [FAWR] adjectif   **quatre**

There are four people in my family.
Il y a quatre personnes dans ma famille.

---

fourteen [fawr-TIN] adjectif   **quatorze**

July 14th is the French national holiday.
Le quatorze juillet est la fête nationale française.

---

fox [FAKS] nom   **le renard**

The fox runs very fast.
Le renard court très vite.

Benjamin Franklin était auteur, inventeur, et
ministre américain à Paris pendant les anées
1776–1785.

Benjamin Franklin was an author, inventor, and
ambassador to Paris for the American
government from 1776–1785.

---

free (no cost) [FRI] adjectif   **gratuit,** masc.
                                                                           gratuite, fém.
It's free. It doesn't cost anything.
Il est gratuit. Ça ne coute rien.

French [FRENCH] adjectif   **français,** masc.
                                                                           française, fém.
I am reading a French book.
Je lis un livre français.

---

fresh (cool) [FRESH] adjectif   **frais,** masc.
                                                                           fraîche, fém.
It is cool at the beach.
Il fait frais à la plage.

Friday [FRAI-dei] nom **vendredi**

What do we eat on Friday? Fish!
Qu'est-ce qu'on mange le vendredi? Du poisson!

---

friend [FREND] nom **l'ami,** masc.
l'amie, fém.
I am your friend.
Je suis ton amie.

---

frightening [FRAIT-ning] adjectif **effrayant,** masc.
effrayante, fém.

Snakes are frightening.
Les serpents sont effrayants.

---

frog [FRAG] nom **la grenouille**

I am trying to catch a frog.
J'essaye d'attraper une grenouille.

---

from [FROM] préposition **de**

Greetings from your friend!
Compliments de la part de votre ami!

---

fruit [FRUT] nom **les fruits**

Here is some fruit. Do you prefer a pear or a banana?
Voici des fruits. Préférez-vous une poire ou une banane?

---

full [FAUHL] adjectif **plein,** masc.
pleine, fém.
The valise is full of clothes.
La valise est pleine de vêtements.

funny [FÚN-i] adjectif

The clown is funny.
Le clown est amusant.

amusant, masc.
amusante, fém.
drôle

---

future [FYU-chér] nom

In the future I'm going to visit France.
Je vais visiter la France dans l'avenir.

l'avenir, masc.

G

game [GEIM] nom

Which game do you prefer?
Quel jeu préférez-vous?

le jeu, masc.
les jeux, pl.

---

garage [gé-RAHZH] nom

le garage

The car is in the garage.
La voiture est dans le garage.

---

garden [GAHR-dén] nom

le jardin

The garden is full of flowers in June.
Le jardin est plein de fleurs au mois de juin.

---

gas [GAS] nom

le gaz

You have a gas stove? We have an electric stove!
Tu as un fourneau à gaz? Nous avons un fourneau électrique!

gasoline [gas-é-LIN] nom **l'essence,** fém.

Daddy says, "We don't have enough gasoline."
Papa dit: "Nous n'avons pas assez d'essence."

---

gas station [GAS STEI-shén] nom **la station-service**

My mother is going to the gas station.
Ma mère va à la station-service.

---

to gather (pick) [GA-thér] verbe **cueillir**

I gather	we gather
you gather	you gather
he, she, it gathers	they gather

He is going to pick some apples.
Il va cueillir des pommes.

---

gentle (soft) [DJEN-tél] adjectif **doux,** masc.
  douce, fém.

This coat is very soft.
Ce manteau est très doux.

---

gentle **gentil**
gently adverbe **doucement**

Walk gently. Mother has a headache.
Marche doucement. Maman a mal à la tête.

---

geography [dji-AG-ré-fi] nom **la géographie**

I study geography in class.
J'étudie la géographie en classe.

---

to get (receive) [GET] verbe **recevoir**

I get	we get
you get	you get
he, she, it gets	they get

I receive a postcard from my sister.
Je reçois une carte postale de ma soeur.

---

to get dressed verbe   **s'habiller**

I get dressed	we get dressed
you get dressed	you get dressed
he, she, it gets dressed	they get dressed

I get up, I get dressed, I go to school.
Je me lève, je m'habille, je vais à l'école.

---

to get up verbe   **se lever**

I get up	we get up
you get up	you get up
he, she, it gets up	they get up

Get up, Edward. You're late.
Lève-toi, Edouard. Tu es en retard.

---

giant [DJAI-ént] nom   **le géant**

Read me the story of "Jack and the Giant."
Lis-moi l'histoire de "Jacques et Le Géant."

---

gift [GIFT] nom   **le cadeau**

A gift for me?
Un cadeau pour moi?

> Comme cadeau, la France a donné la Statue de la Liberté aux Etats-Unis en 1886.
>
> The Statue of Liberty was a gift from France to the United States in 1886.

---

girl [GURL] nom   **la fille**
The girl is wearing an apron.
La petite fille porte un tablier.

---

to give [GIV] verbe   **donner**
I give	we give
you give	you give
he, she, it gives	they give

Please give me the camera.
Donne-moi l'appareil, s'il te plaît.

---

to give back (return) verbe   **rendre**
I give back	we give back
you give back	you give back
he, she, it gives back	they give back

He returns my roller skates.
Il me rend mes patins à roulettes.

---

glad (happy) [GLAD] adjectif

content, masc.
contente, fém.

The little girl is not happy.
La petite fille n'est pas contente.

glad [GLAD] adjectif

heureux, masc.
heureuse, fém.

---

glass [GLAS] nom   **le verre**

I put the glass on the table carefully.
Je mets le verre sur la table avec soin.

made of glass   **en verre**

My glasses are made of glass.
Mes lunettes sont en verre.

---

glasses nom   **les lunettes**

Be careful! You are going to break your glasses.
Attention! Tu vas casser tes lunettes.

---

glove [GLÉV] nom   **le gant**

She is wearing white gloves.
Elle porte des gants blancs.

---

to glue [GLU] verbe   **coller**

I glue	we glue
you glue	you glue
he, she, it glues	they glue

I glue a picture to a page of my notebook.
Je colle une image sur une page de mon cahier.

---

to go (also used with exp. of health) verbe   aller

I go	we go
you go	you go
he, she, it goes	they go

Where are you going? I'm going home.
Où vas-tu? Je vais chez moi.

---

to go back (See to return)   retourner

---

to go down verbe   descendre

I go down	we go down
you go down	you go down
he, she, it goes down	they go down

The man goes down the mountain.
L'homme descend de la montagne.

---

to go into verbe   entrer

They go into the house.
Ils entrent dans la maison.

---

to go out (leave) verbe   sortir

The nurse leaves the hospital.
L'infirmière sort de l'hôpital.

---

to go to bed verbe   coucher

I go to bed	we go to bed
you go to bed	you go to bed
he, she, it goes to bed	they go to bed

I don't like to go to bed early.
Je n'aime pas me coucher de bonne heure.

---

to go up verbe   monter

The kite goes up into the sky.
Le cerf-volant monte dans le ciel.

goat [GOHT] nom   **la chèvre**

The goat eats grass on the mountain.
La chèvre mange de l'herbe à la montagne.

---

gold [GOHLD] nom   **l'or,** masc.
made of gold   **en or**

I would like to have a gold ring.
Je voudrais avoir une bague en or.

> Un proverbe: Tout ce qui brille, n'est pas or.
>
> Proverb: All that glitters is not gold.

---

goldfish   **le poisson rouge**

I have five goldfish.
J'ai cinq poissons rouges.

---

good [GAUHD] adjectif   **bon,** masc.
                                                                                  bonne, fém.
It is an interesting book; it is a good book.
C'est un livre intéressant; c'est un bon livre.

Good afternoon [gauhd af-ter-NUN]   **Bonjour (après-midi)**
expression idiomatique

"Good afternoon, children," says the teacher.
"Bonjour les enfants," dit le professeur.

Good-bye [gauhd BAY] expression idiomatique   **Au revoir**

In the morning Father says "Good-bye" to his family.
Le matin papa dit: "au revoir" à sa famille.

Good evening! [gauhd IV-ning]   **Bonsoir**
expression idiomatique

When father returns home at nine o'clock, he says,
"Good evening!"
Quand papa retourne à la maison à neuf heures, il dit: "Bonsoir!"

Good luck! [gauhd LÜK]   **Bonne chance!**
expression idiomatique

Good morning [gauhd MAWR-NING]   **bonjour**
expression idiomatique

---

good-looking (pretty) adjectif   **joli,** masc.
                                                jolie, fém.
What a pretty sweater! Is it new?
Quel joli chandail! Il est neuf?

Google [GU-g l] nom   **Google**

Google is a search engine.
Google est un moteur de recherche.

to use Google verbe   **chercher sur Google**

---

granddaughter [GRAND-da-tér] nom   **la petite-fille**

I am the engineer's granddaughter.
Je suis la petite-fille de l'ingénieur.

---

grandfather [GRAND-fah-thér] nom   **le grand-père**

My grandfather likes to drive the car.
Mon grand-père aime conduire la voiture.

---

grandmother [GRAND-méth-ér] nom   **la grand-mère**

We are going to my grandmother's house on Sunday.
Dimanche nous allons chez ma grand-mère.

---

grandparents [GRAND-PEHR-énts] nom   **les grands-parents**

I like to go to my grandparents' house.
J'aime aller chez mes grand-parents.

grandson [GRAND-sén] nom   **le petit-fils**

John is the doctor's grandson.
Jean est le petit-fils du médecin.

grape [GREIP] nom   **le raisin**

The fox looks at the grapes.
Le renard regarde les raisins.

grapefruit [GREIP-frut] nom   **le pamplemousse**

The grapefruit is not sweet.
Le pamplemousse n'est pas doux.

grass [GRAS] nom   **l'herbe,** fém.

Grass is green.
L'herbe est verte.

grasshopper [GRAS-hap-ér] nom   **la sauterelle**

The boy tries to catch the grasshopper.
Le garçon essaye d'attraper la sauterelle.

gray [GREI] adjectif   **gris,** masc.
                                                    grise, fém.
The mouse is gray.
La souris est grise.

Great! [GREIT] interjection   **formidable**

You are going to the circus? Great!
Tu vas au cirque? Formidable!

---

great adjectif   **grand,** masc.
     grande, fém.
Madame Curie was a great scientist.
Madame Curie était une grande savante.

---

green [GRIN] adjectif   **vert,** masc.
     verte, fém.
When the banana is not ripe, it is green.
Quand la banane n'est pas mûre, elle est verte.

---

grocer [GROH-sér] nom   **l'épicier**

The grocer sells salt and jam.
L'épicier vend du sel et de la confiture.

---

grocery store nom   **l'épicerie**

You go to the grocery store to buy sugar.
On va à l'épicerie pour acheter du sucre.

---

ground (earth) [GROWND] nom   **la terre**

When the astronaut is on the moon, he sees the earth.
Quand l'astronaute est sur la lune, il voit la terre.

---

ground floor nom   **le rez-de-chaussée**

Our apartment is on the ground floor.
Notre appartement est au rez-de-chaussée.

---

to grow [GROH] verbe   **pousser**

I grow	we grow
you grow	you grow
he, she, it grows	they grow

Flowers grow in the garden.
Les fleurs poussent dans le jardin.

to guard [GAHRD] verbe   **garder**

I guard	we guard
you guard	you guard
he, she, it guards	they guard

The dog guards the house.
Le chien garde la maison.

to guess [GES] verbe   **deviner**

I guess	we guess
you guess	you guess
he, she, it guesses	they guess

Can you guess how much money I have in my hand?
Pouvez-vous deviner combien d'argent j'ai dans la main?

guitar [gi-TAHR] nom   **la guitare**

I know how to play the guitar.
Je sais jouer de la guitare.

gun [GĬN] nom   **le fusil**

The hunter carries a gun.
Le chasseur porte un fusil.

H

hair [HEHR] nom   **le cheveu,** masc.
                              les cheveux, pl.

Students at the university like
long hair.
Les étudiants à l'université aiment les cheveux longs.

hairbrush nom   **la brosse à cheveux**

half [HAF] adjectif   **demi,** masc.
                                                           demie, fém.
half an hour   **la demi-heure**

I have been waiting for you for half an hour!
Voilà une demi-heure que je vous attends!

half nom   **la moitié**

Give me half of the pear, please.
Donnez-moi la moitié de la poire, s'il vous plaît.

---

ham [HAM] nom   **le jambon**

Will you have some ham in your sandwich?
Vous prenez du jambon dans votre sandwich?

---

hammer [HAM-ér] nom   **le marteau**

Albert is working with a hammer.
Albert travaille avec un marteau.

---

hand [HAND] nom   **la main**

My hands are dirty!
J'ai les mains sales!

right hand   **la main droite**
left hand   **la main gauche**

---

handbag [HAND-bag] nom   **le sac**

I am buying a handbag for my mother.
J'achète un sac à main pour ma mère.

---

handkerchief [HANG-kér-chif] nom   **le mouchoir**

I use a handkerchief when I sneeze.
J'emploie un mouchoir quand j'éternue.

---

handsome (beautiful) [HAN-sém] adjectif   **beau,** masc.
                                       beaux, masc., pl.
The actor is handsome;   **belle,** fém.
the actress is beautiful.   **bel,** masc. (before a vowel)
L'acteur est beau; l'actrice
est belle.

to happen [HAP-én] verbe   **arriver**
What is happening?
Qu'est-ce qui arrive?

happy [HAP-i] adjectif   **content**
The little girl is not happy.
La petite fille n'est pas contente.

happy adjectif   **heureux**
Happy Birthday   **Joyeux Anniversaire**

hard [HAHRD] adjectif   **dur,** masc.
                                       dure, fém.
This apple is too hard.
Cette pomme est trop dure.

hat [HAT] nom   **le chapeau**
What a pretty hat!
Quel joli chapeau!

to hate [HEIT] verbe   **détester**
  I hate   we hate
  you hate   you hate
  he, she, it hates   they hate

He hates spinach.
Il déteste les épinards.

to have [HAV] verbe   **avoir**

I have	we have
you have	you have
he, she, it has	they have

She has a pencil.
Elle a un crayon.

to have a good time verbe   **s'amuser**

I have a good time at the circus.
Je m'amuse au cirque.

to have a pain (ache) in the ...   **avoir mal à**
expression idiomatique

I am sick. I have a headache.
Je suis malade. J'ai mal à la tête.

to have a sore ... expression idiomatique   **avoir mal à**

Peter has a sore foot.
Pierre a mal au pied.

to have (food) verbe   **prendre**

Mom has a croissant for breakfast.
Maman prend un croissant pour le petit déjeuner.

to have to verbe   **devoir**

I have to	we have to
you have to	you have to
he, she, it has to	they have to

I have to wash my hands.
Je dois me laver les mains.

hay [HEI] nom   **le foin**

The farmer gives hay to the horses.
Le fermier donne du foin aux chevaux.

he [HI] pronom

il

head [HED] nom

la tête

The soldier turns his head.
Le soldat tourne la tête.

health [HELTH] nom

la santé

Mother says, "Candy is not good for your health."
Maman dit: "Les bonbons ne sont pas bons pour la santé."

to hear [HIR] verbe

entendre

I hear	we hear
you hear	you hear
he, she, it hears	they hear

I hear the telephone ringing.
J'entends le téléphone qui sonne.

heart [HAHRT] nom

le coeur

Look at all the hearts on the (playing) card!
Regardez tous les coeurs sur la carte!

heavy [HEV-i] adjectif

lourd, masc.
lourde, fém.

The valise is very heavy.
La valise est très lourde.

helicopter [HEL-i-kap-tér] nom

l'hélicoptère

The helicopter goes to the airport.
L'hélicoptère va à l'aéroport.

Hello [he-LOH] interjection   **bonjour**

"Hello, children," says the teacher.
"Bonjour, les enfants," dit le professeur.

---

to help [HELP] verbe   **aider**

I help	we help
you help	you help
he, she, it helps	they help

John helps his sister carry the books.
Jean aide sa soeur à porter les livres.

Help! interjection   **Au secours!**

When I fall I cry, "Help!"
Quand je tombe je crie: "Au secours!"

---

her [HUR] pronom   **la**
her pronom   **lui**
her adjectif   **son**

---

here [HIR] adverbe   **ici**

Come here, Pierrot.
Viens ici, Pierrot.

---

here (present) adverbe   **présent,** masc.
                                présente, fém.
My friend Joan is present; my friend
Susan is absent.
Mon amie Jeanne est présente; mon amie
Suzanne est absente.

---

here are adverbe   **voici**

Here are my tops (toys).
Voici mes toupies.

---

here is adverbe   **voici**

Here is my top (toy).
Voici ma toupie.

---

herself [HUR-SELF] pronom   **se**

---

to hide [HAID] verbe   **cacher**

I hide	we hide
you hide	you hide
he, she, it hides	they hide

The boy is hiding the flowers behind him.
Le garçon cache les fleurs derrière lui.

---

to play hide-and-seek   **jouer à cache-cache**
(See **to play**)

---

high [HAI] adjectif   **grand,** masc.
                                                           grande, fém.

high adjectif   **haut**

The Eiffel Tower is very high.
La Tour Eiffel est très haute.

---

highway (road) [HAI-wei] nom   **la route**

What's the name of this road?
Quel est le nom de cette route?

---

him [HIM] pronom   **le,** masc.
                                                     l' (before a vowel)
I like him (her) (it).   **la,** fém.
Je l'aime.
I see her (it).
Je la vois.

I see them.
Je les vois.

him pronom   **lui**

She gives him a cup of coffee.
Elle lui donne un café.

---

himself [HIM-SELF] pronom   **se**

He washes himself.
Il se lave.

---

his [HIZ] adjectif   **son**

---

history [HIS-té-ri] nom   **l'histoire**

I like to study history.
J'aime étudier l'histoire.

---

to hit [HIT] verbe   **battre**
  I hit   we hit
  you hit   you hit
  he, she, it hits they hit

He's hitting me!
Il me bat!

---

hole [HOHL] nom   **le trou**

I have a hole in my sock.
J'ai un trou dans la chaussette.

---

holiday [HAL-i-dei] nom   **le jour de fête**

The holiday is July 18th?
Le jour de fête est le dix-huit juillet?

---

home (house) nom   **la maison**

Here is my uncle's house.
Voici la maison de mon oncle.

---

homework [H<u>OH</u>M-W<u>UR</u>k] nom   **le devoir**

We are going to do our homework together.
Nous allons faire nos devoirs ensemble.

---

hoop [HUP] nom   **le cerceau**

The boy is rolling a big hoop.
Le garçon roule un grand cerceau.

---

to hope [H<u>OH</u>P] verbe   **espérer**

I hope	we hope
you hope	you hope
he, she hopes	they hope

I hope to get a good mark in history.
J'espère recevoir une bonne note en historie.

---

to play hopscotch   **jouer à la marelle**
(See **to play**)

---

horse [H<u>AW</u>RS] nom   **le cheval**

The boy is riding a horse.
Le garçon monte à cheval.

---

hospital [H<u>A</u>S-pi-t<u>é</u>l] nom   **l'hôpital,** masc.

The nurse works at the hospital.
L'infirmière travaille à l'hôpital.

---

hot [H<u>A</u>T] adjectif   **chaud**
It is hot   **Il fait chaud**
to be hot   **avoir chaud**

The boy is hot. He is going to swim.
Le garçon a chaud. Il va nager.

hotel [h<u>oh</u>-TEL] nom   **l'hôtel,** masc.

What is the name of this hotel?
Quel est le nom de cet hôtel?

hour (time) [<u>OW</u>R] nom   **l'heure,** fém.

What time is it?
Quelle heure est-il?

house [H<u>OW</u>S] nom   **la maison**

Here is my uncle's house.
Voici la maison de mon oncle.

how [H<u>OW</u>] adverbe   **comment**

How are you?
Comment allez-vous?

how many [h<u>ow</u> MEN-i] adverbe   **combien**

How many toys do you have?
Combien de jouets as-tu?

how much [H<u>OW</u> M<u>UCH</u>]   **combien**

humid (damp) [HYU-m<u>i</u>d] adjectif   **humide**

My bathing suit is damp.
Mon maillot est humide.

to be hungry [H<u>U</u>NG-gri]   **avoir faim**
expression idiomatique

Poor baby. He is hungry.
Pauvre bébé. Il a faim.

hunter [HÉN-tér] nom   **le chasseur**

The hunter goes into the forest.
Le chasseur entre dans la forêt.

Hurray! [hé-REI] interjection   **Bravo!**

---

to hurry [HÉ-ri] verbe   **se dépêcher**

  I hurry   we hurry
  you hurry   you hurry
  he, she, it hurries they hurry

They hurry because they are late.
Ils se dépêchent parce qu'ils sont en retard.

---

to hurt [HURT] expression idiomatique   **avoir mal à**

My finger hurts.
J'ai mal au doigt.

---

husband [HÉZ-bénd] nom   **le mari**

My aunt's husband is my uncle.
Le mari de ma tante est mon oncle.

I

I [AI] pronom   **je**

I am speaking to my friends.
Je parle à mes amis.

---

ice [AIS] nom   **la glace**

Let's go ice skating.
Allons patiner sur la glace.

---

ice cream [ais KRIM] nom   **la glace**

Do you like vanilla ice cream?
Tu aimes la glace à la vanille?

ice skate [<u>AI</u>S SKEIT] nom   **le patin à glace**
to ice-skate   **patiner**
Let's go ice skating!
Allons patiner!

idea [<u>ai</u>-DI-é] nom   **l'idée,** fém.
What a good idea it is to go swimming!
Quelle bonne idée d'aller nager!

if [<u>I</u>F] préposition   **si**

immediately [<u>i</u>-MI-di-<u>i</u>t-li] adverbe   **tout de suite**
I call the dog and he comes immediately.
J'appelle le chien et il vient tout de suite.

important [<u>i</u>m-P<u>AW</u>R-tént] adjectif   **important**
It is important to eat vegetables.
Il est important de manger des légumes.

impossible [<u>i</u>m-P<u>AS</u>-<u>i</u>-bél] adjectif   **impossible**
It is impossible to roll this rock.
Il est impossible de rouler ce rocher.

in, into [<u>I</u>N] préposition   **en; dans**
They go into the school.
Ils entrent dans l'école.

in front of [<u>I</u>N FR<u>É</u>NT év] préposition   **devant**
There is a table in front of the sofa.
Il y a une table devant le canapé.

in honor of [<u>I</u>N <u>A</u>N-ér év]   **en l'honneur de**
expression idiomatique

We are dining in a restaurant in honor of my daughter.
Nous dînons au restaurant en l'honneur de ma fille.

in order to (to) [IN AWR-dér té] préposition   **pour**

She is going to the store to buy stockings.
Elle va au magasin pour acheter des bas.

---

in the middle of [IN the MI-DÉL év]   **au milieu de**
préposition

Mom puts the candy in the middle of the table.
Maman met les bonbons au milieu de la table.

(in) this way [IN this WEI] adverbe   **ainsi**

The little marionettes dance this way.
Ainsi dansent les petites marionettes.

---

to indicate [IN-di-keit] verbe   **indiquer**

I indicate	we indicate
you indicate	you indicate
he, she, it indicates	they indicate

The policeman indicates that we must go by this road.
L'agent de police indique qu'il faut aller par cette route.

---

inexpensive [in-ik-SPEN-siv] adjectif   **bon marché**

Bread is cheap; it is not expensive.
On vend le pain bon marché; il ne coûte pas cher.

---

insect [IN-sekt] nom   **l'insecte, masc.**

I hate insects!
Je déteste les insectes!

---

intelligent [in-TEL-i-djént] adjectif   **intelligent, masc.**
                                                  intelligente, fém.
The teacher says, "What an
intelligent class!"
Le professeur dit: "Quelle classe intelligente!"

---

intentionally (on purpose)   **exprès**
[in-TEN-shén-él-li] adverbe

My brother teases me on purpose. (intentionally)
Mon frère me taquine exprès.

---

interesting [IN-tér-és-ting] adjectif   **intéressant,** masc.
Do you think the film is interesting?   **intéressante,** fém.
Tu trouves que le film est intéressant?

Internet [IN-ter-neht] nom   **internet**
They are surfing the Internet.
Elles surfent sur internet.

surfing the Internet verbe   **surfer sur internet**

---

into [IN-tu] préposition   **dans**
They go into the school.
Ils entrent dans l'école.

---

to introduce [in-tré-DUS] verbe   **présenter**
   I introduce   we introduce
   you introduce   you introduce
   he, she, it introduces   they introduce

I would like to introduce my grandson to you.
Je vous présente mon petit-fils.

---

to invite [in-VAIT] verbe   **inviter**
   I invite   we invite
   you invite   you invite
   he, she, it invites   they invite

My aunt invites me to her house.
Ma tante m'invite chez elle.

---

i-pod [AI-PAHD] nom | **un ipod,** masc.

Where is my i-pod?
Où est mon ipod?

podcast [PAHD-kast] nom | **le podcast,** masc.

---

iron (appliance) [AI-érn] nom | **le fer**

The iron is not working. I can't iron this dress.
Le fer ne marche pas. Je ne peux pas repasser cette robe.

iron (metal) | **en fer**

The stove is made of iron.
Le fourneau est en fer.

---

to iron verbe | **repasser**

I iron	we iron
you iron	you iron
he, she, it irons	they iron

He irons the shirt with an iron.
Il repasse la chemise avec un fer.

---

island [AI-lénd] nom | **l'île,** fém.

Corsica is a French island.
La Corse est une île française.

Isn't that true? Isn't that so? | **n'est-ce pas?**
Don't you agree? expression idiomatique

The weather is bad, isn't it?
Il fait mauvais, n'est-ce pas?

My teacher is handsome, don't you agree?
Mon professeur est beau, n'est-ce pas?

---

it [ɪT] pronom   **il,** masc.
         elle, fém.

they   **ils,** masc., pl.
         elles, fém., pl.

Here is the pencil. It is yellow.
Voici le crayon. Il est jaune.

Where is my shoe? It's under the bed.
Où est ma chaussure? Elle est sous le lit.

It is forbidden to   **défense de**
it is necessary expression idiomatique   **il faut**

It is necessary to go to school.
Il faut aller à l'école.
(We have to go to school.)

It is raining. (It rains.) verbe   **Il pleut.**

It rains a lot in the month of April.
Il pleut beaucoup au mois d'avril.

It is snowing. verbe   **Il neige.**

Look out the window. It's snowing!
Regardez par la fenêtre. Il neige!

---

its adjectif   **son**

I would like . . . verbe   **je voudrais**
He would like . . .   **il voudrait**
She would like . . .   **elle voudrait**
They would like . . .   **ils, elles voudraient**

I would like to take a walk.
Je voudrais faire une promenade.

She would like to go shopping.
Elle voudrait faire des emplettes.

J

jacket [DJAK-<u>i</u>t] nom   **la veste**

My grandfather wears pants and a jacket.
Mon grand-père porte un pantalon et une veste.

---

jackknife (pocketknife) [DJAK-N<u>AI</u>F] nom   **le canif**

Do you have a pocketknife?
Avez-vous un canif?

---

jam [DJAM] nom   **la confiture**

Please give me a piece of bread with strawberry jam.
Donnez-moi un morceau de pain avec de la confiture
aux fraises, s'il vous plaît.

January [DJAN-yu-er-i] nom   **janvier**

January sixth is a holiday in France.
Le six janvier est un jour de fête en France.

---

jet airplane (See **airplane**) nom   **l'avion à réaction**

---

jewel [DJU-<del>é</del>l] nom   **le bijou**
jewelry (jewels) nom   **le bijou**
                                                                les bijoux, pl.

There are many jewels in the trunk.
Il y a beaucoup de bijoux dans la malle.

---

juice [DJUS] nom   **le jus**
orange juice nom   **le jus d'orange**

I like orange juice.
J'aime le jus d'orange.

July [dju-L̲A̲I̲] nom **juillet**

July 14th is the French national holiday.
Le quatorze juillet est la fête nationale française.

> **Le 4 juillet est la fête nationale des Etats-Unis.**
>
> **July 4th is the national holiday of the United States.**

to jump [DJ̲MP] verbe **sauter**

I jump	we jump
you jump	you jump
he, she, it jumps	they jump

The boy jumps from the stairs.
Le garçon saute de l'escalier.

June [DJUN] nom **juin**

How many days are there in June?
Combien de jours y a-t-il en juin?

K

kangaroo [kang-g̲é̲-RU] nom **le kangourou**

The kangaroo is a strange animal.
Le kangourou est un animal bizarre.

to keep [KIP] verbe **garder**

I keep	we keep
you keep	you keep
he, she, it keeps	they keep

I keep a dog.
Je garde un chien.

key [KI] nom   **la clef**

Where is my key?
Où est ma clef?

---

to kick [KIK]   **donner un coup de pied à**
expression idiomatique

He kicks the ball.
Il donne un coup de pied à la balle.

---

to kill [KIL] verbe   **tuer**

  I kill   we kill
  you kill   you kill
  he, she, it kills   they kill

My mother kills the fly.
Maman tue la mouche.

---

kilometer [KIL-é-mi-tér] nom   **le kilomètre**

I live five kilometers from the school.
J'habite à cinq kilomètres de l'école.

---

kind [KAIND] adjectif   **gentil,** masc.
                                                     gentille, fém.

The teacher is very kind.
La maîtresse est très gentille.

---

kind nom   **la sorte**

What kind of meat is this?
Quelle sorte de viande est-ce?

---

king [KĬNG] nom   **le roi**

Is there a king in France? No, there is a president.
Est-ce qu'il y a un roi en France? Non, il y a un président.

> Martin Luther King était un grand dirigeant du
> mouvement des droits civils aux Etats-Unis.
>
> Martin Luther King, Jr. was a great leader of the
> civil rights movement in the United States.

kiss [KĬS] nom   **le baiser**

Mother is kissing the child.
Maman donne un baiser à l'enfant.

kitchen [KĬCH-én] nom   **la cuisine**

Mother prepares meals in the kitchen.
Maman prépare les repas dans la cuisine.

to cook   **faire la cuisine**

kite [KĀIT] nom   **le cerf-volant**
                                                         les cerfs-volants, pl.

Good, it's windy. Let's play with a kite.
Bon, il fait du vent. Allons jouer avec un cerf-volant.

kitten [KĬT-én] nom   **le petit chat, le chaton**

My kitten is black.
Mon petit chat est noir.

knee [NĬ] nom   **le genou,** masc.

You have a sore knee? That's too bad!   **les genous,** pl.
Tu as mal au genou? C'est triste.

knife [N<u>AI</u>F] nom   le couteau; le canif
(kitchen or table) knife   le couteau, masc.
She puts a knife at each place   les couteaux, pl.
at the table.
Elle met un couteau à chaque place à la table.

---

to knit [N<u>I</u>T] verbe   tricoter
  I knit   we knit
  you knit   you knit
  he, she, it knits   they knit
I am learning how to knit.
J'apprends à tricoter.

---

knob (See **door**) nom   **le bouton**

---

knock [N<u>A</u>K] nom   **le coup**
There are two knocks on the door. Who's there?
Il y a deux coups à la porte. Qui est là?

---

to knock verbe   **frapper**
Mommy, someone is knocking at the door.
Maman, on frappe à la porte.

---

to know [N<u>OH</u>] verbe   **connaître**
  I know   we know
  you know   you know
  he, she, it knows they know
Do you know my teacher?
Connais-tu mon maître?

---

to know verbe   ·   **savoir**
I know that he is there.
Je sais qu'il est là.

to know how to verbe   **savoir**

I know how to ride a bicycle.
Je sais monter à bicyclette.

L

lady [LEI-di] nom   **la dame**

Who is this lady?
Qui est cette dame?

lake [LEIK] nom   **le lac**

There is a boat in the middle of the lake.
Il y a un bateau au milieu du lac.

lamp [LAMP] nom   **la lampe**

The lamp is in the living room.
La lampe est dans le salon.

large (See **elephant**) adjectif   **grand**

last [LAST] adjectif   **dernier,** masc.
                                                    dernière, fém.
*Paul is the last one to sit down
at the table.*
Paul est le dernier à s'asseoir à table.

last one nom   **le dernier**

late [LEIT] adverbe   **tard**

It is late. Let's hurry.
Il est tard. Dépêchons-nous.

late adverbe   **retard; en retard**

Frank comes late to school.
François arrive à l'école en retard.

---

later adverbe   **plus tard**

It is eight o'clock now. The mailman comes later.
Il est huit heures maintenant. Le facteur arrive plus tard.

---

to laugh [LAF] verbe   **rire**

I laugh	we laugh
you laugh	you laugh
he, she, it laughs	they laugh

She laughs when she looks at the clown.
Elle rit quand il regarde les ours.

---

lawyer [LAW-yér] nom   **l'avocat**

My uncle is a lawyer.
Mon oncle est avocat.

---

lazy [LEI-zi] adjectif   **paresseux**, masc.
                                              paresseuse, fém.

My teacher says I am lazy.
Ma maîtresse dit que je suis paresseuse.

---

to lead [LID] verbe   **mener**

I lead	we lead
you lead	you lead
he, she, it leads	they lead

He leads his dog outside.
Il mène son chien dehors.

---

leader [LI-dér] nom   **le chef**

No! You're always playing the leader.
Mais non! Tu joues toujours le rôle du chef.

---

leaf [LIF] nom   **la feuille**
leaves [LEEVZ]

There are so many leaves on the ground in autumn!
Il y a tant de feuilles sur terre en automne!

---

to leap [LIP] verbe   **sauter**
   I leap   we leap
   you leap   you leap
   he, she, it leaps   they leap

to play leap-frog   **jouer à saute-mouton**

---

to learn [LURN] verbe   **apprendre**
   I learn   we learn
   you learn   you learn
   he, she, it learns   they learn

She likes to learn French.
Elle aime apprendre le français.

---

leather [LETH-ér] nom   **le cuir**
made of leather   **en cuir**

My brother's jacket is made of leather.
La veste de mon frère est en cuir.

---

to leave [LIV] verbe   **laisser**
   I leave   we leave
   you leave   you leave
   he, she, it leaves   they leave

I often leave my books at Michael's house.
Je laisse souvent mes livres chez Michel.

---

to leave verbe   **partir**

My aunt is leaving at 5 o'clock.
Ma tante part à cinq heures.

---

to leave verbe   **quitter**

We leave the museum at 5 o'clock.
Nous quittons le musée à cinq heures.

---

to leave verbe   **sortir**

The nurse leaves the hospital.
L'infirmière sort de l'hôpital.

---

left [LEFT] adjectif   **gauche**
left hand nom   **la main gauche**

I raise my left hand.
Je lève la main gauche.

---

to the left expression idiomatique   **à gauche**

The tree is to the left of the house.
L'arbre est à gauche de la maison.

---

leg [LEG] nom   **la jambe**

Birds have two legs; animals have four paws.
L'oiseau a deux jambes; l'animal a quatre pattes.

---

lemon [LEM-én] nom   **le citron**

Lemons are yellow.
Les citrons sont jaunes.

---

to lend [LEND] verbe   **prêter**

I lend	we lend
you lend	you lend
he, she, it lends	they lend

Can you lend me your bicycle?
Peux-tu me prêter ta bicyclette?

---

leopard [LEP-érd] nom   **le léopard**
The leopard is in the forest.
Le léopard est dans la fôret.

less (before, to) [LES] adverbe   **moins**
We are leaving at twenty minutes to two.
Nous partons à deux heures moins vingt.

lesson [LES-én] nom   **la leçon**
Today's lesson is difficult, isn't it?
La leçon d'aujourd'hui est difficile, n'est-ce pas?

to let [LET] verbe   **laisser**

I let	we let
you let	you let
he, she, it lets	they let

My brother lets me wash the car.
Mon frère me laisse laver la voiture.

letter [LET-ér] nom   **la lettre**
I put the letter in the envelope.
Je mets la lettre dans l'enveloppe.

letter box; mailbox   **la boîte aux lettres**

lettuce [LET-is] nom   **la laitue**
Mom makes a salad with lettuce.
Maman prépare une salade avec la laitue.

library [LAI-brer-i] nom   **la bibliothèque**

There are so many books in the library!
Il y a tant de livres dans la bibliothèque!

---

lie [LAI] nom   **le mensonge**

He tells lies!
Il dit des mensonges!

---

light (See **clear**)   **clair**

---

light [LAIT] nom   **la lumière**

The moon does not give much light.
La lune ne donne pas beaucoup de lumière.

light (traffic) nom   **le feu**

You cross the street when you see the green light.
On traverse la rue quand on voit le feu vert.

light (weight) [LAIT] adjectif   **léger,** masc.
                                            légère, fém.
This box is light.
Cette boîte est légère.

---

lightning [LAIT-ning] nom   **l'éclair,** masc.

I am afraid of lightning.
J'ai peur de l'éclair.

(light) switch **le bouton**

to like [L<u>AI</u>K] verbe **aimer**

  I like   we like
  you like   you like
  he, she, it likes   they like

Mother likes her children.
Maman aime ses enfants.

Le président Abraham Lincoln a signé
"l'Emancipation Proclamation," le document qui a
affranchi les esclaves aux Etat-Unis.

President Abraham Lincoln signed the
"Emancipation Proclamation," the document that
freed the slaves in the United States.

---

lion [L<u>AI</u>-én] nom **le lion**

The lion is not a gentle animal.
Le lion n'est pas un animal doux.

---

lip [L<u>I</u>P] nom **la lèvre**

Look! The doll is opening its lips.
Regarde! La poupée ouvre les lèvres.

---

to listen [L<u>I</u>S-én] verbe **écouter**

  I listen   we listen
  you listen   you listen
  he, she, it listens   they listen

The boy is listening to the radio.
Le garçon écoute la radio.

---

little [LIT-él] adjectif   **petit,** masc.
The bird is small.   **petite,** fém.
L'oiseau est petit.

---

little adverbe   **un peu**

Do you want any soup? A little, please.
Voulez-vous de la soupe? Un peu, s'il vous plaît.

---

to live (dwell) verbe   **habiter**

  I live   we live
  you live   you live
  he, she, it lives   they live

Where do you live?
Où habitez-vous?

---

to live (reside) [LIV] verbe   **demeurer**

Where do you live?
Où demeurez-vous?

---

to live verbe   **vivre**

Do any wild animals live in this forest?
Est-ce que des animaux sauvages vivent dans cette forêt?

---

living room [LIV-ing rum] nom   **le salon**

Who is in the living room?
Qui est dans le salon?

---

lollipop [LAL-i-PAP] nom   **la sucette**

Mmm, I like the lollipop.
Mmm, j'aime la sucette.

---

long [LAWNG] adjectif   **long,** masc.
                                                      longue, fém.
She is wearing a long dress.
Elle porte une robe longue.

---

look [LAUHK] nom   **l'air**

The tiger has a ferocious look.
Le tigre a l'air féroce.

---

to look (at), watch verbe   **regarder**

I look	we look
you look	you look
he, she, it looks	they look

I like to watch television.
J'aime regarder la télévision.

---

to look after verbe   **surveiller**

The cat looks after the kittens.
Le chat surveille les petits (chats).

---

to look for verbe   **chercher**

Father is always looking for his keys.
Papa cherche toujours ses clefs.

---

to lose [LUZ] verbe   **perdre**

I lose	we lose
you lose	you lose
he, she, it loses	they lose

Jack always loses his hat.
Jacques perd toujours son chapeau.

---

a lot (of) [L<u>A</u>T] adverbe   **beaucoup de (d')**

Bertha has a lot of books.
Berthe a beaucoup de livres.

---

loud [L<u>OW</u>D] adjectif   **haut,** masc.
                                                        haute, fém.
My dog's voice is very loud.
La voix de mon chien est très haute.

in a loud voice   **à haute voix**

loudly adverbe   **fort**

He plays the drum too loudly.
Il joue trop fort au tambour.

---

love [L<u>Ǝ</u>V] nom   **l'amour,** masc.

The boy loves his dog.
Le garçon a un grand amour pour son chien.

---

to love verbe   **aimer**

I love	we love
you love	you love
he, she, it loves	they love

I love my cat.
J'aime mon chat.

---

low (See **short**) adjectif   **bas**
to lower (put down) [L<u>OH</u>-ér] verbe   **baisser**

I lower	we lower
you lower	you lower
he, she, it lowers	they lower

The teacher says, "Put your hands down!"
Le professeur dit: "Baissez les mains!"

luck [LŰK] nom   **la chance**
Good luck! interjection   **Bonne chance!**

Before the examination my friend says, "Good luck!"
Avant l'examen mon ami dit: "Bonne chance!"

---

to be lucky expression idiomatique   **avoir de la chance**
The boy wins a prize. He is lucky.
Le garçon gagne un prix. Il a de la chance.

---

luggage (baggage) [LŰG-idj] nom   **les bagages,**
The luggage is ready for the trip.   **masc., pl.**
Les bagages sont prêts pour le voyage.

---

lunch [LŰNCH] nom   **le déjeuner**
I eat lunch at noon.
Je prends le déjeuner à midi.

lunchtime   **l'heure du déjeuner**

M

machine [mé-SHIN] nom   **la machine**
washing machine nom   **la machine à laver**
Mother wants a washing machine.
Maman désire une machine à laver.

---

mad (See **crazy**) adjectif   **fou**

---

made of adjectif   **en**

---

maid [MEID] nom   **la bonne**
The maid cleans the house.
La bonne nettoie la maison.

---

mail a letter (See **letter**)   **mettre une lettre à la poste**
mailbox (See **letter**)   **la boîte aux lettres**
mail carrier nom   **le facteur**

The mail carrier brings letters and packages.
Le facteur apporte des lettres et des paquets.

---

to make [MEIK] verbe   **former**

I make a snowball with the snow.
Je forme une balle avec la neige.

---

to make (do) verbe   **faire**

I make	we make
you make	you make
he, she, it makes	they make

He does his homework.
Il fait ses devoirs.

Mama [MA-mé] nom   **maman**

Mom, where are my socks?
Maman, où sont mes chaussettes?

---

man [MAN] nom   **l'homme**
men [MEN] pl.

The man comes to fix the television set.
L'homme vient pour réparer le téléviseur.

---

many (a lot) [MEN-i] adverbe   **beaucoup de (d')**

Bertha has a lot of books.
Berthe a beaucoup de livres.

---

map [MAP] nom   **la carte**

Do you have a road map of France?
Avez-vous une carte des routes de la France?

---

marbles [MAHR-bélz] nom   **les billes,** fém., pl.

Boys like to play marbles.
Les garçons aiment jouer aux billes.

March [MAHRCH] nom   **mars**

It is windy in March.
Il fait du vent en mars.

---

marionette [ma-ri-é-NET] nom   **la marionnette**

The marionettes are funny.
Les marionnettes sont drôles.

---

mark (in school) [MAHRK] nom   **la note**

Do you have good marks?
Tu as de bonnes notes?

---

market [MAHR-kit] nom   **le marché**

What do they sell at the market?
Qu'est-ce qu'on vend au marché?

---

to marry [MAR-i] verbe   **épouser**

I marry	we marry
you marry	you marry
he, she, it marries	they marry

The prince marries the princess.
Le prince épouse la princesse.

Marvelous! (Great!) [MAHR-vé-lés] interjection   **formidable**

You are going to the circus? Great!
Tu vas au cirque? Formidable!

---

marvelous adjectif   **sensationnel**

You're going to the theater? Marvelous!
Tu vas au théâtre? Sensationnel!

---

match [MACH] nom   **l'allumette,** fém.

Matches are dangerous for children.
Les allumettes sont dangereuses pour les enfants.

May [MEI] nom   **mai**

There are thirty-one days in May.
Il y a trente et un jours en mai.

---

may verbe   **pouvoir**

I may	we may
you may	you may
he, she, it may	they may

May I go fishing?
Puis-je aller à la pêche?

---

maybe [MEI-bi] adverbe   **peut-être**

Are we going horseback riding this morning? Maybe.
Nous montons à cheval ce matin? Peut-être.

---

me [MI] pronom   **me**

He gives me some bread.
Il me donne du pain.

---

me pronom   **moi**

Who is knocking at the door? It's me, Michael.
Qui frappe à la porte? C'est moi, Michel.

---

meal [MIL] nom   **le repas**

Which meal do you prefer?
Quel repas préférez-vous?

---

to mean [MIN] verbe   **vouloir dire**

What does this word mean?
Que veut dire ce mot?

---

meat [MIT] nom   **la viande**

The woman goes to the butcher shop to buy meat.
La femme va à la boucherie pour acheter de la viande.

mechanic [mé-KAN-ik] nom   **le mécanicien**

I would like to become a mechanic.
Je voudrais devenir mécanicien.

medicine [MED-i-sin] nom   **le médicament**

I don't like this medicine.
Je n'aime pas ce médicament.

to meet [MIT] verbe   **rencontrer**

I meet	we meet
you meet	you meet
he, she, it meets	they meet

Who meets Little Red Riding Hood in the forest?
Qui rencontre Le Petit Chaperon Rouge dans la forêt?

member [MEM-bér] nom   **le membre**

He is a member of our team.
Il est membre de notre équipe.

menu [MEN-yu] nom   **la carte**

merry-go-round [MER-i-goh-rownd] nom   **le manège**

Look at the horses on the merry-go-round!
Regarde les chevaux du manège!

midnight [MID-n<u>ai</u>t] nom   **minuit**

It is midnight. Why aren't you sleeping?
Il est minuit. Pourquoi ne dors-tu pas?

---

mile [M<u>AI</u>L] nom   **le mille**

My friend lives one mile from here.
Mon ami demeure un mille d'ici.

---

milk [M<u>I</u>LK] nom   **le lait**

I drink milk and Daddy drinks coffee with milk.
Je bois du lait et Papa boit du café avec du lait.

---

million [M<u>I</u>L-yén] nom   **le million**

How many books do you have? A million!
Combien de livres as-tu? Un million!

---

minute [M<u>I</u>N-<u>i</u>t] nom   **la minute**

How many minutes are there in an hour?
Combien de minutes y a-t-il dans une heure?

---

mirror [M<u>I</u>R-ér] nom   **le miroir**

There is a mirror in the bedroom.
Il y a un miroir dans la chambre.

mirror nom   **la glace**

Do you have a mirror?
Est-ce que vous avez une glace?

Miss [MIS] nom   **mademoiselle**
young ladies nom   **mesdemoiselles,** pl.

Miss Duval? She is a good teacher.
Mademoiselle Duval? Elle est un bon professeur.

---

mistake [mis-TEIK] nom   **la faute**

I make mistakes when I write in French.
Je fais des fautes quand j'écris en français.

Mister [MIS-ter] nom   **monsieur**
gentlemen   **messieurs**

The man's name is Mr. Montand.
L'homme s'appelle monsieur Montand.

---

to mix [MIKS] verbe   **mélanger**

I mix	we mix
you mix	you mix
he, she, it mixes	they mix

When you play dominoes, you mix the dominoes.
Quand on joue aux dominos, on mélange les dominos.

---

moist (damp) [MOIST] adjectif   **humide**

My bathing suit is damp.
Mon maillot est humide.

Mom, Mommy [MAM, MA-mi] nom   **Maman**

Mom, where are my socks?
Maman, où sont mes chaussettes?

---

moment [MOH- mént] nom   **le moment**

I am going into the post office for a moment.
J'entre dans la poste pour un moment.

Monday [MÉN-dei] nom   **lundi,** masc.

What do you do on Mondays?
Que faites-vous le lundi?

---

money [MÉN-i] nom   **l'argent,** masc.

He doesn't have enough money.
Il n'a pas assez d'argent.

---

money box (piggy bank) nom   **la tirelire**

I do not have much money in my piggy bank.
Je n'ai pas beaucoup d'argent dans ma tirelire.

---

monkey [MÉNG-ki] nom   **le singe**

The monkey is eating a banana.
Le singe mange une banane.

---

month [MÉNTH] nom   **le mois**

We have two months of vacation.
Nous avons deux mois de vacances.

---

moon [MUN] nom   **la lune**

The astronaut walks on the moon.
L'astronaute marche sur la lune.

---

more [MAWR] adverbe   **encore**

Do you want more bread?
Tu désires encore du pain?

---

more adverbe   **plus**

morning [MAWR-ning] nom   **le matin**
What do you eat in the morning?
Que mangez-vous le matin?
Good morning   **Bonjour**

mosquito [més-KI-toh] nom   **le moustique**
Daddy, catch the mosquito! It's going to bite me.
Papa, attrapez le moustique. Il va me piquer!

mother [MÉTH-ér] nom   **la mère**
Today is my mother's birthday.
C'est l'anniversaire de ma mère aujourd'hui.

mountain [MOWN-tén] nom   **la montagne**
The mountains near Spain are the Pyrenees.
Les montagnes près de l'Espagne sont les Pyrénées.

mouse [MOWS] nom   **la souris**
mice pl.
There are mice in the field.
Il y a des souris dans ce champ.

mouth [MOWTH] nom   **la bouche**
The child opens his mouth when he cries.
L'enfant ouvre la bouche quand il pleure.

to move [MUV] verbe   **remuer**
  I move   we move
  you move   you move
  he, she, it moves   they move
She moves her fingers quickly when she plays the piano.
Elle remue vite ses doigts quand elle joue du piano.

movie [MU-vi] nom   **le film**

Are they playing a good film at the movies?
On joue un bon film au cinéma?

movies nom   **le cinéma**

There is a good film at the movies.
Il y a un bon film au cinéma.

Mr. [MIS-tér] nom   **M.**

Mrs. [MIS-és] nom   **Mme, madame**

Say "Good morning, Mrs. Jones" to your teacher.
Dis "Bonjour, Madame" à ta maîtresse.

much (See **many**)   **beaucoup de (d')**

mud [MÉD] nom   **la boue**

My hands are covered with mud!
Mes mains sont couvertes de boue!

museum [myu-ZI-ém] nom   **le musée**

The museum is open from 2 o'clock to 5 o'clock.
Le musée est ouvert de deux heures jusqu'à cinq heures.

music [MYU-zik] nom   **la musique**

Do you know how to read musical notes?
Est-ce que vous savez lire les notes de musique?

Irving Berlin était un compositeur américain qui a écrit beaucoup de belles chansons comme *God Bless America.*

Irving Berlin was an American composer who wrote many beautiful songs such as "God Bless America."

---

musical note   **la note**

musician [myu-ZI-shén] nom   **le musicien**

The musician is handsome.
Le musicien est beau.

my [MAI] pronom   **mon,** masc.
                                                   ma, fém.
My brother is handsome.   **mes,** pl.
Mon frère est beau.

My sister is pretty.
Ma soeur est jolie.

My cousins are always cheerful.
Mes cousins sont toujours gais.

myself [mai-SELF] pronom   **me; moi-même**

N

nail (finger) (See **fingernail**)   **l'ongle**

nail (metal) [NEIL] nom   **le clou**
My brother plays with nails and a hammer.
Mon frère joue avec des clous et un marteau.

name [NEIM] nom   **le nom**
What is the name of this building?
Quel est le nom de ce bâtiment?

— name is verbe   **s'appeler**

my name is	our name is
your name is	your name is
his, her, its name is	their name is

What is your name? My name is Henry.
Comment vous appelez-vous? Je m'appelle Henri.

surname [SUR-neim] nom   **le nom de famille**

---

napkin [NAP-kin] nom   **la serviette**

There are four napkins on the table.
Il y a quatre serviettes sur la table.

---

narrow [NAR-oh] adjectif   **étroit,** masc.
                                           étroite, fém.

The drawer is too narrow for the papers.
Le tiroir est trop étroit pour les papiers.

---

nation [NEI-shén] nom   **la nation**

There are many flags at the United Nations.
Il y a beaucoup de drapeaux aux Nations Unies.

---

national [NASH-én-él] adjectif   **national,** masc.
                                           nationale, fém.

The Fourth of July is the national
holiday of the United States.
Le quatre juillet est la fête nationale des États-Unis.

naughty [naw-ti] adjectif   **méchant,** masc.
Robert cannot go out. He is naughty.   **méchante,** fém.
Robert ne peut pas sortir. Il est méchant.

---

near [NIR] préposition   **près de**
Bordeaux is near the Atlantic Ocean.
Bordeaux est près de l'océan Atlantique.

---

neck [NEK] nom   **le cou**
My grandmother says, "My neck hurts."
Ma grand-mère dit: "J'ai mal au cou."

---

to need [NID] expression idiomatique   **avoir besoin de (d')**
The fish needs water.
Le poisson a besoin d'eau.

---

needle [NID-él] nom   **l'aiguille,** fém.
Here is a sewing needle.
Voici une aiguille à coudre.

---

neighbor [NEI-bér] nom   **le voisin,** masc.
My neighbor Bernard lives near me.   **la voisine,** fém.
Mon voisin Bernard demeure près de moi.

---

nephew [NEF-yu] nom   **le neveu**
He is Mr. Duval's nephew.
Il est le neveu de monsieur Duval.

---

nest [NEST] nom   **le nid**
How many eggs do you see in the nest?
Combien d'oeufs vois-tu dans le nid?

---

never [NEV-ér] adverbe   **jamais**
I never want to play with you!
Je ne veux jamais jouer avec toi!

never adverbe   **ne ... jamais**

I go to school. My sister never goes to school.
Je vais à l'école. Ma soeur ne va jamais à l'école.

---

new [NU] adjectif   **neuf,** masc.
                                         neuve, fém.
My bicycle is new.
Ma bicyclette est neuve.

---

new adjectif   **nouveau,** masc.
                                         nouveaux, masc., pl.
Look at my new turtle!   **nouvel,** masc., before a vowel
Regarde ma nouvelle tortue!   **nouvelle,** fém.

---

newspaper [NUZ-pei-pér] nom   **le journal**
                                         les journaux, pl.
After dinner my uncle reads
the newspaper.
Après le dîner mon oncle lit le journal.

---

next [NEKST] adjectif   **prochain,** masc.
                                         prochaine, fém.
The teacher says, "Next week we
will have an examination."
Le professeur dit: "La semaine prochaine
nous avons un examen."

---

next to préposition   **à côté de**

At the restaurant Peter is seated next to Carolyn.
Dans le restaurant Pierre est assis à côté de Caroline.

---

nice (pleasant) [NAIS] adjectif   **agréable**

Spring is a pleasant (nice) season.
Le printemps est une saison agréable.

---

nice adjectif   **gentil,** masc.
                                         gentille, fém.
The teacher is nice. She doesn't scold.
La maîtresse est gentille. Elle ne gronde pas.

---

niece [NIS] nom   **la nièce**

She is the lawyer's niece.
Elle est la nièce de l'avocat.

---

night [NAIT] nom   **la ˌnuit**

At night you can see the stars.
La nuit on peut voir des étoiles.

---

nine [NAIN] adjectif   **neuf**

How much are nine and two?
Combien font neuf et deux?

I am nine years old.
J'ai neuf ans.

---

nineteen [nain-TIN] adjectif   **dix-neuf**

Today is September 19th.
C'est aujourd'hui le dix-neuf septembre.

---

ninety [NAIN-ti] adjectif   **quatre-vingt-dix**

Somebody is ninety years old?
Quelqu'un a quatre-vingt-dix ans?

---

no [NOH] adverbe   **non**

Get up! No, I don't want to get up!
Lève-toi! Non, je ne veux pas me lever!

No ... expression idiomatique   **défense de**
No admittance   **défense d'entrer**
expression idiomatique

No admittance. We cannot enter.
Défense d'entrer. Nous ne pouvons pas entrer.

No smoking expression idiomatique   **défense de fumer**

No smoking in school.
Défense de fumer à l'école.

noise [N<u>OI</u>Z] nom   **le bruit**

Thunder makes a loud noise.
Le tonnerre fait un grand bruit.

no longer [noh-L<u>AWNG</u>-ér] adverbe   **ne ... plus**

I go to school.
Je vais à l'école.

My brother no longer goes to school.
Mon frère ne va plus a l'école.

No matter!—never mind   **N'importe!**
expression idiomatique

You don't have a pen? No matter! Here is a pencil.
Vous n'avez pas de stylo? N'importe! Voici un crayon.

noon [N<u>U</u>N] nom   **midi,** masc.

It is noon. It's time for lunch.
Il est midi. C'est l'heure du déjeuner.

north [N<u>AW</u>RTH] nom   **le nord**

When I go from Marseilles to Paris, I go toward the north.
Quand je vais de Marseille à Paris, je vais vers le nord.

nose [N<u>OH</u>Z] nom   **le nez**

My doll's nose is cute.
Le nez de ma poupée est mignon.

not [N<u>A</u>T] adverbe   **ne ... pas**

I go to school. My grandfather does not go to school.
Je vais à l'école. Mon grand-père ne va pas à l'école.

note [N<u>OH</u>T] nom   **le billet**

I have notes in my pocket.
J'ai des billets dans la poche.

note (musical) nom (See **music**)   **la note**

---

notebook [NOHT-bauhk] nom   **le cahier**

She writes her homework in a notebook.
Elle écrit ses devoirs dans un cahier.

---

nothing [NÉTH-ing] pronom   **rien**

What do you have in your pocket? Nothing!
Qu'est-ce que tu as dans la poche? Rien!

> Un proverbe: Qui ne risque rien, n'a rien.
>
> Proverb: Nothing ventured, nothing gained.

November [noh-VEM-bér] nom   **novembre**

November is not the last month of the year.
Novembre n'est pas le dernier mois de l'année.

---

now [NOW] adverbe   **maintenant**

You have to take a bath now!
Tu dois prendre un bain maintenant!

---

number [NÚM-bér] nom   **le numéro**

What is your telephone number?
Quel est votre numéro de téléphone?

---

number (quantity) nom   **le nombre**

You have a great number of books!
Tu as un grand nombre de livres!

nurse [NURS] nom   **l'infirmière**

My neighbor is a nurse.
Ma voisine est infirmière.

O

to obey [oh-BEI] verbe   **obéir**

I obey	we obey
you obey	you obey
he, she, it obeys	they obey

When I am well-behaved, I obey my parents.
Quand je suis sage, j'obéis à mes parents.

occupied, busy [AK-yu-paid] adjectif   **occupé**, masc.
                                                         occupée, fém.
My brother is busy now; he is doing
his homework.
Mon frère est occupé maintenant; il fait ses devoirs.

ocean [OH-shén] nom   **l'océan**

Is the Atlantic Ocean to the west of France?
L'océan Atlantique est à l'ouest de la France?

ocean liner nom   **le paquebot**

The ocean liner crosses the Atlantic Ocean.
Le paquebot traverse l'Océan Atlantique.

October [ak-TOH-bér] nom   **octobre**
It is cool in October.
Il fait frais en octobre.

odd [AD] adjectif   **bizarre**
Here is an odd animal.
Voici un animal bizarre!

odd (funny) adjectif   **drôle**
The marionettes are funny.
Les marionnettes sont drôles.

of [év] préposition   **de**

office [AW-fis] nom   **le bureau**
Here is the office of a large company.
Voici le bureau d'une grande compagnie.

post office nom   **le bureau de poste**
You go to the post office to mail a package.
On va au bureau de poste pour mettre un colis à la poste.

often [AW-fén] adverbe   **souvent**
I often go by bus.
Je vais souvent en autobus.

oil [OIL] nom   **l'huile,** fém.

Mother, are you putting oil in the salad?
Maman, tu mets de l'huile dans la salade?

That's funny. You put oil in the car.
C'est drôle. On met de l'huile dans l'auto.

OK (okay) [oh-KEI] expression idiomatique   **accord**
                                                       d'accord!
Do you want to play with me? OK!
Veux-tu jouer avec moi? D'accord!

---

old [OHLD] adjectif   **vieux,** masc.
                                                       vieille, fém.
The book is old and the watch   **vieil,** masc. before vowel
is old.
Le livre est vieux et la montre est vieille.

---

on [AHN] préposition   **sur**

The ruler is on the desk.
La règle est sur le pupitre.

---

once again [wéns é-GEN] adverbe   **encore une fois**

---

one (we, they, you) [wÍN] pronom   **on**

Are we playing now?
On joue maintenant?

one adjectif   **un**

One monkey is in the tree.
Un singe est dans l'arbre.

one (number) adjectif   **une**
one hundred adjectif   **cent**

There are a hundred people at the fair!
Il y a cent personnes à la foire!

one must expression idiomatique   **il faut**

It is necessary (one must) to go to school.
Il faut aller à l'école.

one's son

one that (who) pronom   **celui,** masc.
Here is a red pen. The one that belongs   **ceux,** masc., pl.
to my father is yellow.   **celle,** fém.
Voici un stylo rouge. Celui de mon père   **celles,** fém., pl.
est jaune.

Here is a red ruler. Those that are on the table are
yellow.
Voici une règle rouge. Celles qui sont sur la table sont jaunes.

---

onion [ÉN-yén] nom   **l'oignon**
I am going to the store to buy some onions.
Je vais au marché pour acheter des oignons.

---

online [AHN-LAIN] adjectif   **en ligne**
I have it . . . I am online.
Voilà . . . je suis en ligne.

---

only [OHN-li] adjectif   **seul**

---

only adverbe   **seulement**
I have only one goldfish.
J'ai seulement un poisson rouge.

---

on purpose adverbe   **exprès**
My brother teases me on purpose.
Mon frère me taquine exprès.

---

open [OH-pén] adjectif   **ouvert,** masc.
The window is open.   **ouverte,** fém.
La fenêtre est ouverte.

to open verbe   **ouvrir**

I open	we open
you open	you open
he, she, it opens	they open

I open my desk to look for an eraser.
J'ouvre mon pupitre pour chercher une gomme.

to operate [A-pé-reit] verbe   **marcher**

This lamp is not working (operating).
Cette lampe ne marche pas.

or [AWR] conjonction   **ou**

What would you like, peaches or apples?
Que désirez-vous, des pêches ou des pommes?

orange [AR-indj] nom   **l'orange,** fém.

What color is the orange?
De quelle couleur est l'orange?

orange adjectif   **orange**

I need an orange skirt.
J'ai besoin d'une jupe orange.

orange juice [AR-indj DJUS] nom   **le jus d'orange**

to order [AWR-dér] verbe   **commander**

I order	we order
you order	you order
he, she, it orders	they order

In the restaurant Father orders dinner.
Dans le restaurant Papa commande le dîner.

in order to préposition   **pour**

other (another) [*ŁTH-ér*] adjectif   **autre**

Here is another pencil.
Voici un autre crayon.

---

our [OWR] adjectif   **notre**

Our teacher is scolding us today.   **nos,** pl.
Notre maîtresse nous gronde aujourd'hui.

---

out of [OWT év] préposition   **par**

My grandfather looks out of the window.
Mon grand-père regarde par la fenêtre.

---

outside [OWT-said] préposition   **dehors**

My friend is waiting for me outside.
Mon ami m'attend dehors.

---

over there [oh-vér THEHR] adverbe   **là-bas**

Do you see your brother coming down (over) there?
Tu vois ton frère qui arrive, là-bas?

---

to overturn [oh-vér-TURN] verbe   **renverser**

I overturn	we overturn
you overturn	you overturn
he, she, it overturns	they overturn

The baby overturns the plate.
Le bébé renverse l'assiette.

---

owl [OWL] nom   **le hibou**

You hear the owl during the night.   **hiboux,** pl.
On entend le hibou pendant la nuit.

---

own [OHN] adjectif   **propre**

It is not my sister's book; it is my own book.
Ce n'est pas le livre de ma soeur; c'est mon propre livre.

P

package [PAK-idj] nom
Oh, good! A package for me!
Ah, bon! Un colis pour moi!

le colis
le paquet

page [PEIDJ] nom
The map of France is on page ten.
La carte de la France est à la page dix.

la page

pail (See **bucket**) nom

le seau

to paint [PEINT] verbe

peindre

I paint	we paint
you paint	you paint
he, she, it paints	they paint

My sister is an artist. She likes to paint.
Ma soeur est artiste. Elle aime peindre.

pair [PEHR] nom
I would like to buy a pair of gloves.
Je voudrais acheter une paire de gants.

la paire

pajamas [pé-DJAH-méz] nom
I put on my pajamas at ten o'clock at night.
Je mets le pyjama à dix heures du soir.

le pyjama

palace [PAL-is] nom
palace nom
The king arrives at the palace.
Le roi arrive au palais.

le château
le palais

pants [PANTS] nom   **le pantalon**

The boy's pants are dirty.
Le pantalon du garçon est sale.

Papa (Daddy) [PA-PA] nom   **papa**
Daddy, I'm afraid!
Papa, j'ai peur!

paper [PEI-pér] nom   **le papier**
There is some paper in my notebook.
Il y a du papier dans mon cahier.

sheet of paper   **la feuille de papier**

parachute [PAR-é-shut] nom   **le parachute**
Is it dangerous to jump with a parachute?
Est-ce qu'il est dangereux de sauter en parachute?

parade [pé-REID] nom   **le défilé**

We walk in the parade.
Nous marchons dans le défilé.

parakeet [PAR-é-kit] nom   **la perruche**
We have two pretty parakeets.
Nous avons deux jolies perruches.

pardon me (excuse me) [PAHR-dén MI] **pardon**
expression idiomatique

Excuse me! It's your pocketbook, isn't it?
Pardon! C'est votre sac, n'est-ce pas?

---

parents [PEHR-énts] nom **les parents**

My parents go to work in the morning.
Mes parents vont au travail le matin.

---

park [PAHRK] nom **le parc**

The park is near by.
Le parc est tout près d'ici.

---

parrot [PAR-ét] nom **le perroquet**

My pet is a parrot.
Un perroquet est mon animal favori.

---

part [PAHRT] nom **le rôle**

I want to play the part of the prince.
Je veux jouer le rôle du prince.

---

party [PAHR-ti] nom **la fête**

The party is July 18th?
Le jour de la fête est le dix-huit juillet?

---

to pass [PAS] verbe **dépasser**

I pass	we pass
you pass	you pass
he, she, it passes	they pass

The car passes the truck.
L'auto dépasse le camion.

---

to pass (spend) verbe **passer**

She spends two weeks in the country.
Elle passe deux semaines à la compagne.

---

passenger [PAS-én-gér] nom   **le passager,** masc.
There are six passengers on the bus.   **la passagère,** fém.
Il y a six passagers dans l'autobus.

---

to paste (paste) [PEIST] verbe   **coller**
  I paste   we paste
  you paste   you paste
  he, she, it pastes   they paste

I paste a picture to a page of my notebook.
Je colle une image sur une page de mon cahier.

---

path [PATH] nom   **le sentier**
This path leads to the bridge.
Ce sentier mène au pont.

---

paw [PAW] nom   **la patte**
The dog has four paws.
Le chien a quatre pattes.

---

to pay [PEI] verbe   **payer**
  I pay   we pay
  you pay   you pay
  he, she, it pays   they pay

Mother pays the butcher for the meat.
Maman paye la viande au boucher.

---

peach [PICH] nom   **la pêche**
People eat peaches in summer.
On mange des pêches en été.

---

peanut [PI-nét] nom   **la cachuète**
The elephant likes to eat peanuts.
L'éléphant aime manger les cacahuètes.

---

pear [PEHR] nom   **la poire**

Is the pear ripe?
Est-ce que la poire est mûre?

---

peas [PIZ] nom   **les petits pois**

I like to eat peas.
J'aime bien manger les petits pois.

---

pen [PEN] nom   **le stylo**

I always leave my pen at home.
Je laisse toujours mon stylo à la maison.

ballpoint pen nom   **le stylo à bille**

I am writing with a ballpoint pen.
J'écris avec un stylo à bille.

---

pencil [PEN-sil] nom   **le crayon**

Please give me a pencil.
Donnez-moi un crayon, s'il vous plaît.

---

people [PI-pél] nom   **les personnes**
                                                           les gens
There are seven people in my family.
Il y a sept personnes dans ma famille.

---

perhaps (maybe) [pur-HAPS] adverbe   **peut-être**

Are we going horseback riding this morning? Maybe.
Nous montons à cheval ce matin? Peut-être.

---

permission [pur-MISH-én] nom   **la permission**

Do you have permission to go to the country?
Tu as la permission d'aller à la campagne?

to permit [pur-MIT] verbe   **laisser**
   I permit   we permit
   you permit   you permit
   he, she, it permits   they permit

My brother lets me wash the car.
Mon frère me laisse laver la voiture.

---

person, people [PUR-SON] nom   **la personne**

There are seven people in my family.
Il y a sept personnes dans ma famille.

---

pet [PET] nom   **l'animal favori,** masc.

My dog is my pet.
Mon chien est mon animal favori.

---

pharmacy [FAHR-mé-si] nom   **la pharmacie**

The pharmacy is located close to the park.
La pharmacie se trouve près du parc.

---

photograph (picture) [FOH-té-GRAF] nom   **la photo**

Look at my picture. It's funny, isn't it?
Regarde ma photo! Elle est drôle, n'est-ce pas?

---

piano [PYA-noh] nom   **le piano**
to play the piano   **jouer du piano**

Who plays the piano in your family?
Qui joue du piano dans votre famille?

---

to pick [PIK] verbe   **cueillir**
   I pick   we pick
   you pick   you pick
   he, she, it picks   they pick

He is going to pick some apples.
Il va cueillir des pommes.

---

picnic [PIK-nĭk] nom   **le pique-nique**

We have a picnic in the country.
Nous faisons un pique-nique à la campagne.

---

picture [PIK-chér] nom   **la photo**
picture   **l'image,** fém.

There are many pictures in this book.
Il y a beaucoup d'images dans ce livre.

---

pie [PAI] nom   **la tarte**

Do you like apple pie?
Aimez-vous la tarte aux pommes?

> La plupart des américains aiment la tarte aux pommes.
>
> Most Americans like apple pie.

---

piece [PIS] nom   **le morceau**

I want a piece of cheese.
Je désire un morceau de fromage.

---

pig [PIG] nom   **le cochon**

The farmer has three pigs.
Le fermier a trois cochons.

piggy bank nom   **la tirelire**
I do not have much money in my piggy bank.
Je n'ai pas beaucoup d'argent dans ma tirelire.

pillow [PIL-<u>oh</u>] nom   **l'oreiller,** fém.
The pillow is comfortable.
L'oreiller est comfortable.

pilot (See **airplane**) [P<u>AI</u>-lét] nom   **le pilote**

pin [P<u>IN</u>] nom   **l'épingle,** fém.
What a pretty flower pin!
Quelle jolie épingle en forme de fleurs!

pineapple [P<u>AI</u>-na-pél] nom   **l'ananas,** masc.
The pineapple is big.
L'ananas est grand.

pink [P<u>IN</u>GK] adjectif   **rose**
I like to wear my pink ribbon in my hair.
J'aime porter mon ruban rose dans les cheveux.

place (table setting) [PLEIS] nom   **la place**
My cousin puts a knife at each setting.
Ma cousine met un couteau à chaque place.

planet [PLAN-<u>i</u>t] nom   **la planète**
Do you know the names of all the planets?
Savez-vous les noms de toutes les planètes?

plant [PLANT] nom   **la plante**
There are five plants in the classroom.
Il y a cinq plantes dans la salle de classe.

plate [PLEIT] nom **l'assiette,** fém.

The plate is on the table.
L'assiette est sur la table.

---

to play [PLEI] verbe **jouer**

I play	we play
you play	you play
he, she, it plays	they play

Let's play ball.
Jouons à la balle.

Laura plays the piano.
Laure joue du piano.

to play (a game) **jouer à ...**
to play (a musical instrument) **jouer de ...**
to play checkers **jouer aux dames**
expression idiomatique

My friend and I play checkers.
Mon ami et moi, nous jouons aux dames.

to play chess expression idiomatique **jouer aux échecs**

My father and my uncle play chess.
Mon père et mon oncle jouent aux échecs.

to play blindman's buff **jouer à colin-maillard**
expression idiomatique

Yes, I'd like to play blindman's buff.
Oui, je voudrais jouer à colin-maillard.

to play hide-and-seek **jouer à cache-cache**
expression idiomatique

The children are playing hide-and-seek.
Les enfants jouent à cache-cache.

to play hopscotch   **jouer à la marelle**
expression idiomatique
I don't know how to play hopscotch.
Je ne sais pas jouer à la marelle.

to play leapfrog   **jouer à saute-mouton**
expression idiomatique
We play leapfrog.
Nous jouons à saute-mouton.

playground [PLEI-gr<u>ow</u>nd] nom   **le terrain de jeux**
We play ball in the playground.
Nous jouons à la balle au terrain de jeux.

playing card nom   **la carte**
Do you know how to play cards?
Savez-vous jouer aux cartes?

pleasant [PLEZ-ént] adjectif   **agréable**
Spring is a pleasant season.
Le printemps est une saison agréable.

please [PLIZ] expression idiomatique   **s'il vous plaît**
                                                  s'il te plaît (familiar)
Please give me a pencil, Mr. Duval.
Donnez-moi un crayon, s'il vous plaît, monsieur Duval.

Please give me a pencil, Petey.
Donne-moi un crayon, s'il te plaît, Pierrot.

pleasure [PLEZH-ér] nom   **le plaisir**
Are you coming with us? With pleasure!
Tu viens avec nous? Avec plaisir!

pocket [PAK-it] nom   **la poche**

I have some marbles in my pocket.
J'ai des billes dans la poche.

---

pocketbook (bag, purse) nom   **le sac**
handbag   **le sac à main**

I am buying a handbag for mother.
J'achete un sac à main pour maman.

---

pocketknife nom   **le canif**

Do you have a pocketknife?
Avez-vous un canif?

---

to point to (out) (indicate) [POINT] verbe   **indiquer**
  I point   we point
  you point   you point
  he, she, it points   they point

The policeman indicates that we must go by this road.
L'agent de police indique qu'il faut aller par cette route.

---

police officer   **l'agent (de police)**, masc.
[pé-LIS AW-fis-er] nom

The police officer directs traffic.
L'agent de police dirige la circulation.

---

polite [pé-LAIT] adjectif   **poli**

Mother says, "A polite child does not speak
with a full mouth."
Maman dit: "L'enfant poli ne parle pas la bouche pleine."

---

poor [PUR] adjectif   **pauvre**

This poor boy does not have much money.
Ce garçon pauvre n'a pas beaucoup d'argent.

postcard (See **postman**) nom   **la carte**

---

postman (mail carrier) [P<u>OH</u>ST-mén] nom   **le facteur**
The mail carrier brings letters, packages, and postcards.
Le facteur apporte des lettres, des paquets, et des cartes.

---

post office nom   **la poste**
I go to the post office to send   **le bureau de poste**
a package.
Je vais au bureau de poste pour envoyer un paquet.

---

potato [pé-TEI-t<u>oh</u>] nom   **la pomme de terre**
Do you like potatoes?
Aimez-vous les pommes de terre?

---

to pour [P<u>AWR</u>] verbe   **verser**

I pour	we pour
you pour	you pour
he, she, it pours	they pour

Margaret pours coffee into a cup.
Marguerite verse le café dans une tasse.

---

to prefer [pré-F<u>UR</u>] verbe   **préférer**

I prefer	we prefer
you prefer	you prefer
he, she, it prefers	they prefer

Do you prefer the city or the country?
Préfères-tu la ville ou la campagne?

---

to prepare [pré-PEHR] verbe   **préparer**
  I prepare   we prepare
  you prepare   you prepare
  he, she, it prepares they prepare
My brother prepares the salad.
Mon frère prépare la salade.

present (gift) [PREZ-ént] nom   **le cadeau**
Here is a birthday gift.   **les cadeaux**, pl.
Voici un cadeau pour votre anniversaire.

present (See **here**) adjectif   **présent**

president [PREZ-i-dént] nom   **le président**
Who is the president of France?
Qui est le président de la France?

> On célèbre en février, la journée de la fête du président George Washington et du président Abraham Lincoln.
>
> Presidents' Day in February celebrates the birthdays of Presidents George Washington and Abraham Lincoln.

pretty (See **good-looking**) adjectif   **joli**

price [PRAIS] nom   **le prix**
What is the price of this suit?
Quel est le prix de ce complet?

386

prince [PRINS] nom   **le prince**
princess [prin-SES] nom   **la princesse**

The prince is playing in the garden.
Le prince joue dans le jardin.

---

to promise [PRAM-is] verbe   **promettre**
   I promise   we promise
   you promise   you promise
   he, she, it promises they promise

I promise to do my homework.
Je promets de faire mes devoirs.

---

to pull (drag) [PAUHL] verbe   **tirer**
   I pull   we pull
   you pull   you pull
   he, she, it pulls   they pull

He is pulling a bag of potatoes.
Il tire un sac de pommes de terre.

---

pumpkin [PUM-kin] nom   **la citrouille**

This is a big pumpkin.
C'est une grande citrouille.

---

to punish [PUN-ish] verbe   **punir**
   I punish   we punish
   you punish   you punish
   he, she, it punishes they punish

When I am naughty, Mommy punishes me.
Quand je suis méchant, Maman me punit.

---

pupil [PYU-pil] nom   **l'élève**
                                                         les élèves, pl.
The pupils are in the classroom.
Les élèves sont dans la salle de classe.

puppy (See **dog**) nom   **le petit chien**

---

purple [PUR-pél] ajdectif   **violet,** masc.
Are there any purple flowers?   **violette,** fém.
Est-ce qu'il y a des fleurs violettes?

---

purse (See **handbag**) nom   **le sac**

---

to push [PAUHSH] verbe   **pousser**
   I push   we push
   you push   you push
   he, she, it pushes   they push

He's pushing me!
Il me pousse!

---

to put (down) verbe   **baisser**
   I put   we put
   you put   you put
   he, she, it puts   they put

The teacher says, "Put your hands down!"
Le professeur dit, "Baissez les mains."

to put (on) verbe   **mettre**
My sister puts on her gloves.
Ma soeur met les gants.

Q

quarrel [KWAR-él] nom   **la querelle**
My father sometimes has a quarrel with my mother.
Mon père a une querelle quelquefois avec ma mère.

---

quarter [KW<u>AW</u>-tér] nom   **le quart**
It is a quarter after seven.
Il est sept heures et quart.

queen [KWIN] nom   **la reine**
The queen is seated near the king.
La reine est assise près du roi.

question [KWES-chén] nom   **la question**
The teacher asks, "Are there any questions?"
Le professeur demande: "Est-ce qu'il y a des questions?"

quickly (fast) [KW<u>I</u>K-li] adverbe   **vite**
My brother walks too fast. (quickly)
Mon frère marche trop vite.

quiet [KW<u>AI</u>-ét] adjectif   **silencieux**
quiet (calm) adjectif   **tranquille**
I like to go fishing when the water is calm. (quiet)
J'aime aller à la pêche quand l'eau est tranquille.

R

rabbit [RAB-<u>i</u>t] nom   **le lapin**

The rabbit runs and jumps.
Le lapin court et saute.

radio [REI-di-<u>oh</u>] nom   **la radio**

The radio is not working.
La radio ne marche pas.

---

railroad (See **road**) nom   **le chemin de fer**

---

to rain [REIN] verbe   **pleuvoir**

Do you think it's going to rain?
Vous pensez qu'il va pleuvoir?

It is raining   **Il pleut**

---

rainbow [REIN-b<u>oh</u>] nom   **l'arc-en-ciel,** masc.

I like the colors of the rainbow.
J'aime les couleurs de l'arc-en-ciel.

---

raincoat [REIN-k<u>oh</u>t] nom   **l'imperméable**

He is wearing his raincoat because it is raining.
Il porte son imperméable parce qu'il pleut.

---

to raise [REIZ] verbe   **lever**

I raise	we raise
you raise	you raise
he, she, it raises	they raise

The policeman raises his right hand.
L'agent de police lève la main droite.

---

rapid (See **fast**) adjectif   **rapide**

---

rat [RAT] nom   **le rat**

I am afraid of rats!
J'ai peur des rats!

---

to read [RID] verbe   **lire**

I read	we read
you read	you read
he, she, it reads	they read

We are going to read in the library.
Nous allons lire dans la bibliotèque.

---

ready [RED-i] adjectif   **prêt,** masc.

Are you ready? We are late.   **prête,** fém.
Es-tu prêt? Nous sommes en retard.

---

really [RI-LI] adverbe   **vraiment**

Do you know that I would like to become an astronaut?
Really!
Vous savez que je voudrais devenir astronaute? Vraiment!

---

to receive [ri-SIV] verbe   **recevoir**

I receive	we receive
you receive	you receive
he, she, it receives	they receive

I receive a postcard from my sister.
Je reçois une carte postale de ma soeur.

---

red [RED] adjectif   **rouge**

The cars stop when the light is red.
Les voitures s'arrêtent quand le feu est rouge.

---

refrigerator [ri-FRIDJ-é-rei-tér] nom   **le réfrigérateur**
The refrigerator is in the kitchen.
Le réfrigérateur est dans la cuisine.

---

relatives [RE-lé-tivz] nom   **les parents**

to remain (stay) [ri̱-MEIN] verbe   **rester**

I remain	we remain
you remain	you remain
he, she, it remains	they remain

to remember [ri̱-MEM-bér] verbe   **se rappeler**

I remember	we remember
you remember	you remember
he, she, it remembers	they remember

I cannot remember the name of this building.
Je ne peux pas me rappeler le nom de ce bâtiment.

to remove (take off) [ri̱-MUV] verbe   **ôter**

I remove	we remove
you remove	you remove
he, she, it removes	they remove

Take off your hat in the house.
Ôte le chapeau dans la maison.

to repair (fix) [ri̱-PEHR] verbe   **réparer**

I repair	we repair
you repair	you repair
he, she, it repairs	they repair

My brother is fixing the machine.
Mon frere répare la machine.

to repeat [ri̱-PIT] verbe   **répéter**

I repeat	we repeat
you repeat	you repeat
he, she, it repeats	they repeat

The teacher says, "Repeat after me."
Le maître dit: "Répétez après moi."

to reply (answer) [ri-PLAI] verbe   **répondre**

I reply	we reply
you reply	you reply
he, she, it replies	they reply

The little girl cannot answer the question.
La petite fille ne peut pas répondre à la question.

---

to rescue (save) [RES-kyu] verbe   **sauver**

I rescue	we rescue
you rescue	you rescue
he, she, it rescues	they rescue

My uncle saves me when I fall into the water.
Mon oncle me sauve quand je tombe dans l'eau.

---

to rest [REST] verbe   **se reposer**

I rest	we rest
you rest	you rest
he, she, it rests	they rest

The child runs. He does not want to rest.
L'enfant court. Il ne veut pas se reposer.

---

restroom [REST-rum] nom   **les toilettes**

Where is the restroom?
Où sont les toilettes?

---

restaurant [RES-tér-ént] nom   **le restaurant**

The waiter works in this restaurant.
Le garcon travaille dans ce restaurant.

---

to return (to give back) [ri-TURN] verbe   **rendre**

He returns my roller skates.
Il me rend mes patins à roulettes.

---

to return [ri-TURN] verbe   **retourner**

I return	we return
you return	you return
he, she, it returns	they return

He goes to the blackboard and then he returns to his seat.
Il va au tableau noir et puis il retourne à sa place.

---

ribbon [RIB-én] nom   **le ruban**

She is wearing a pretty ribbon.
Elle porte un joli ruban.

---

rice [RAIS] nom   **le riz**

The rice is delicious.
Le riz est délicieux.

---

rich [RICH] adjectif   **riche**

The rich lady wears jewels.
La femme riche porte des bijoux.

---

to ride [RAID] verbe   **monter**

He rides a horse.
Il monte à cheval.

---

right [RAIT] adjectif   **droit,** masc.
                                                    droite, fém.
right hand nom   **la main droite**

I raise my right hand.
Je lève la main droite.

---

ring [RING] nom   **l'anneau,** masc.
                                                    la bague
Helen is wearing a pretty ring.
Hélène porte une jolie bague.

---

to ring verbe   **sonner**

I ring	we ring
you ring	you ring
he, she, it rings	they ring

The telephone is ringing.
Le téléphone sonne.

---

ripe [RAIP] adjectif   **mûr,** masc.
                                                    mûre, fém.
When the banana is yellow, it is ripe.
Quand la banane est jaune, elle est mûre.

---

river [RIV-ér] nom   **la rivière**

How can we cross the river?
Comment peut-on traverser la rivière?

---

road [ROHD] nom   **le chemin**

Is this the road to town?
C'est le chemin de la ville?

railroad [REIL-rohd] nom   **le chemin de fer**

To go to Marseilles, I take the railroad.
Pour aller à Marseille, je prends le chemin de fer.

---

roast beef [ROHST-bif] nom   **le rosbif**

I would like a roast beef sandwich, please.
Je voudrais un sandwich de rosbif, s'il vous plaît.

---

robber (thief) [RA-BÉ] nom   **le voleur**

They are looking for the thief at the bank.
On cherche le voleur à la banque.

---

rock [RAK] nom   **le rocher**

What a large rock over there!
Quel grand rocher là-bas!

---

role [ROHL] nom   **le rôle**

I want to play the role of the prince.
Je veux jouer le rôle du prince.

---

roll [ROHL] nom   **la brioche**
     la petit pain

Susan eats a roll for breakfast.
Suzanne prend une brioche pour le petit déjeuner.

to roll verbe   **rouler**

I roll	we roll
you roll	you roll
he, she, it rolls	they roll

The roller skate is rolling into the street.
Le patin à roulettes roule dans la rue.

---

roller skate (See **skate**) nom   **le patin à roulettes**

---

roof [RUF] nom   **le toit**

I look at the city from the roof of the house.
Je regarde la ville du toit de la maison.

---

room [RUM] nom   **la pièce**

There are two rooms in our apartment.
Il y a deux pièces dans notre appartement.

---

room nom   **la salle**
bathroom nom   **la salle de bain**

The bathroom is small.
La salle de bain est petite.

---

classroom nom   **la salle de classe**

The classroom is empty.
La salle de classe est vide.

dining room nom   **la salle à manger**

Mother enters the dining room.
Maman entre dans la salle à manger.

---

rooster [RUS-tér] nom   **le coq**

The rooster gets up early.
Le coq se lève de bonne heure.

rope [ROHP] nom   **la corde**
to jump rope expression idiomatique   **sauter à la corde**

Mary, Joan and I are jumping rope.
Marie, Jeanne et moi, nous sautons à la corde.

---

round [ROWND] adjectif   **rond,** masc.
                                ronde, fém.
The plate is round.
L'assiette est ronde.

---

route [RUT] nom   **la route**

What's the name of this road? (route)
Quel est le nom de cette route?

---

row [ROH] nom   **le rang**

The teacher says, "Children in the first row, stand."
La maîtresse dit: "Les enfants du premier rang, levez-vous."

---

rubber [RUB-ér] nom   **le caoutchouc**

It is raining. I have to put on my rubbers.
Il pleut. Il faut mettre mes caoutchoucs.

made of rubber   **en caoutchouc**

---

rug [RUG] nom   **le tapis**

The rug is on the floor.
Le tapis est sur le plancher.

---

rule [RUL] nom   **la règle**

We have to obey the rules at school and at home.
Il faut obéir aux règles à l'école et à la maison.

---

ruler [RUL-ér] nom   **la règle**

The ruler is long.
La règle est longue.

to run [R∅N] verbe   **courir**

I run	we run
you run	you run
he, she, it runs	it runs

They are running to the station because they are late.
Ils courent à la gare parce qu'ils sont en retard.

S

sack (See **bag**) nom   **le sac**

---

sad [SAD] adjectif   **triste**

Why are you sad?
Pourquoi es-tu triste?

---

safe and sound [SEIF-and-S<u>OW</u>ND]   **sain et sauf**
expression idiomatique

I come home safe and sound.
Je retourne à la maison sain et sauf.

---

salad [SAL-éd] nom   **la salade**

My cousin puts the salad in the middle of the table.
Ma cousine met la salade au milieu de la table.

---

salesperson [SEILZ-p<u>ur</u>-sohn] nom   **le vendeur**
                                                              la vendeuse

The salesperson shows
me a sweater.
Le vendeur me
montre un chandail.

---

salt [SAWLT] nom   **le sel**

Please pass me the salt.
Passez-moi le sel, s'il vous plaît.

same [SEIM] adjectif; adverbe   **même**

My friend and I are wearing the same dress.
Mon amie et moi, nous portons la même robe.

sand [SAND] nom   **le sable**

At the beach I sit on the sand.
A la plage, je m'assieds sur le sable.

sandwich [SAND-wich] nom   **le sandwich**

Do you want a sandwich or a salad?
Veux-tu un sandwich ou une salade?

Saturday [SAT-ér-dei] nom   **samedi**

Let's have a picnic Saturday.
Faisons un pique-nique samedi.

saucer [SAW-sér] nom   **la soucoupe**

The woman puts the cup on the saucer.
La femme met la tasse sur la soucoupe.

to save [SEIV] verbe   **sauver**

I save	we save
you save	you save
he, she, it saves	they save

My uncle saves me when I fall into the water.
Mon oncle me sauve quand je tombe dans l'eau.

to say [SEI] verbe   **dire**

I say	we say
you say	you say
he, she, it says	they say

The teacher says "Good Morning" each morning.
Le professeur dit: "Bonjour" chaque matin.

Say! Well! interjection   **Tiens!**

Say! It's beginning to snow.
Tiens! Il commence à neiger.

---

school [SKUL] nom   **l'école,** fém.

We don't go to school on Thursdays.
Le jeudi nous n'allons pas à l'école.

---

science [S<u>AI</u>-éns] nom   **la science**

I like to go to my science class.
J'aime aller à ma classe de science.

---

scientist [S<u>AI</u>-en-t<u>i</u>st] nom   **le savant,** masc.
                                 la savante, fém.

I would like to become a scientist.
Je voudrais devenir savant.

---

scissors [S<u>I</u>Z-érz] nom   **les ciseaux**

I cut the paper with scissors.
Je coupe le papier avec les ciseaux.

---

to scold [SK<u>OH</u>LD] verbe   **gronder**

I scold	we scold
you scold	you scold
he, she, it scolds	they scold

He is ashamed because his mother is scolding him.
Il a honte parce que sa mère le gronde.

---

to scream (shout) [SKRIM] verbe   **crier**

I scream	we scream
you scream	you scream
he, she, it screams	they scream

Mom shouts, "Come quickly!"
Maman crie: "Viens vite!"

---

sea [SI] nom   **la mer**

Are there many fish in the sea?
Est-ce qu'il y a beaucoup de poissons dans la mer?

---

season [SI-zén] nom   **la saison**

How many seasons are there?
Combien de saisons y a-t-il?

---

seat [SIT] nom   **la place**

I go to the blackboard and I return to my seat.
Je vais au tableau noir et je retourne à ma place.

seated adjectif   **assis,** masc.
         assise, fém.

He is seated in an armchair.
Il est assis dans un fauteuil.

---

second [SEK-énd] adjectif   **deuxième**

What is the name of the second month of the year?
Quel est le nom du deuxième mois de l'année?

---

secret [SI-krit] nom   **le secret**

Tell me the secret!
Dis-moi le secret!

---

secretary [SEK-ré-ter-i] nom   **la dactylo,** fém.
         le dactylo, masc.

There are three secretaries in this office.
Il y a trois dactylos dans ce bureau.

---

to see [SI] verbe   **voir**

I see	we see
you see	you see
he, she, it sees	they see

I see the airplane in the sky.
Je vois l'avion dans le ciel.

to see again verbe   **revoir**

I am going to see the film again.
Je vais revoir le film.

---

seesaw [SI-s<u>aw</u>] nom   **la balançoire**

The boys are on the seesaw.
Les garçons sont sur la balançoire.

---

to sell [SEL] verbe   **vendre**

I sell	we sell
you sell	you sell
he, she, it sells	they sell

They sell medicine in this store.
On vend des médicaments dans ce magasin.

---

to send [SEND] verbe   **envoyer**

I send	we send
you send	you send
he, she, it sends	they send

My uncle is going to send me a present.
Mon oncle va m'envoyer un cadeau.

---

sentence [SEN-téns] nom   **la phrase**

I am writing a sentence in my notebook.
J'écris une phrase dans mon cahier.

September [sep-TEM-bér] nom   **septembre**

Do we go back to school on the first of September?
Est-ce qu'on retourne à l'école le premier septembre?

---

serious [SIR-i-és] adjectif   **sérieux,** masc.
                                sérieuse, fém.
*They are playing a serious film
at the movies.*
On joue un film sérieux au cinéma.

---

to serve [SURV] verbe   **servir**

I serve	we serve
you serve	you serve
he, she, it serves	they serve

I serve my dog his dinner.
Je sers le dîner à mon chien.

---

server (waiter, waitress) [SURV-ér] nom   **le serveur,** masc.
                                        la serveuse, fém.

The server brings us ice cream.
Le serveur nous apporte la glace.

to set [SET] verbe   **mettre**
> I set   we set
> you set   you set
> he, she, it sets   they set

My mother sets the table.
Ma mère met le couvert.

setting (table) nom   **la place**

My cousin puts a knife at each setting.
Ma cousine met un couteau à chaque place.

---

to set (sun) verbe   **se coucher**

The sun is setting.
Le soleil se couche.

---

seven [SEV-én] adjectif   **sept**

There are seven apples.
Voilà sept pommes.

---

seventeen [sev-én-TIN] adjectif   **dix-sept**

Nine and eight are seventeen.
Neuf et huit font dix-sept.

---

seventy [SEV-én-ti] adjectif   **soixante-dix**

Nancy's grandmother is seventy years old.
La grand-mère de Nanette a soixante-dix ans.

---

several [SEV-rél] adjectif   **plusieurs**

There are several cars on the road.
Il y a plusieurs autos sur la route.

---

to sew [SOH] verbe   **coudre**

I sew	we sew
you sew	you sew
he, she, it sews	they sew

Mother sews with a sewing needle.
Maman coud avec une aiguille à coudre.

shadow [SHAD-oh] nom   **l'ombre,** fém.

Do you see the shadow?
Voyez-vous l'ombre?

to shake (move) [SHEIK] verbe   **remuer**

I shake	we shake
you shake	you shake
he, she, it shakes	they shake

She moves her fingers quickly when she plays the piano.
Elle remue vite ses doigts quand elle joue du piano.

to shake hands verbe   **serrer la main à**

Alan, shake hands with your neighbor.
Alain, serre la main à ton voisin.

to share [SHEHR] verbe   **partager**

I share	we share
you share	you share
he, she, it shares	they share

Let's share the cake!
Partageons le gâteau.

she [SHI] pronom　　　　　　　　　　　　　　　　**elle**

sheep [SHIP] nom　　　　　　　　　　　　　**le mouton**
The sheep is in the field.
Le mouton est dans le champ.

sheet of paper [shit-év-PEI-pér] nom　　　　**la feuille**
Give me a sheet of paper, please.
Donne-moi une feuille de papier, s'il te plaît.

shell [SHEL] nom　　　　　　　　　　**le coquillage**
I am looking for shells at the beach.
Je cherche des coquillages à la plage.

ship [SHIP] nom　　　　　　　　　**le bateau,** masc.
You cross the ocean by ship.　　　　　**les bateaux,** pl.
On traverse l'océan en bateau.

shirt [SHURT] nom　　　　　　　　　　**la chemise**
The boy is wearing a white shirt.
Le garçon porte une chemise blanche.

shoe [SHU] nom　　　　　　　　　　**la chaussure**
I don't like these shoes!　　　　　　　　**le soulier**
Je n'aime pas ces chaussures!

shop [SHAP] nom　　　　　　　　　　**la boutique**
Excuse me. Where is Mr. Le Blanc's shop?
Pardon. Où se trouve la boutique de monsieur Le Blanc?

to go shopping　　　　　　**faire des emplettes**

shore [SHAWR] nom　　　　　　　　　　**le bord**
I am seated on the shore of the lake.
Je suis assis au bord du lac.

short (length) [SH<u>AW</u>RT] adjectif

One ruler is short; the other is long.
Une règle est courte; l'autre est longue.

court, masc.
courte, fém.

---

short (height) adjectif

The tree at the left is short; the tree at the right is tall.
L'arbre à gauche est bas; l'arbre à droite est haut.

bas, masc.
basse, fém.

---

shoulder [SHOHL-dér] nom

The ball hits Claude's shoulder.
La balle frappe l'épaule de Claude.

l'épaule, fém.

---

to shout [SH<u>OW</u>T] verbe

I shout	we shout
you shout	you shout
he, she, it shouts	they shout

Mom shouts, "Come quickly!"
Maman crie: "Viens vite!"

crier

---

shovel [SH<u>U</u>V-él] nom

My brother plays with a shovel.
Mon frère joue avec une pelle.

la pelle

---

to show [SH<u>OH</u>] verbe

I show	we show
you show	you show
he, she, it shows	they show

Show me your new pen.
Montre-moi ton nouveau stylo.

montrer

---

shower [SH<u>OW</u>-ér] nom

I take a shower every morning.
Je prends une douche chaque matin.

la douche

sick [sɪk] adjectif   **malade**

What's the matter? I am sick.
Qu'as-tu? Je suis malade.

---

sideboard (cupboard, closet) [sᴀɪᴅ-bawrd] nom   **le buffet**

There are plates in the cupboard.
Il y a des assiettes dans le buffet.

---

sidewalk [sᴀɪᴅ-wawk] nom   **le trottoir**

The sidewalk is very narrow.
Le trottoir est très étroit.

---

silent [sᴀɪ-lént] adjectif   **silencieux,** masc.
                     silencieuse, fém.

The city street is never quiet.
La rue dans la ville n'est jamais silencieuse.

---

silly [sɪʟ-i] adjectif   **bête**

The puppy is silly.
Le petit chien est bête.

---

silver [sɪʟ-vér] adjectif   **l'argent,** masc.
made of silver   **en argent**

The pin is made of silver.
L'épingle est en argent.

---

similar (See **alike**) adjectif   **pareil**

---

to sing [sɪɴɢ] verbe   **chanter**

I sing	we sing
you sing	you sing
he, she, it sings	they sing

I am singing and the birds are singing.
Je chante et les oiseaux chantent.

---

sink (bathroom) (See **bathroom**) nom | **le lavabo**

---

sister [SIS-tér] nom | **la soeur**

My aunt is my mother's sister.
Ma tante est la soeur de ma mère.

---

to sit (down) [SIT DOWN] verbe | **s'asseoir**

I sit	we sit
you sit	you sit
he, she, it sits	they sit

Grandmother sits down on a chair.
Grand-mère s'assied sur une chaise.

---

six [SIKS] adjectif | **six**

How many pencils do you have? Six.
Combien de crayons avez-vous? Six.

He has six friends.
Il a six amis.

He has six nails.
Il a six clous.

---

sixteen [siks-TIN] adjectif | **seize**

I have to read sixteen pages this evening!
Je dois lire seize pages ce soir!

---

sixty [SIKS-ti] adjectif | **soixante**

There are sixty minutes in an hour.
Il y a soixante minutes dans une heure.

---

size [SAIZ] nom | **la taille**

In a store they ask me, "What is your size?"
Dans un magasin on me demande: "Quelle est votre taille?"

---

skate [SKEIT] nom   **le patin**
ice skate   **le patin (à glace)**
roller skate   **le patin à roulettes**

---

to skate verbe   **patiner**

I skate	we skate
you skate	you skate
he, she, it skates	they skate

Let's go skating!
Allons patiner!

---

skin [SKIN] nom   **la peau**

The sun burns my skin when I take a sun bath.
Le soleil me brûle la peau quand je prends un
bain de soleil.

---

skinny (thin) [SKIN-i] adjectif   **maigre**

You are too thin. You must eat.
Vous êtes trop maigre. Il faut manger.

---

skirt [SKURT] nom   **la jupe**

I can't choose. Which skirt do you prefer?
Je ne peux pas choisir. Quelle jupe préférez-vous?

---

sky [SKAI] nom   **le ciel**

I see the moon in the sky.
Je vois la lune dans le ciel.

---

skyscraper nom   **le gratte-ciel**

New York City has many skyscrapers.
La ville de New York a beaucoup de gratte-ciel.

---

sled [SLED] nom

la luge
le traîneau

I have a good time
with the sled.
Je m'amuse avec la luge.

---

to sleep [SLIP] verbe   **dormir**

I sleep	we sleep
you sleep	you sleep
he, she, it sleeps	they sleep

Are you sleeping? I would like to talk to you.
Tu dors? Je voudrais te parler.

---

to slide (slip) [SLAID] verbe   **glisser**

I slide	we slide
you slide	you slide
he, she, it slides	they slide

We slip on the ice in winter.
Nous glissons sur la glace en hiver.

to slip [SLIP] verbe   **glisser**
slowly [SLOH-li] adverbe   **lentement**

Grandfather walks slowly.
Grand-père marche lentement.

---

small [SMAWL] adjectif   **petit,** masc.
                                                              petite, fém.
The bird is small.
L'oiseau est petit.

---

to smell (to feel) [SMEL] verbe   **sentir**

I smell	we smell
you smell	you smell
he, she, it smells	they smell

The cake smells good.
Le gâteau sent bon.

---

to smile [SMAIL] verbe   **sourire**

I smile	we smile
you smile	you smile
he, she, it smiles	they smile

You always smile when I give you a cookie.
Tu souris toujours quand je te donne un petit gâteau.

---

smoke [SMOHK] nom   **la fumée**

Look at the smoke!
Regarde la fumée!

---

to smoke verbe   **fumer**

I smoke	we smoke
you smoke	you smoke
he, she, it smokes	they smoke

Dad says that it is dangerous to smoke.
Papa dit qu'il est dangereux de fumer.

no smoking   **défense de fumer**

---

snack [SNAK] nom   **le goûter**

Hello, Mother. Do you have a snack for us?
Bonjour, Maman. Tu as un goûter pour nous?

---

snake [SNEIK] nom   **le serpent**

Are there any snakes in France?
Est-ce qu'il y a des serpents en France?

---

to sneeze [SNIZ] verbe   **éternuer**

I sneeze	we sneeze
you sneeze	you sneeze
he, she, it sneezes	they sneeze

You're sneezing. Do you have a cold?
Tu éternues. Tu as un rhume?

---

snow [SNOH] nom   **la neige**

I like to play in the snow.
J'aime jouer dans la neige.

---

to snow verbe   **neiger**

Is it going to snow tomorrow?
Il va neiger demain?

It is snowing   **Il neige**

---

snowman [SNOH-man] nom   **le bonhomme de neige**

The snowman is wearing a hat.
Le bonhomme de neige porte
un chapeau.

---

so [SOH] adverbe   **si**

The baby eats so slowly!
Le bébé mange si lentement!

---

so many adverbe   **tant**

So many grapes!
Tant de raisins!

---

so much adverbe   **tant**

So much work!
Tant de travail!

---

soap [SOHP] nom   **le savon**

Don't forget to use soap!
N'oublie pas d'employer le savon!

soccer [SAK-ér] nom   **le football**

Here is our soccer team.
Voici notre équipe de football.

sock [SAK] nom   **la chaussette**

I would like to buy a pair of socks.
Je voudrais acheter une paire de chaussettes.

soda [SOH-dé] nom   **le soda**

I am drinking soda.
Je bois du soda.

sofa [SOH-fé] nom   **le canapé**

The sofa is very comfortable.
Le canapé est très confortable.

soft (See **gentle**) adjectif   **doux**

softly [SAWFT-li] adverbe   **doucement**

Walk softly. Mother has a headache.
Marche doucement. Maman a mal à la tête.

soldier [SOHL-djér] nom   **le soldat**

My cousin is a soldier.
Mon cousin est soldat.

some [sᴧᴍ] nom   **de**

some pronom   **quelque**

somebody, someone pronom   **quelqu'un,** masc.

Somebody is in the restaurant.   **quelqu'une,** fém.
Quelqu'un est dans le restaurant.

something pronom   **quelque chose**

Is there something in this drawer?
Est-ce qu'il y a quelque chose dans ce tiroir?

sometimes adverbe   **quelquefois**

Sometimes I am not well-behaved.
Quelquefois je ne suis pas sage.

---

son [sᴧɴ] nom   **le fils**

I should like to introduce my son, George.
Je vous présente mon fils, Georges.

---

song [sᴀɴɢ] nom   **la chanson**

Which song do you prefer?
Quelle chanson préférez-vous?

> La chanson *Star Spangled Banner* est la chanson
> nationale américaine.
>
> The "Star Spangled Banner" is the American
> national anthem.

---

soon [sᴜɴ] adverbe   **bientôt**

The mailman will come soon.
Le facteur arrive bientôt.

See you soon! expression idiomatique   **à bientôt**

I am going shopping. See you soon!
Je vais faire des emplettes. A bientôt!

---

sort (See **kind**) nom   **la sorte**

---

soup [sup] nom   **la soupe**
My sister serves soup to my brother.
Ma soeur sert la soupe à mon frère.

---

south [s<u>ow</u>th] nom   **le sud**
Marseilles is in the south of France.
Marseille est au sud de la France.

---

space [speis] nom   **l'espace,** masc.

The astronauts travel in space.
Les astronautes voyagent dans l'espace.

---

spaceship [speis-sh<u>i</u>p] nom   **la fusée**
They are going to the moon in a spaceship.
On va à la lune en fusée.

---

to speak (talk) [spik] verbe   **parler**
  I speak   we speak
  you speak   you speak
  he, she, it speaks   they speak
We are talking about the movie on television.
Nous parlons du film à la télévision.

---

to spend (time) [SPEND] verbe   **passer**

I spend	we spend
you spend	you spend
he, she, it spends	they spend

She spends two weeks in the country.
Elle passe deux semaines à la campagne.

---

spider [SPAI-dér] nom   **l'araignée,** fém.

Who's afraid of a spider?
Qui a peur d'une araignée?

---

to spill (overturn) [SPIL] verbe   **renverser**

I spill	we spill
you spill	you spill
he, she, it spills	they spill

The baby overturns the plate.
Le bébé renverse l'assiette.

---

spinach [SPIN-éch] nom   **les épinards**

Spinach is green.
Les épinards sont verts.

---

spoon [SPUN] nom   **la cuiller**

I don't have a spoon.
Je n'ai pas de cuiller.

---

sport [SPAWRT] nom   **le sport**

What is your favorite sport?
Quel est votre sport favori?

---

spot (stain) [SPAT] nom   **la tache**

There is a stain on the rug.
Il y a une tache sur le tapis.

spotted adjectif

My turtle is spotted.
Ma tortue est tachetée.

tacheté, masc.
tachetée, fém.

---

spring [SPRING] nom

You see a lot of flowers in the spring.
Au printemps on voit beaucoup de fleurs.

le printemps

---

square [SKWEHR] adjectif

The box is square.
La boîte est carrée.

carré, masc.
carrée, fém.

---

staircase [STEHR-keis] nom

I like to jump over the last step of the staircase.
J'aime sauter la dernière marche de l'escalier.

l'escalier, masc.

---

stamp (postage) [STAMP] nom

I put a stamp on the envelope.
Je mets un timbre sur l'enveloppe.

le timbre

---

standing [STAN-ding] adverbe

In the classroom the teacher is standing.
Dans la salle de classe la maîtresse est debout.

debout

---

to stand (See **to get up**) [STAND] verbe

se lever

---

star [STAHR] nom

How many stars are there in the sky?
Combien d'étoiles y a-t-il dans le ciel?

l'étoile, fém.

---

to start (begin) [STAHRT] verbe

I start	we start
you start	you start
he, she, it starts	they start

The French class begins at nine o'clock.
La classe de français commence à neuf heures.

commencer

---

state [STEIT] nom · **l'état,** masc.

From which state do you come?
De quel état venez-vous?

---

station [STEI-shén] nom · **la gare**

The train is in the station.
Le train est à la gare.

---

to stay [STEI] verbe · **rester**

I stay	we stay
you stay	you stay
he, she, it stays	they stay

I would like to stay at my grandmother's house.
Je voudrais rester chez ma grand-mère.

---

to steal [STIL] verbe · **voler**

I steal	we steal
you steal	you steal
he, she, it steals	they steal

Who has just stolen my spoon?
Qui vient de voler ma cuiller?

---

steamship [STIM-ship] nom · **le paquebot**

The steamship crosses the Atlantic Ocean.
Le paquebot traverse l'océan Atlantique.

---

step [STEP] nom · **la marche**

There are many steps in front of this building.
Il y a beaucoup de marches devant ce bâtiment.

---

stereo [STE-re-o] nom · **la stéréo,** fém.

The stereo is not working.
La stéréo ne marche pas.

---

stick [STIK] nom   **le bâton**

The policeman carries a stick.
L'agent de police porte un bâton.

---

still [STIL] adverbe   **encore**

Are you still at home?
Es-tu encore à la maison?

---

to sting (bite) [STING] verbe   **piquer**
he, she, it stings   they sting

The mosquitoes like to bite me.
Les moustiques aiment me piquer.

---

stocking [STAK-ing] nom   **les bas**

Women wear nylon stockings.
Les femmes portent des bas de nylon.

---

stomach (See **to have a ...**) nom   **le ventre**

---

stone [STOHN] nom   **la pierre**

There are many stones in the playground.
Il y a beaucoup de pierres dans le terrain de jeux.

---

to stop [STAP] verbe   **arrêter**
   I stop   we stop
   you stop   you stop
   he, she, it stops   they stop

The policeman stops the car.
L'agent arrête les autos.

---

to stop (oneself) verbe   **s'arrêter**
The train stops at the station.
Le train s'arrête à la gare.

---

store [STAWR] nom   **le magasin**

I'm going to the store with my friend.
Je vais au magasin avec mon amie.

---

store (market) nom   **le marché**

What do they sell at the market?
Qu'est-ce qu'on vend au marché?

---

store window [STAWR WIN-doh] nom   **la vitrine**

We are going to look at the things in the store windows.
Nous allons regarder les choses dans les vitrines.

---

storm [STAWRM] nom   **l'orage,** masc.

It is windy during a storm.
Il fait du vent pendant l'orage.

---

story [STAWR-i] nom   **le conte,**
l'histoire, fém.

Read me the story of the
"Three Little Kittens."
Lisez-moi le conte des "Trois petits chatons."

---

stove [STOHV] nom   **le fourneau**

Mother cooks on a stove.
Maman fait la cuisine sur un fourneau.

---

strange [STREINDJ] adjectif   **bizarre**

Here is a strange animal!
Voici un animal bizarre!

---

stranger [STREIN-djér] nom   **étranger, masc.**
Mother says, "Don't speak to strangers."   **étrangère, fém.**
Maman dit: "Ne parlez pas aux étrangers."

---

strawberry [STRAW-ber-i] nom   **la fraise**
Strawberries are red.
Les fraises sont rouges.

---

street [STRIT] nom   **la rue**
It is dangerous to play ball in the street.
Il est dangereux de jouer à la balle dans la rue.

street cleaner nom   **le balayeur des rues**
The street cleaner is carrying a broom.
Le balayeur des rues porte un balai.

---

string [STRING] nom   **la ficelle**
I am looking for a string for my kite.
Je cherche une ficelle pour mon cerf-volant.

---

string beans [STRING-binz] nom   **les haricots verts**
We have string beans for dinner.
Nous avons des haricots verts pour le dîner.

---

strong [STRAWNG] adjectif   **fort, masc.**
My father is very strong.   **forte, fém.**
Mon père est très fort.

---

student [STUD-ént] nom   **l'étudiant, masc.**
My cousin is a student at the university. **l'étudiante, fém.**
Mon cousin est étudiant à l'université.

to study [STŬD-i] verbe   **étudier**

I study	we study
you study	you study
he, she, it studies	they study

I have to study this evening. I have an examination tomorrow.
Je dois étudier ce soir. J'ai un examen demain.

---

stupid [STU-pĭd] adjectif   **stupide, bête**

Is the elephant intelligent or stupid?
Est-ce que l'éléphant est intelligent ou stupide?

---

subway [SŬB-wei] nom   **le métro**

We take the subway to go to the museum.
Pour aller au musée nous prenons le métro.

---

to succeed [sék-SID] verbe   **réussir**

I succeed	we succeed
you succeed	you succeed
he, she, it succeeds	they succeed

He succeeds in catching a fish.
Il réussit à attraper un poisson.

---

suddenly [SŬD-én-li] adverbe   **tout à coup**

Suddenly the doctor enters.
Tout à coup le médecin entre.

---

sugar [SHAUHG-ér] nom   **le sucre**

He serves sugar with tea.
Il sert du sucre avec le thé.

---

suit [SUT] nom   **le complet**

Father wears a suit when he goes to work.
Papa porte un complet quand il va au travail.

bathing suit   **le maillot**

suitcase [SUT-keis] nom   **la valise**

I put my clothes in the suitcase.
Je mets mes vêtements dans la valise.

summer [SÉM-ér] nom   **l'été,** masc.

Do you prefer summer or winter?
Préférez-vous l'été ou l'hiver?

sun [SÉN] nom   **le soleil**

What time does the sun rise?
A quelle heure se lève le soleil?

sunbath [SÉN-bath] nom   **le bain de soleil**

I take a sunbath on the grass.
Je prends un bain de soleil sur l'herbe.

It is sunny. expression idiomatique   **Il fait du soleil.**

Sunday [SÉN-dei] nom   **dimanche**

We go to the park on Sundays.
Le dimanche nous allons au parc.

supermarket [SU-pér-MAHR-két] nom   **le supermarché**

The supermarket is a large market.
Le supermarché est un grand marché.

---

sure (See **certain**) adjectif   **sur**

---

surprise [sér-PRAIZ] nom   **la surprise**

A surprise for me?
Une surprise pour moi?

---

surprising adjectif   **étonnant,** masc.
                              étonnante, fém.
*It is surprising to receive a letter from
an actress.*
Il est étonnant de recevoir une lettre d'une actrice.

---

sweater [SWET-ér] nom   **le chandail**

I am wearing a sweater because it is cool.
Je porte un chandail parce qu'il fait frais.

---

sweet [SWIT] adjectif   **doux**

This dessert is very sweet.
Ce dessert est très doux.

---

to swim [SWIM] verbe   **nager**

I swim	we swim
you swim	you swim
he, she, it swims	they swim

I go swimming in summer.
Je vais nager en été.

swimming pool (pool) nom   **la piscine**

We are swimming in the pool.
Nous nageons dans la piscine.

---

swing [SWING] nom   **la balançoire**
In the park the children are having a good time on the swings.
Dans le parc les enfants s'amusent sur les balançoires.

---

switch (See **to turn off**) nom   **le bouton**

T

---

table [TEI-bél] nom   **la table**
The brush is on the table.
La brosse est sur la table.

---

tablecloth [TEI-bél-clath] nom   **la nappe**
My aunt puts the tablecloth on the table.
Ma tante met la nappe sur la table.

---

tail [TEIL] nom   **la queue**
My dog wags his tail when I return home.
Mon chien remue la queue quand je retourne à la maison.

---

tailor [TEI-lér] nom   **le tailleur**
My neighbor is a tailor.
Mon voisin est tailleur.

---

to take (has) [TEIK] verbe   **prendre**
  I take   we take
  you take   you take
  he, she, it takes   they take
Mom has a croissant for breakfast.
Maman prend un croissant pour le petit déjeuner.

to take a bath   **prendre un bain**
to take a walk verbe   **se promener**

They are walking in the park.
Elles se promènent dans le parc.

take care! interjection   **attention!**

The teacher says, "Take care!"
Le professeur dit: "Attention!"

to take off (clothing) verbe   **ôter**
  I take off   we take off
  you take off   you take off
  he, she, it takes off   they take off

Take off your hat in the house.
Ôte le chapeau dans la maison.

to take a trip   **faire un voyage**

tale (See **story**) nom   **le conte**
fairy tale   **le conte de fées**

to talk [TAK] verbe   **parler**
  I talk   we talk
  you talk   you talk
  he, she, it talks   they talk

We are talking about the movie on television.
Nous parlons du film à la télévision.

tall [LOWD] adjectif   **haut,** masc.
                                                          haute, fém.
The Eiffel Tower is very tall.
La Tour Eiffel est très haute.

tape recorder [teip ré-KAWR-dér] nom   **le magnétophone**

The teacher uses a tape recorder in class.
Le professeur emploie un magnétophone dans la classe.

taxi [tak-si] nom   **le taxi**
My brother drives a taxi.
Mon frère conduit un taxi.

tea [ti] nom   **le thé**
Do you want tea or coffee?
Tu veux du thé ou du café?

teacher [ti-cher] nom   **la maîtresse,** fém.
The teacher is kind.   **le maître,** masc.
La maîtresse est gentille.

teacher nom   **le professeur**
The teacher is in the classroom.
Le professeur est dans la salle de classe.

to teach [tich] verbe   **enseigner**
  I teach   we teach
  you teach   you teach
  he, she, it teaches   they teach
Who teaches music to this class?
Qui enseigne la musique dans cette classe?

team [tim] nom   **l'équipe,** fém.
We are all members of the same team.
Nous sommes tous membres de la même équipe.

tear [tir] nom   **la larme**
Grandpa says, "Enough tears!"
Grand-père dit: "Assez de larmes!"

to tease [TIZ] verbe   **taquiner**

I tease	we tease
you tease	you tease
he, she, it teases	they tease

My brother always teases me!
Mon frère me taquine toujours!

---

teeth (See **tooth**) nom, pl.   **les dents**

---

telephone [TEL-é-fohn] nom   **le téléphone**

I like to talk on the telephone.
J'aime parler au téléphone.

cell phone [SEL-FOHN] nom   **le portable**, masc.

I keep my cell phone in my pocket.
Je garde mon portable dans la poche.

---

television [TEL-é-vizh-én] nom   **la télévision**
                                        la télé

My brother and I watch television.
Mon frère et moi, nous regardons la télévision.

television antenna nom   **l'antenne de télévision**

Television antennas are on the roof of the building.
Les antennes de télévision sont sur le toit du bâtiment.

television set nom   **le téléviseur**

The television set is not working.
Le téléviseur ne marche pas.

cable television (TV) nom   **le cable**, masc.

to tell [TEL] verbe   **raconter**

Tell me a story, Mom.
Raconte-moi une histoire, Maman.

ten [TEN] adjectif   **dix**

How many fingers do you have? Ten.
Combien de doigts avez-vous? Dix.

tent [TENT] nom   **la tente**

When I am at camp I sleep in a tent.
Quand je suis à la colonie de vacances je dors dans
une tente.

test (See **examination**) nom   **l'examen,** masc.

text message [TEXT-MES-adj] nom   **le texto,** masc.

She is texting her friend.
Elle envoie un message par texto à son amie.

to text verbe   **envoyer par texto**

thank you [THANGK-yu] nom   **merci**

When my grandmother gives me a cookie I say,
"Thank you."
Quand ma grand-mère me donne un petit gâteau je dis:
"Merci."

> On célèbre, en novembre, La Journée de la Fête
> de Thanksgiving, l'arrivée des Pilgrims à
> l'Amérique.
>
> Thanksgiving Day, in November, celebrates the
> arrival of the Pilgrims in America.

that [THAT] pronom **cela**

I don't like that!
Je n'aime pas cela!

---

that pronom **que**
That's too bad! **C'est dommage!**
expression idiomatique

You don't like chocolate? That's too bad!
Vous n'aimez pas le chocolat? C'est dommage!

---

the [THE] article **le, la, les**

---

theater [THI-é-tér] nom **le théâtre**

What are they performing at the theater?
Qu'est-ce qu'on joue au théâtre?

---

their [THEHR] adjectif **leur**

---

them [THEM] pronom **eux**

I go to school with them.
Je vais à l'école avec eux.

---

them pronom **leur**

I give them a card.
Je leur donne une carte.

---

then [THEN] adverbe **ensuite**

I read the book; then I return the book to the library.
Je lis le livre; ensuite je rends le livre à la bibliothèque.

---

then adverbe **puis**

I write a letter; then I go to my friend's house.
J'écris une lettre; puis, je vais chez mon ami.

there [THEHR] adverbe   **là-bas**
there is [THEHR iz] adverbe   **il y a**

they [THEI] pronom   **ils, elles, on**

thick [THIK] adjectif   **épais,** masc.
The lemon's skin is very thick.   **épaisse,** fém.
La peau du citron est très épaisse.

thief [THIF] nom   **le voleur**
They are looking for the thief at the bank.
On cherche le voleur à la banque.

thin [THIN] adjectif   **maigre**
You are too thin. You must eat.
Vous êtes trop maigre. Il faut manger.

thing [THING] nom   **la chose**
They sell all kinds of things in this store.
On vend toutes sortes de choses dans cette boutique.

to think [THINGK] verbe   **penser**
  I think   we think
  you think   you think
  he, she, it thinks   they think
I think I'll go to my friend's house. All right?
Je pense que je vais chez mon ami. D'accord?

thirsty (to be) (See **to drink**) verbe   **avoir soif**

thirteen [thur-TIN] adjectif   **treize**
There are thirteen steps in the staircase.
Il y a treize marches dans l'escalier.

thirty [THU̱R-ti] adjectif   **trente**

Which months have thirty days?
Quels mois ont trente jours?

---

this [THIS] adjectif   **ce**
                                                         cette, fém.
This little girl is well-behaved.   **ces,** pl.
Cette petite fille est sage.
                                    cet, masc. form before a vowel

---

this pronom   **ceci**

Mmm, this is good!
Mmm, ceci est bon!

---

thousand [THO̱W-zénd] adjectif   **mille**

How much does a car cost? A thousand francs?
Combien coûte une auto? Mille francs?

---

three [THRI] adjectif   **trois**

There are three glasses on the table.
Il y a trois verres sur la table.

---

throat [THRO̱HT] nom   **la gorge**

The teacher says softly, "I have a sore throat."
La maîtresse dit doucement: "J'ai mal à la gorge."

---

to throw [THRO̱H] verbe   **lancer**

  I throw   we throw
  you throw   you throw
  he, she, it throws they throw

He's throwing a pillow at me!
Il me lance un oreiller!

---

thunder [THÉ̱N-dér] nom   **le tonnerre**

After the lightning you hear the thunder.
Après l'éclair on entend le tonnerre.

Thursday [THURZ-dei] nom   **jeudi**
My birthday is Thursday.
Jeudi est mon anniversaire.

---

ticket [TIK-it] nom   **le billet**
Here is my ticket, sir.
Voici mon billet, monsieur.

---

tie [TAI] nom   **la cravate**
Daddy's tie is too big for me.
La cravate de Papa est trop grande pour moi.

---

time (hour) [TAIM] nom   **l'heure**
What time is it?
Quelle heure est-il?

It is dinner time. It is seven thirty. (It is half past seven.)
C'est l'heure du dîner. Il est sept heures et demie.

---

time (repeated action) [TAIM] nom   **la fois**
They knock three times at the door.
On frappe trois fois à la porte.

---

tip [TIP] nom   **le pourboire**
The man leaves a tip for the waiter.
L'homme laisse un pourboire pour le garçon.

---

tired [TAIRD]   **fatigué,** masc.
                                                                  fatiguée, fém.
After two hours of work in the garden,
I am tired.
Après deux heures de travail dans le jardin,
je suis fatigué.

---

to [TÉ] préposition   **à**

They are going to Paris.
Ils vont à Paris.

---

toast [TOHST] nom   **le pain grillé**

My sister prefers toast.
Ma soeur préfère le pain grillé.

---

today [té-DEI] adverbe   **aujourd'hui**

Today is January 12th.
Aujourd'hui c'est le douze janvier.

---

toe [TOH] nom   **l'orteil,** masc.

The baby looks at his toes.
Le bébé regarde ses orteils.

---

together [té-GETH-ér] adverbe   **ensemble**

We are going to the grocery store together.
Nous allons à l'épicerie ensemble.

---

tomato [té-MEI-toh] nom   **la tomate**

The tomato is red when it is ripe.
La tomate est rouge quand elle est mûre.

---

tomorrow [té-MAR-oh] adverbe   **demain**

Tomorrow I am going to camp.
Demain je vais à la colonie de vacances.

---

tongue [TÉNG] nom   **la langue**

I burn my tongue with hot soup.
Je me brûle la langue avec la soupe chaude.

---

too [TU] adverbe   **aussi**

I want some candy too!
Moi aussi, je veux des bonbons!

436

too (many) (much) adverbe   **trop**

The little girl says, "This is too much for me!"
La petite fille dit: "C'est trop pour moi!"

tooth [TUTH] nom   **la dent**

I have a toothache.
J'ai mal aux dents.

toothache nom   **mal aux dents**
toothbrush nom   **la brosse aux dents**
toothpaste nom   **le dentifrice**

Mom, I don't like this toothpaste.
Maman, je n'aime pas ce dentifrice.

top (toy) [TAP] nom   **la toupie**

Do you have a top?
As-tu une toupie?

tortoise (turtle) [TAWR-tis] nom   **la tortue**

The turtle walks slowly.
La tortue marche lentement.

to touch [TĔCH] verbe   **toucher**

I touch	we touch
you touch	you touch
he, she, it touches	they touch

"Do not touch the flowers."
"Défense de toucher les fleurs."

toward [TAWRD] préposition   **vers**

We are going toward the hotel.
Nous allons vers l'hôtel.

towel [TOW-ĕl] nom   **la serviette**

My towel is in the bathroom.
Ma serviette est dans la salle de bain.

tower [TOW-ér] nom   **la tour**

The Eiffel Tower is very tall.
La Tour Eiffel est très haute.

---

toy [TOI] nom   **le jouet**

What kind of toys do you have?
Quelle sorte de jouets as-tu?

---

traffic [TRAF-ik] nom   **la circulation**

The traffic stops for the red light.
La circulation s'arrête au feu rouge.

---

train [TREIN] nom   **le train**

Let's play with my electric trains.
Allons jouer avec mon train électrique.

---

to travel [TRAV-él] verbe   **voyager**

  I travel   we travel
  you travel   you travel
  he, she, it travels they travel

Are you traveling by car or by airplane?
Vous voyagez en auto ou en avion?

---

traveler nom   **le voyageur**

The traveler is tired.
Le voyageur est fatigué.

---

tree [TRI] nom   **l'arbre,** masc.

We are sitting under a tree.
Nous sommes assis sous l'arbre.

---

trip [TRIP] nom   **le voyage, le tour**
to take a trip expression idiomatique   **faire un voyage**
We are taking a trip to the castle.
Nous faisons un voyage au château.

---

trousers (pants) [TROW-zérs] nom   **le pantalon**
The boy's pants are dirty.
Le pantalon du garçon est sale.

---

truck [TRÉK] nom   **le camion**

The truck is carrying vegetables.
Le camion porte des légumes.

---

true [TRU] adjectif   **vrai,** masc.
It's a true story!   **vraie,** fém.
C'est une histoire vraie!

---

trunk [TRÉNGK] nom   **la malle**
It is difficult to carry this trunk.
Il est difficile de porter cette malle.

---

truth [TRUTH] nom   **la vérité**
It's true. I only tell the truth.
C'est vrai. Je ne dis que la vérité.

to try [TRAI] verbe   **essayer**

I try	we try
you try	you try
he, she, it tries	they try

She tries to carry the heavy package.
Elle essaye de porter le paquet lourd.

Tuesday [TUZ-dei] nom   **mardi**

Is Tuesday a day off?
Est-ce que mardi est un jour de congé?

---

turkey [TUR-ki] nom   **la dinde**

Do you like to eat turkey?
Tu aimes manger la dinde?

---

turn [TURN] nom   **le tour**
to turn verbe   **tourner**

I turn	we turn
you turn	you turn
he, she, it turns	they turn

I turn the page of the dictionary.
Je tourne la page du dictionnaire.

to turn off verbe   **éteindre**

I turn off the light.
J'éteins la lumière.

to turn on   **allumer**

turtle [TUR-tél] nom   **la tortue**

The turtle likes the sun.
La tortue aime le soleil.

---

twelve [TWELV] adjectif   **douze**

There are twelve bananas in a dozen.
Il y a douze bananes dans une douzaine.

---

twenty [TWEN-ti] adjectif   **vingt**

Ten and ten are twenty.
Dix et dix font vingt.

---

twice [TWHAIS] adverbe   **deux fois**

---

two [TU] adjectif   **deux**

I see two cats.
Je vois deux chats.

U

ugly [ŒG-li] adjectif   **laid,** masc.
                                                                laide, fém.
I don't like this hat; it's ugly.
Je n'aime pas ce chapeau; il est laid.

---

umbrella [ém-BREL-é] nom   **le parapluie**

That's a pretty umbrella.
C'est un joli parapluie.

---

uncle [ÚNG-kél] nom   **l'oncle**

My uncle is my mother's brother.
Mon oncle est le frère de ma mère.

---

under [ÚN-dér] préposition   **sous**

The carrot grows under the ground.
La carotte pousse sous la terre.

---

to understand [én-dér-STAND] verbe   **comprendre**

I understand	we understand
you understand	you understand
he, she, it understands	they understand

Do you understand today's lesson?
Tu comprends la leçon d'aujourd'hui?

---

unhappy [én-HAP-i] adjectif   **malheureux,** masc.
                                                              malheureuse, fém.
He is unhappy because he can't
play ball.
Il est malheureux parce qu'il ne peut pas jouer à la balle.

---

united [u-NAIT-éd]   **uni,** masc.
The boy lives in the United States.   **unie,** fém.
Le garçon habite les Etats-Unis.

The United Nations building is located in New York City.
Le bâtiment des Nations Unies se trouve dans la ville de
New York.

United Nations [u-NAIT-éd NEI-shénz]   **Les Nations Unies**
United States [u-NAIT-éd STEITS]   **Les Etats-Unis**

---

university (See **student**) nom   **l'université,** fém.

---

until [én-TIL] préposition   **jusqu'à**
We are in school until three o'clock.
Nous sommes à l'école jusqu'à trois heures.

---

unusual (See **extraordinary**) adjectif   **extraordinaire**

---

upstairs   **en haut**
Where are you? Upstairs.
Où es-tu? En haut.

---

us [ŕs] pronom   **nous**

---

to use [YUZ] verbe   **employer**
  I use   we use
  you use   you use
  he, she, it uses   they use
She uses scissors to cut the ribbon.
Elle emploie les ciseaux pour couper le ruban.

---

useful adjectif   **utile**
Some insects are useful.
Quelques insectes sont utiles.

V

vacation [vei-KEI-shén] nom   **les vacances**
summer vacation   **les grandes vacances**

Where are you going during the summer vacation?
Où allez-vous pendant les grandes vacances?

---

to vaccinate [VAK-si̱n-eit] verbe   **vacciner**
  I vaccinate   we vaccinate
  you vaccinate   you vaccinate
  he, she, it vaccinates   they vaccinate

I am afraid when the doctor vaccinates me.
J'ai peur quand le médecin me vaccine.

---

vacuum cleaner   **l'aspirateur,** masc.
[VAK-yu-ém-kli-nér] nom

Mother uses the vacuum cleaner to clean the house.
Pour nettoyer la maison, Maman emploie l'aspirateur.

---

valise [vé-LIS] nom   **la valise**

I put my clothes in the valise.
Je mets mes vêtements dans la valise.

---

valley [VAL-i] nom   **la vallée**

There are many flowers in the valley.
Il y a beaucoup de fleurs dans la vallée.

---

vanilla [vé-NI̱L-é] nom   **la vanille**

I like vanilla ice cream.
J'aime la glace à la vanille.

---

vegetable [VEDJ-té-bél] nom   **le légume**

Vegetables are delicious with meat.
Les légumes sont délicieux avec la viande.

---

very [VER-i] adverbe   **très**

The castle is very big.
Le château est très grand.

---

village [VIL-idj] nom   **le village**

My cousin lives in a village in the country.
Mon cousin habite un village à la campagne.

---

violet (See **purple**) nom   **violet**

---

violin [VAI-oh-lin] nom   **le violon**

The musician plays the violin.
Le musicien joue du violon.

---

to visit [VIZ-it] verbe   **visiter**
  I visit   we visit
  you visit   you visit
  he, she, it visits   they visit

My parents visit my camp.
Mes parents visitent ma colonie de vacances.

---

voice [VOIS] nom   **la voix**

My aunt's voice is sweet.
La voix de ma tante est douce.

in a loud voice   **à haute voix**
aloud   **à haute voix**
in a low voice   **à voix basse**

W

to wag [WAG] verbe **remuer**
The dog wags the tail.
Le chien remue la queue.

---

waist (size) [WEIST] nom **la taille**
In a store they ask me, "What is your size?"
Dans un magasin on me demande: "Quelle est votre taille?"

---

waiter [WEI-tér] nom **le garçon**
The waiter brings the dessert.
Le garçon apporte le dessert.

---

to wait for [WEIT fér] verbe **attendre**

I wait for	we wait for
you wait for	you wait for
he, she, it waits for	they wait for

She is waiting for her friend.
Elle attend son amie.

---

waitress [WEI-trés] nom **la serveuse**
The waitress is in the restaurant.
La serveuse est dans le restaurant.

---

to wake up [WEIK ép] verbe **se réveiller**

I wake up	we wake up
you wake up	you wake up
he, she, it wakes up	they wake up

We wake up early.
Nous nous réveillons de bonne heure.

to walk (energetically) [wAWK] verbe   **marcher**

I walk	we walk
you walk	you walk
he, she, it walks	they walk

We walk in the parade.
Nous marchons dans le défilé.

to walk (to stroll) verbe   **se promener**

They are strolling in the park.
Elles se promènent dans le parc.

---

wall [wAL] nom   **le mur**

There is a picture of a rocket ship on my bedroom wall.
Il y a une image d'une fusée au mur de ma chambre.

---

to want verbe   **vouloir**

I want	we want
you want	you want
he, she, it wants	they want

The baby is crying because he wants his toy.
Le bébé pleure parce qu'il veut son jouet.

See also: to wish

---

war [wAWR] nom   **la guerre**

My uncle is a soldier in the war.
Mon oncle est soldat à la guerre.

---

warm (See **hot**) adjectif   **chaud**

to wash (something or someone) [WAHSH] verbe   **laver**

I wash	we wash
you wash	you wash
he, she, it washes	they wash

She is washing the car.
Elle lave la voiture.

to wash (oneself) verbe   **se laver**

I wash my hands before eating.
Je me lave les mains avant de manger.

washing machine   **la machine à laver**

washstand nom   **le lavabo**

The washstand is in the bathroom.
Le lavabo est dans la salle de bain.

---

watch [WACH] nom   **la montre**

What a shame, my watch doesn't work.
Hélas, ma montre ne marche pas.

---

to watch verbe   **regarder**

I watch	we watch
you watch	you watch
he, she, it watches	they watch

I like to watch television.
J'aime regarder la télévision.

to watch over (look after)   **surveiller**
[WACH-<u>oh</u>-vér] verbe

I watch over	we watch over
you watch over	you watch over
he, she, it watches over	they watch over

The cat looks after the kittens.
Le chat surveille les petits (chats).

---

water [W<u>A</u>-tér] nom   **l'eau,** fém.
There is water in the swimming pool.   **les eaux,** pl.
Il y a de l'eau dans la piscine.

---

watermelon [W<u>A</u>-tér-mel-én] nom   **la pastèque**
Watermelon is a delicious fruit.
La pastèque est un fruit délicieux.

---

wave [WEIV] nom   **la vague**
I see waves at the beach.
Je vois des vagues à la plage.

---

we [WI] pronom   **nous**
We are going to the beach.
Nous allons à la plage.

---

we pronom   **on**
Are we playing now?
On joue maintenant?

---

weak [WIK] adjectif   **faible**
The poor boy is weak because he is sick.
Le pauvre garçon est faible parce qu'il est malade.

---

wealthy (rich) [WEL-thi] adjectif   **riche**
The rich lady wears jewels.
La femme riche porte des bijoux.

---

to wear [WEHR] verbe   **porter**

I wear	we wear
you wear	you wear
he, she, it wears	they wear

She is wearing a hat.
Elle porte un chapeau.

---

weather [WETH-ér] nom   **le temps**

What is the weather? The sun is shining.
Quel temps fait-il? Il fait du soleil.

Wednesday [WENZ-dei] nom   **mercredi**

Today is Wednesday—they are serving chicken.
C'est aujourd'hui mercredi—on sert du poulet.

---

week [WIK] nom   **la semaine**

The calendar shows us the seven days of the week.
Le calendrier nous montre les sept jours de la semaine.

---

to weep (cry) [WIP] verbe   **pleurer**

I weep	we weep
you weep	you weep
he, she, it weeps	they weep

I cry when somebody teases me.
Je pleure quand on me taquine.

You're welcome.   **il n'y a pas de quoi,**
[YUR-WEL-kém] expression idiomatique   **Je vous en prie.**

---

well [WEL] adverbe   **bien**

I'm feeling very well, thank you.
Je vais très bien, merci.

---

well-behaved [WEL-bi-HEIVD] adjectif   **sage**

Little girls are better behaved than little boys.
Les petites filles sont plus sages que les petits garçons.

Well done! Hurray! [wel-DÉN] interjection   **bravo**

Arnold answers the question well. "Well done!"
says the teacher.
Arnaud répond bien à la question. Le professeur dit: "Bravo!"

---

west [WEST] nom   **l'ouest,** masc.

When I go from Lyons to Bordeaux, I go toward the west.
Quand je vais de Lyon à Bordeaux, je vais vers l'ouest.

---

wet [WET] adjectif   **mouillé,** masc.
                                         mouillée, fém.
My notebook is falling into the water.
Oh, it is wet!
Mon cahier tombe dans l'eau. Oh, il est mouillé!

---

what? [WHAT] adverbe   **comment?**
What?
Comment?

---

what adverbe   **quoi**

What? You don't have the change for the bus?
Quoi? Tu n'as pas la monnaie pour l'autobus?

what   **que**
what   **quel**
what a . . . !   **quel,** masc.
                                      quelle, fém.
What a beautiful dress!
Quelle belle robe!

---

wheat [WHIT] nom   **le blé**

I see wheat in the fields.
Je vois le blé dans les champs.

---

wheel [WHIL] nom   **la roue**

My uncle fixes the wheel of my bicycle.
Mon oncle répare la roue de ma bicyclette.

---

when [WHEN] adverbe   **quand**

I read a book when it rains.
Je lis un livre quand il pleut.

---

where [WHEHR] adverbe   **où**

Where are my glasses?
Où sont mes lunettes?

---

whether (if) [WHETH-ér] adverbe   **si**
                                      s' (before il)
I am going to the window to
see if it is raining.
Je vais à la fenêtre pour voir s'il pleut.

---

which [WHICH] adjectif, pronom   **que**
which adjectif   **quel,** masc.
which pronoun   **quelle,** fém.
                                      qui
I am looking for my pen, which is on the rug.
Je cherche mon stylo qui est sur le tapis.

---

to whistle [WHIS-él] verbe   **siffler**

I whistle	we whistle
you whistle	you whistle
he, she, it whistles	they whistle

When I whistle, my friend knows that I'm at the door.
Quand je siffle, mon ami sait que je suis à la porte.

---

white [WHAIT] adjectif   **blanc,** masc.
                                  blanche, fém.
My shoes are white.
Mes souliers sont blancs.

who [HU] pronom   **qui**

Who is coming to visit us?
Qui vient chez nous?

---

whole [HOHL] adjectif   **entier,** masc.
                                                                entière, fém.
Of course I would like to eat the whole cake!
Bien sûr je voudrais manger le gâteau entier!

---

whom [HUM] pronom   **que**
                                                        qu' (before a vowel)

The woman whom I see is my aunt.
La femme que je vois est ma tante.

---

why? [WHAI] adverbe   **pourquoi**

Why are you late?
Pourquoi êtes-vous en retard?

---

wide [WAID] adjectif   **large**

The boulevard is a wide street.
Le boulevard est une large rue.

---

wide street [WAID-STRIT] nom   **le boulevard**

Students walk on the Boulevard St. Michel in Paris.
Les étudiants se promènent sur le boulevard St-Michel à Paris.

---

wife [WAIF] nom   **la femme**

Mother is my father's wife.
Maman est la femme de mon père.

---

wild [WAILD] adjectif   **féroce, sauvage**

Who is afraid of a wild tiger?
Qui a peur d'un tigre féroce?

---

to win [WIN] verbe   **gagner**
  I win   we win
  you win   you win
  he, she, it wins they win

Our team wins!
C'est notre équipe qui gagne!

---

wind [WIND] nom   **le vent**

It is windy and I lose my hat.
Il fait du vent et je perds mon chapeau.

---

window [WIN-doh] nom   **la fenêtre**

The dog likes to look out the window.
Le chien aime regarder par la fenêtre.

store window   **la vitrine**

---

wine [WAIN] nom   **le vin**

The waiter brings the wine.
Le garçon apporte le vin.

---

wing [WING] nom   **l'aile,** fém.

The airplane has two wings.
L'avion a deux ailes.

---

winner [WIN-ér] nom   **le gagnant,** masc.
                                               la gagnante, fém.
I like to be the winner!
J'aime être la gagnante!

---

winter [wɪn-tér] nom   **l'hiver,** masc.
It is cold in winter.
En hiver il fait froid.

---

wise [wa̱iz] adjectif   **sage**
Grandfather is wise.
Grand-père est sage.

---

wish [wɪsh] nom   **le souhait**
When I go to bed I make a wish.
Quand je me couche je fais un souhait.

---

to wish verbe   **désirer**
  I wish   we wish
  you wish   you wish
  he, she, it wishes   they wish
What do you wish, sir?
Monsieur désire?
See also: to want

---

with [wɪth] préposition   **avec**
Mary is at the beach with her friends.
Marie est à la plage avec ses amies.
with care   **avec soin**
Paul pours water into the glass carefully.
Paul verse l'eau dans le verre avec soin.

---

without [with-o̱wt] préposition   **sans**
I'm going to class without my friend. He is sick.
Je vais à mes classes sans mon ami. Il est malade.

---

wolf [WAUHLF] nom   **le loup**

Who's afraid of the bad wolf?
Qui a peur du méchant loup?

woman [WAUHM-en] nom   **la femme**
These two women are going shopping.
Ces deux femmes vont faire des emplettes.

wonderful [WÍN-dér-fél] adjectif   **extraordinaire**
We are going to take a wonderful trip in a spaceship.
Nous allons faire un voyage extraordinaire en fusée.

Wonderful! (Great!) interjection   **formidable**
You are going to the circus? Great!
Tu vas au cirque? Formidable!

woods [WAUHDZ] nom   **la forêt, le bois**
I am going into the woods.
Je vais dans le bois.

wool [WAUHL] nom   **la laine**
made of wool, woolen   **en laine**
My coat is made of wool.
Mon manteau est en laine.

word [WURD] nom   **le mot**
I'm thinking of a word that begins with the letter "a."
Je pense à un mot qui commence avec la lettre "a."

work [WURK] nom   **le travail**

My mother has a lot of work to do.
Ma mère a beaucoup de travail.

---

to work verbe   **travailler**

  I work   we work
  you work   you work
  he, she, it works   they work

The farmer works outside.
Le fermier travaille dehors.

---

to work (things) [WURK] verbe   **marcher**

This lamp is not working.
Cette lampe ne marche pas.

---

world [WURLD] nom   **le monde**

How many nations are there in the world?
Combien de nations y a-t-il dans le monde?

---

worm [WURM] nom   **le ver**

There's a worm in the apple.
Il y a un ver dans la pomme.

---

to write [R<u>AI</u>T] verbe   **écrire**

I write	we write
you write	you write
he, she, it writes	they write

The teacher says, "Write the date on the blackboard."
La maîtresse dit: "Écrivez la date au tableau noir."

> Mark Twain était un écrivain américain qui a écrit des histoires à propos de la rivière Mississippi.
>
> Mark Twain was an American writer who wrote stories about the Mississippi River.

(to be) wrong [RONG] expression   **avoir tort**

Y

year [YIR] nom   **l'année,** fém.

There are twelve months in a year.
Il y a douze mois dans une année.

year nom   **l'an,** masc.

I'm nine years old.
J'ai neuf ans.

yellow [YEL-<u>oh</u>] adjectif   **jaune**

Corn is yellow.
Le maïs est jaune.

yes [YES] adverbe   **oui**

Do you want some candy? Yes, of course!
Veux-tu des bonbons? Oui, bien sûr!

yesterday [YES-tér-dei] adverbe **hier**
Today is May 10; yesterday (was) May 9.
C'est aujourd'hui le dix mai; hier, le neuf mai.

you [YU] pronom **on**
When you look out of the window, you see the Eiffel Tower.
Quand on regarde par la fenêtre, on voit la Tour Eiffel.

you pronom (familiar) **te**
I give you some milk.
Je te donne du lait.

you pronom (familiar) **toi**
Do you have my stick, Jack?
C'est toi, Jacques, qui as mon bâton?

you pronom **vous**
How are you?
Comment allez-vous?

I am giving you a ticket.
Je vous donne un billet.

you (familiar) pronom **tu**
How are you?
Comment vas-tu?

you have to expression idiomatique **il faut**
It is necessary to go to school.
(We have to go to school.)
Il faut aller à l'école.

young [YŬNG] adjectif   **jeune**

The puppy is young. It is six weeks old.
Le petit chien est jeune. Il a six semaines.

your [YAWR] adjectif   **ton,** masc.
                               ta, fém.
Your cousin is handsome.   **tes,** pl.
Ton cousin est beau.

Your neighbor is kind.   **votre**
Ta voisine est gentille.   **vos,** pl.

Your parents are tall.
Tes parents sont grands.

Where is your tape recorder?
Où est votre magnétophone?

Where are your stamps?
Où sont vos timbres?

you're welcome   **de rein; je vous en prie;**
[YUR-WEL-kém]   **il n'y a pas de quoi; pas de quoi**

Z

zebra [ZI-bré] nom   **le zèbre**

Is it a zebra or a horse?
Est-ce un zèbre ou un cheval?

zero [ZIR-<u>oh</u>] nom   **le zéro**

There is a zero in the number ten.
Il y a un zéro dans le numéro dix.

---

zoo [ZU] nom   **le zoo**

I like to watch the tigers at the zoo.
J'aime regarder les tigres au zoo.

bear	**l'ours**	**lion**	**le lion**
elephant	**l'éléphant**	**monkey**	**le singe**
fox	**le renard**	**snake**	**le serpent**
kangaroo	**le kangourou**	**tiger**	**le tigre**
leopard	**le léopard**	**wolf**	**le loup**

Les Verbes Anglais
English Verb Supplement

Regular Verbs
Verbes Réguliers

Present (Présent)	Past (Passé Simple)	Future (Futur)

TO ARRANGE (arranger)

Present	Past	Future
I arrange	I arranged	I will arrange
you arrange	you arranged	you will arrange
he, she, it arranges	he, she, it arranged	he, she, it, will arrange
we arrange	we arranged	we will arrange
you arrange	you arranged	you will arrange
they arrange	they arranged	they will arrange

TO TALK (parler)

Present	Past	Future
I talk	I talked	I will talk
you talk	you talked	you will talk
he, she, it talks	he, she, it talked	he, she, it will talk
we talk	we talked	we will talk
you talk	you talked	you will talk
they talk	they talked	they will talk

Irregular Verbs
Verbes Irréguliers

TO BE (être)

Present	Past	Future
I am	I was	I will be
you are	you were	you will be
he, she, it is	he, she, it was	he, she, it will be
we are	we were	we will be

| you are | you were | you will be |
| they are | they were | they will be |

TO DO (faire)

I do	I did	I will do
you do	you did	you will do
he, she, it does	he, she, it did	he, she, it will do
we do	we did	we will do
you do	you did	you will do
they do	they did	they will do

TO BECOME (devenir)

I become	I became	I will become
you become	you became	you will become
he, she, it becomes	he, she, it became	he, she, it will become
we become	we became	we will become
you become	you became	you will become
they become	they became	they will become

TO BEGIN (commencer)

I begin	I began	I will begin
you begin	you began	you will begin
he, she, it begins	he, she, it began	he, she, it will begin
we begin	we began	we will begin
you begin	you began	you will begin
they begin	they began	they will begin

TO CARRY (porter)

I carry	I carried	I will carry
you carry	you carried	you will carry
he, she, it carries	he, she, it carried	he, she, it will carry
we carry	we carried	we will carry
you carry	you carried	you will carry
they carry	they carried	they will carry

TO HAVE (avoir)

I have	I had	I will have
you have	you had	you will have
he, she, it has	he, she, it had	he, she, it will have
we have	we had	we will have
you have	you had	you will have
they have	they had	they will have

TO FEEL (sentir)

I feel	I felt	I will feel
you feel	you felt	you will feel
he, she, it feels	he, she, it felt	he, she, it will feel
we feel	we felt	we will feel
you feel	you felt	you will feel
they feel	they felt	they will feel

TO HURRY (dépêcher)

I hurry	I hurried	I will hurry
you hurry	you hurried	you will hurry
he, she, it hurries	he, she, it hurried	he, she, it will hurry
we hurry	we hurried	we will hurry
you hurry	you hurried	you will hurry
they hurry	they hurried	they will hurry

TO LEAVE (partir)

I leave	I left	I will leave
you leave	you left	you will leave
he, she, it leaves	he, she, it left	he, she, it will leave
we leave	we left	we will leave
you leave	you left	you will leave
they leave	they left	they will leave

TO SAY (dire)

I say	I said	I will say
you say	you said	you will say
he, she, it says	he, she, it said	he, she, it will say

we say	we said	we will say
you say	you said	you will say
they say	they said	they will say

TO SEE (voir)

I see	I saw	I will see
you see	you saw	you will see
he, she, it sees	he, she, it saw	he, she, it will see
we see	we saw	we will see
you see	you saw	you will see
they see	they saw	they will see

TO WIN (gagner)

I win	I won	I will win
you win	you won	you will win
he, she, it wins	he, she, it won	he, she, it will win
we win	we won	we will win
you win	you won	you will win
they win	they won	they will win

DAYS OF THE WEEK
Les Jours de la Semaine

English/Anglais	Français/French
Monday	lundi
Tuesday	mardi
Wednesday	mercredi
Thursday	jeudi
Friday	vendredi
Saturday	samedi
Sunday	dimanche

MONTHS OF THE YEAR
Les Mois de L'Année

English/Anglais	Français/French
January	janvier
February	février
March	mars
April	avril
May	mai
June	juin
July	juillet
August	août
September	septembre
October	octobre
November	novembre
December	décembre

PERSONAL NAMES
Prénoms

Boys/*Les Garçons*

English/Anglais	Français/French
Allen	Alain [a-LAIN]
Albert	Albert [al-BEHR]
Andrew	André [ahn-DRAY]
Anthony	Antoine [ahn-TWAN]
Arnold	Arnaud [ar-NOH]
Arthur	Arthur [ar-TEWR]
Charles	Charles [SHARL]
Claud	Chaude [KLOHD]
David	David [da-VEED]
Edward	Edouard [eh-DWAR]
Eugene	Eugène [euh-ZHEHN]
Frank	Francois [frahn-SWA]
Frederick	Frédéric [fray-day-REEK]
George	Georges [ZHUHRZH]
Henry	Henri [ahn-REE]
James, Jack	Jacques [ZHAK]
Jerome	Jérôme [zhay-ROHM]
John	Jean [ZHAHN]
Lawrence	Laurent [luh-RAHN]
Leo	Léon [lay-OHN]
Mark	Marc [MARK]
Michael	Michel [mee-SHEHL]
Paul	Paul [PUHL]
Peter	Pierre [PYEHR]
Philip	Philippe [fee-LEEP]
Ralph	Raoul [ra-OOL]
Robert	Robert [ruh-BEHR]
William	Guillaume [gee-OHM]

Girls/*Les Jeunes Filles*	
English/Anglais	Français/French
Amy	Aimée [ay-MAY]
Ann	Anne [AN]
Beatrice	Béatrice [bay-a-TREES]
Bertha	Berthe [BEHRT]
Carolyn	Caroline [ca-ruh-LEEN]
Claire	Claire [KLEHR]
Colette	Colette [kuh-LEHT]
Denise	Denise [dé-NEEZ]
Dorothy	Dorothée [duh-ruh-TAY]
Elizabeth	Elisabeth [ay-lee-za-BEHT]
Elsie	Elise [ay-LEEZ]
Emily	Emilie [ay-mee-LEE]
Frances	Françoise [frahñ-SWAZ]
Harriet	Henriette [ahñ-ree-EHT]
Helen	Hélène [ay-LEHN]
Jacquelyn	Jacqueline [zha-KLEEN]
Jane, Jean, Joan	Jeanne [ZHAN]
Laura	Laure [LUHR]
Louise	Louise [LWEEZ]
Margaret	Marguerite [mar-guh-REET]
Martha	Marthe [MART]
Mary	Marie [ma-REE]
Nancy	Nanette [na-NEHT]
Susan	Suzanne [sew-zan]
Sylvia	Sylvie [seel-VEE]
Theresa	Thérèse [tay-REHZ]
Virginia	Virginie [veer-zhee-NEE]
Yvonne	Yvonne [EE-VUHN]

CLASSROOM EXPRESSIONS
Expressions de Classe

English/Anglais	Français/French
again	encore une fois
aloud	à haute voix
Answer the question.	Répondez à la question. (Réponds)
Begin.	Commencez. (Commence.)
Bring me the book.	Apportez-moi le livre. (Apporte-moi)
Close the door.	Fermez la porte. (Ferme)
Count from one to five.	Comptez de un à cinq. (Compte)
Excellent!	Excellent! Bravo!
Draw a flower.	Dessinez une fleur. (Dessine)
Give me a pencil.	Donnez-moi un crayon. (Donne-moi)
Go to the window.	Allez à la fenêtre. (Va)
Go back to your seat.	Retournez à votre place. (Retourne à ta place.)
Good-bye.	Au revoir.
Hello.	Bonjour.
Let us sing.	Chantons.
Listen.	Ecoutez. (Ecoute)
Look at the blackboard.	Regardez le tableau noir. (Regarde)
Open the door.	Ouvrez la porte. (Ouvre)
Pay attention!	Faites attention! (Fais)
Please	S'il vous plaît (S'il te plaît)

CLASSROOM EXPRESSIONS (continued)
Expressions de Classe

English/Anglais	Français/French
Repeat!	Répétez! (Répète!)
See you tomorrow.	A demain.
Sit down.	Asseyez-vous. (Assieds-toi.)
Stand up.	Levez-vous. (Lève-toi.)
Thank you.	Merci.
You're welcome.	De rien. Je vous en prie. (Je t'en prie.)

NUMBERS
Nombres

English Anglais	Français French
one	un
two	deux
three	trois
four	quatre
five	cinq
six	six
seven	sept
eight	huit
nine	neuf
ten	dix
eleven	onze
twelve	douze
thirteen	treize
fourteen	quatorze
fifteen	quinze
sixteen	seize
seventeen	dix-sept
eighteen	dix-huit
nineteen	dix-neuf
twenty	vingt
twenty-one	vingt et un
twenty-two	vingt-deux
twenty-three	vingt-trois
twenty-four	vingt-quatre
twenty-five	vingt-cinq
twenty-six	vingt-six

twenty-seven	vingt-sept
twenty-eight	vingt-huit
twenty-nine	vingt-neuf
thirty	trente
thirty-one	trente et un
thirty-two	trente-deux
thirty-three	trente-trois
thirty-four	trente-quatre
thirty-five	trente-cinq
thirty-six	trente-six
thirty-seven	trente-sept
thirty-eight	trente-huit
thirty-nine	trente-neuf
forty	quarante
forty-one	quarante et un
forty-two	quarante-deux
forty-three	quarante-trois
forty-four	quarante-quatre
forty-five	quarante-cinq
forty-six	quarante-six
forty-seven	quarante-sept
forty-eight	quarante-huit
forty-nine	quarante-neuf
fifty	cinquante
fifty-one	cinquante et un
fifty-two	cinquante-deux
fifty-three	cinquante-trois
fifty-four	cinquante-quatre
fifty-five	cinquante-cinq
fifty-six	cinquante-six
fifty-seven	cinquante-sept

fifty-eight	cinquante-huit
fifty-nine	cinquante-neuf
sixty	soixante
sixty-one	soixante et un
sixty-two	soixante-deux
sixty-three	soixante-trois
sixty-four	soixante-quatre
sixty-five	soixante-cinq
sixty-six	soixante-six
sixty-seven	soixante-sept
sixty-eight	soixante-huit
sixty-nine	soixante-neuf
seventy	soixante-dix
seventy-one	soixante et onze
seventy-two	soixante-douze
seventy-three	soixante-treize
seventy-four	soixante-quatorze
seventy-five	soixante-quinze
seventy-six	soixante-seize
seventy-seven	soixante-dix-sept
seventy-eight	soixante-dix-huit
seventy-nine	soixante-dix-neuf
eighty	quatre-vingts
eighty-one	quatre-vingts-un
eighty-two	quatre-vingts-deux
eighty-three	quatre-vingts-trois
eighty-four	quatre-vingts-quatre
eighty-five	quatre-vingts-cinq
eighty-six	quatre-vingts-six
eighty-seven	quatre-vingts-sept
eighty-eight	quatre-vingts-huit

eighty-nine	quatre-vingts-neuf
ninety	quatre-vingts-dix
ninety-one	quatre-vingts-onze
ninety-two	quatre-vingts-douze
ninety-three	quatre-vingts-treize
ninety-four	quatre-vingts-quatorze
ninety-five	quatre-vingts-quinze
ninety-six	quatre-vingts-seize
ninety-seven	quatre-vingts-dix-sept
ninety-eight	quatre-vingts-dix-huit
ninety-nine	quatre-vingts-dix-neuf
one hundred	cent
two hundred	deux cents
three hundred	trois cents
four hundred	quatre cents
five hundred	cinq cents
six hundred	six cents
seven hundred	sept cents
eight hundred	huit cents
nine hundred	neuf cents
one thousand	mille
one million	un million

CONVERSION TABLES
Tables de Conversion

CURRENCY, WEIGHTS, AND MEASURES
Monnaies, Poids, Mesures

Français French	English Anglais
1 euro	$1.50*
2 euros	$3.00*
3 euros	$4.50*
1 centimeter	0.39 inches**
1 kilometer	0.62 miles**
10 kilometers	6.21 miles**
1 gram	0.035 ounces**
1 kilogram	2.20 pounds**
English **Anglais**	**Français** **French**
$1	0.66 euro
$2	1.32 euros
$3	1.98 euros
1 inch	2.54 centimeters**
1 foot	30.5 centimeters**
1 yard	91.4 centimeters**
1 mile	1.61 kilometers**
1 ounce	28.3 grams**
1 pound	453.6 grams**

* Because of fluctuations in exchange rates, it is necessary to consult the Internet, the finance section of your daily newspaper, or the foreign currency exchange section of your local bank.
** Approximately

476

PARTS OF SPEECH
Mots Grammaticaux

English / Anglais	Français / French
adjective (adj.)	l'adjectif
article	l'article
adverb (adv.)	l'adverbe
conjunction	la conjonction
idiomatic expression	l'expression idiomatique
interjection	l'interjection
noun, feminine (fem.)	le nom (féminin)
noun, masculine (masc.)	le nom (masculin)
preposition	la préposition
pronoun (pron.)	le pronom
verb	le verbe
verb form	la forme du verbe

English/Anglais	Français/French

Introductions

Présentations

Hello/Good-bye/ See you later	Bonjour/Au revoir/ A bientôt
How are you?	Comment allez-vous?
I'm sorry	Je suis désolé (désolée)
Miss/Mr./Mrs./Ms.	Mademoiselle (Mlle)/Monsieur (M) Madame (Mme)/ Mme ou Mlle
My name is...	Je m'appelle...
Please/Thank you/ You're welcome	S'il vous plaît/ Merci/De rien
Pleased to meet you	Enchanté (Enchantée)
What's your home address?	Quelle est votre adresse personnelle?
What's your e-mail address?	Quelle est votre adresse électronique?

Useful Expressions

Do you speak English? French?	On parle anglais?/français?
I don't understand...	Je ne comprends pas
straight ahead/ to the right/ to the left	droit devant/à droite/ à gauche

English/Anglais	French/Français
Please speak slowly	Parlez lentement, s'il vous plaît
What does ... mean?	Que veut dire...?
What time is it?	Quelle heure est-il?
What's today's date?	Quelle est la date aujourd'hui?
What's the weather?	Quel temps fait-il?
Where is...?	Où est...?

Questions

How...?	Comment...?
How much...?	Combien...?
What...?	Que...?/quoi?
At what time...?	A quelle heure...?
When...?	Quand...?
Where is...? Where are...?	Où est ...?/Où sont...?
Who...?	Qui...?
Why...?	Pourquoi...?

Basic Needs

Help!	Au secours!
I have a toothache... where is a dentist?	J'ai mal au dent... où est le dentiste?
I'm hot/cold	J'ai chaud/J'ai froid
I'm lost	Je suis perdu (perdue)
I need...	J'ai besoin de...
I'm sick...where is the doctor?	Je suis malade...où es le médecin?

English/Anglais	French/Français
My purse has been stolen... where are the police?	On a volé mon sac à main...où est la police?
Today, tomorrow, yesterday	Aujourd'hui, demain, hier
Where is the bathroom?	Où sont les toilettes?

Activities

I would like...	Je voudrais...
to eat in a restaurant	prendre un repas dans un restaurant
to go fishing	aller à la pêche
to go shopping	aller faire des courses
to go skating	aller patiner
to go to a park	aller au parc
to go to the university	aller à l'université
to swim at the beach (at a lake)	nager à la plage (à un lac)
to take a trip (by plane/ train/taxi/ on foot)	faire un voyage (en avion/ en train/en taxi/à pied)
to visit City Hall	visiter la mairie
to visit a monument	visiter un monument

Signs

Danger	Danger
Entrance/Exit	Entrée/Sortie
Information	Renseignements
Open/Closed	Ouvert/Fermé
Prohibited	Interdit
Push/Pull	Poussez/Tirez

English/Anglais	French/Français
No Smoking	Défense de fumer
No Vacancies	Complet
Restroom	les Toilettes
Sale	Solde

Food

Breakfast/lunch/dinner/ snack	Le petit déjeuner/ le déjeuner/le dîner/ le casse-croûte
Bread/rolls	Le pain, les petits pains
Cheese	Le fromage
Water/bottled water/ coffee/hot chocolate	L'eau/l'eau minérale/ un café/du chocolat/
Juice/milk/soda	Du jus/du lait/un soda
Fish/meat/poultry	Le poisson/la viande/ les volailles
Vegetables	Les légumes
The check, please	L'addition, s'il vous plaît
The tip	Le pourboire
Fast-food restaurant	Le fast-food

Shopping

To go shopping at the market/supermarket	Aller faire des courses au marché/ au supermarché
boutique/bakery	à la boutique/ à la pâtisserie

English/Anglais	French/Français
drugstore/bookstore	à la pharmacie/ à la librairie
department store	au grand magasin
What's the price?	C'est combien?
That's too expensive	C'est trop cher
Do you accept credit cards?	Je peux payer avec une carte de crédit?
I need a receipt, please	Je voudrais un reçu, s'il vous plaît

ICI PARLE FRANÇAIS

French spoken here

Algeria
Andorra
Cambodia
Djibouti
Haiti
Laos
Lebanon
Luxembourg
Mauritania
Mauritius
Morocco
Rwanda
Switzerland
Syria
Tunisia
Vanuatu
Vietnam

Belgium
Benin
Burkina Faso
Cameroon
Canada
Central African Republic
Chad
Congo
Côte D'Ivoire
France
French Guiana
Guadelupe
Martinique
Réunion
St. Pierre & Miquelon
French Polynesia
Gabon
Guinea
Mali
Monaco
Niger
Senegal
Seychelles
Togo
Zaire

Countries where French is the official language, or one of the main languages.

Countries where French is widely spoken.

3 Foreign Language Series From Barron's!

The **VERB SERIES** offers more than 300 of the most frequently used verbs.
The **GRAMMAR SERIES** provides complete coverage of the elements of grammar.
The **VOCABULARY SERIES** offers more than 3500 words and phrases with their foreign language translations. Each book: paperback.

FRENCH GRAMMAR
ISBN: 978-0-7641-1351-2

GERMAN GRAMMAR
ISBN: 978-0-8120-4296-2

ITALIAN GRAMMAR
ISBN: 978-0-7641-2060-2

JAPANESE GRAMMAR
ISBN: 978-0-7641-2061-9

RUSSIAN GRAMMAR
ISBN: 978-0-8120-4902-2

SPANISH GRAMMAR
ISBN: 978-0-7641-1615-5

FRENCH VERBS
ISBN: 978-0-7641-1356-7

GERMAN VERBS
ISBN: 978-0-8120-4310-5

ITALIAN VERBS
ISBN: 978-0-7641-2063-3

SPANISH VERBS
ISBN: 978-0-7641-1357-4

FRENCH VOCABULARY
ISBN: 978-0-7641-1999-6

GERMAN VOCABULARY
ISBN: 978-0-8120-4497-3

ITALIAN VOCABULARY
ISBN: 978-0-7641-2190-6

JAPANESE VOCABULARY
ISBN: 978-0-7641-3973-4

RUSSIAN VOCABULARY
ISBN: 978-0-7641-3970-3

SPANISH VOCABULARY
ISBN: 978-0-7641-1985-9

Barron's Educational Series, Inc.
250 Wireless Blvd., Hauppauge, NY 11788
Call toll-free: 1-800-645-3476

In Canada: Georgetown Book Warehouse
34 Armstrong Ave., Georgetown, Ontario L7G 4R9
Call toll-free: 1-800-247-7160

Please visit **www.barronseduc.com**
to view current prices and to order books

(#26) R 12/08

LANGUAGE PACKAGES FOR BUSY PEOPLE

LANGUAGES ON THE GO–Level 1

Developing language skills is easy and fun with the *On The Go* program! Two—three CDs in each package feature a friendly, English-speaking narrator who teaches language fundamentals step-by-step. All that's needed is a CD player. The ideal course for people *on the go!*

  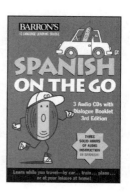

Each package comes in a handy plastic case:

French	Italian	Spanish
ISBN: 978-0-7641-7755-2	ISBN: 978-0-7641-7756-9	ISBN: 978-0-7641-7757-6

Please visit **www.barronseduc.com** to view current prices and to order books.

Barron's Educational Series, Inc.
250 Wireless Blvd., Hauppauge, NY 11788
In Canada: Georgetown Book Warehouse
34 Armstrong Ave., Georgetown, Ont. L7G 4R9

(#30a) R 2/08

Helpful Guides for Mastering a Foreign Language

2001 Idiom Series

Indispensable resources, these completely bilingual dictionaries present the most frequently used idiomatic words and phrases to help students avoid stilted expression when writing in their newly acquired language. Each book includes illustrative sentences. Each feature is easy to locate and designed with clarity in mind.

2001 French and English Idioms, 3rd
978-0-7641-3750-1

2001 German and English Idioms
978-0-8120-9009-3

2001 Italian and English Idioms, 2nd
978-0-8120-9030-7

2001 Russian and English Idioms
978-0-8120-9532-6

2001 Spanish and English Idioms, 3rd
978-0-7641-3744-0

Barron's Bilingual Dictionaries

These dictionaries each present 100,000 entries with translations into English and headwords in color for easy reference. Added features include full-color atlas-style maps, a concise grammar guide, verb conjugation lists, example phrases, pronunciation guides, and much more. Of special value to students and travelers, each book comes with an electronic bilingual dictionary that can be downloaded to all PCs and nearly all PDAs and smartphones!

Barron's French-English Dictionary
978-0-7641-3330-5

Barron's German-English Dictionary
978-0-7641-3763-1

Barron's Italian-English Dictionary
978-0-7641-3764-8

Barron's Spanish-English Dictionary
978-0-7641-3329-9

501 Verb Series

Here is a series to help the foreign language student successfully approach verbs and all their details. Complete conjugations of the verbs are arranged one verb to a page in alphabetical order. Verb forms are printed in boldface type in two columns, and common idioms using the applicable verbs are listed at the bottom of the page in each volume.
Some titles include a CD-ROM.

501 Arabic Verbs
978-0-7641-3622-1

501 English Verbs, 2nd, with CD-ROM
978-0-7641-7985-3

501 French Verbs, 6th, with CD-ROM
978-0-7641-7983-9

501 German Verbs, 4th, with CD-ROM
978-0-7641-9393-4

501 Hebrew Verbs, 2nd
978-0-7641-3748-8

501 Italian Verbs, 3rd, with CD-ROM
978-0-7641-7982-2

501 Japanese Verbs, 3rd
978-0-7641-3749-5

501 Latin Verbs, 2nd
978-0-7641-3742-6

501 Portuguese Verbs, 2nd
978-0-7641-2916-2

501 Russian Verbs, 3rd
978-0-7641-3743-3

501 Spanish Verbs, 6th, with CD-ROM
978-0-7641-7984-6

Barron's Educational Series, Inc.
250 Wireless Boulevard, Hauppauge, NY 11788
In Canada: Georgetown Book Warehouse
34 Armstrong Avenue, Georgetown, Ont. L7G 4R9

Please visit **www.barronseduc.com**
to view current prices and to order books

(#33) R 2/08